Contents

List of Illustrations

TEACHING GEOGRAPHY

TEACHING SERIES

General Editor: Professor E. C. Wragg

Teaching Modern Languages David Webb
Teaching Teaching E. C. Wragg

in preparation

Teaching Art John Lancaster and Ron George
Teaching Mixed-Ability Groups E. C. Wragg (editor)

TEACHING GEOGRAPHY

PATRICK BAILEY
University of Leicester
School of Education

DAVID & CHARLES
NEWTON ABBOT LONDON VANCOUVER

0 7153 6860 5

© Patrick Bailey 1974 ✓

All rights reserved. No part of this
publication may be reproduced, stored
in a retrieval system, or transmitted,
in any form or by any means, electronic,
mechanical, photocopying, recording or
otherwise, without the prior permission
of David & Charles (Holdings) Limited

Set in 11 on 13pt Times
and printed in Great Britain
by John Sherratt and Son Ltd
at the St Ann's Press Park Road
Altrincham Cheshire WA14 5QQ
for David & Charles (Holdings) Limited
South Devon House   Newton Abbot   Devon

Published in Canada by Douglas David &
Charles Limited 3645 McKechnie Drive
West Vancouver BC

Preface

The world is changing, and the schools and what we teach in them must change. We need to look critically at the purposes, content and processes of the whole curriculum, and at the subjects which contribute to that curriculum. Of all subjects, geography needs to take note of a changing world.

This book is founded on the conviction that geography has an irreplaceable part to play in the process of education; and that this will always be so, even though the subject may not always appear separately on school timetables. The process of curriculum development will continue to improve the educational contributions of subjects, and explore ways of relating them to one another, but it will not cause subjects to merge or disappear. The present needs are for geographers to clarify their ideas about the nature of their subject, to make explicit its distinctive contribution to education and to learn how to co-operate with other specialists both at the content and the conceptual levels.

The book emphasises that geography is concerned first and foremost with ideas, not with factual information. Of course facts are important – no-one can reason without knowledge – but they are to be regarded as the means by which ideas are introduced, developed and applied. The subject also involves specific skills, which are needed to make its ideas effective.

The first part of the book is devoted to a discussion of the distinctive ideas and skills of geography – including a review of recent developments in the subject – and of their applications in schools. The second part deals with practical matters such as syllabus and course planning, lesson preparation, the making of audio-visual aids, planning and equipping the geography room, and field work.

Consideration is also given to the problems of running geography departments. As comprehensive reorganisations proceed, more and more teachers of geography find themselves in large and complex schools, where they meet problems of organisation and management which were almost unknown to teachers until very recently. Teachers are unused to thinking in management terms; yet, unless the management functions of a school are mastered, its educational objectives will never be achieved. Developments in curriculum content and process, for example, nearly always require a parallel managerial development.

Teachers have to ask themselves continually why they teach their subject in the ways they do. Geographers must be prepared to answer this question about their own subject, its branches, their own courses and their ways of teaching. In this period of educational re-appraisal, everything will be questioned. A first requirement is, therefore, that geographers should know the nature of their subject and why it is worthwhile to teach it.

. . . the most important thing is the love of ideas.

Rudolf Kjellén

Acknowledgements

A book of this kind owes much to many people. It is impossible to thank every person that has contributed to it, directly or indirectly, except in general terms, which I now do. However, I am aware of having learned a great deal from a relatively small number of people whom I wish to thank by name. They are: Professor F. Kenneth Hare, then of McGill University, Montreal, and the staff which he assembled for the Stanstead Summer School 1950; Professor Harry Thorpe and Alan Tubbs, both of the University of Birmingham; Professor W. R. Mead, for Scandinavian inspirations; Dr Gareth Lewis and Dr Peter Mounfield of the University of Leicester Department of Geography; Dr P. T. Wheeler of the University of Nottingham, and leaders and members of successive Geographical Field Group expeditions, 1960–71, for a continuing education in field work; Dr Richard Odingo of the University of Nairobi for an unforgettable introduction to Kenyan landscapes; John Talbot White; and Marguerita Oughton, who helped prepare the book for publication and who contributed many useful ideas in the process.

I wish most particularly to thank George Clements and Sue Massey of the University of Leicester School of Education, for taking endless trouble with my photographs; also Terry Garfield and David Orme of the Geography Department map room, Leicester University, for cartographic advice. Thanks are due to the Geographical Field Group for permission to use materials gathered on our visit to East Africa in 1971; to Shannon Free Airport Development Company Ltd for Plate 7 (top picture); to Mr Joseph F. Grinnell of IDS Properties Inc for the air photograph of Minneapolis, Plate 8; and to the Trustees of the Frederick Soddy Trust for a grant in support of field work in Orkney, 1968, on which the farm study outline on p 216 is based.

10

1 Geography in the Schools

Before starting to discuss any aspect of the teaching of geography in secondary schools, one might ask 'Why teach geography at all?' This leads to other questions: What is geography? What are its limits? What are its distinctive contributions to the process of education?

DEFINITIONS OF GEOGRAPHY

There have been many attempts to define geography, and much teaching, frequently excellent, not based upon any clearly understood definition. Probably it is true to say that all definitions proposed by geographers, as opposed to those suggested by non-geographers and sometimes included in dictionaries, include reference to four things: (1) the distribution of natural and man-related phenomena on the earth's surface; (2) the spatial organisation of such phenomena; (3) location or place; and (4) man-and-environment relationships. No recent definition of geography has even suggested that the subject is mainly descriptive; yet many people still think of it in this way, possibly because of the 'geography' they were taught at school.

Three definitions of geography warrant special attention. Alexander von Humboldt (1769–1859), one of geography's founding fathers, defined his field of study as 'that which exists areally together'. Alfred Hettner (1859–1941) wrote that 'geography is concerned to study the areas of the earth according to their causally related differences'. And in 1925 the distinguished Swedish scientist Sten de Geer defined geography as 'the science of the present-day distribution phenomena on the surface of the earth'.

These definitions, and especially de Geer's, bring out two

11

important ideas. First, that geography is a distinctive way of looking at the earth's surface – the subject has in fact been described as a point of view. Second, that geography is concerned with spatial relationships between surface phenomena, rather than with those phenomena *per se*. In this sense, therefore, geography has no special subject matter. It is to be assigned to the general sciences, such as mathematics, statistics, philosophy and perhaps also history. This freeing of geography from the constraints of narrowly defined subject matter has been crucial to its development.

The geographer studies distribution phenomena: what does this mean? All phenomena on the earth's surface, eg towns, trade routes, tropical forests, either occupy areas or are located at points, or take the form of lines or links between points and areas.

The geographer is therefore concerned to study and explain the position, size, shape, distribution and limits of distinctive areas, and the interactions between them; the position and distribution of points on the surface, together with the nature, size, intensity and value of developments at points; and the position, length and distribution of lines and links of all kinds between points and areas, also the nature, frequency and strength of connections along these lines.

Implicit in such studies is a consideration of events and processes. Thus, a point on the earth's surface may be static, but its relative position may be affected by events elsewhere: the relative positions of New York and Valparaiso changed dramatically when the Panama Canal was opened. Then again, a moraine is produced in a particular place by a combination of physical events and processes; other processes, related to subsequent events, may remove it. Event and process are involved in the explanation of all distributions and areal differentiations, and all relationships along lines.

All surface phenomena exist within and themselves form part of an environment. Thus, development at one point, eg the deposition of a moraine or the establishment of a new town, changes the environment for all other points and also the pattern and strength of lines in that area. The moraine may act as a new watershed and so alter the drainage pattern; some streams may gain in volume, others may be reduced as a result. The new town will probably affect the status of other towns and villages, and produce changes in the transport network. Geography is, therefore, always an environmental study. It deals with surface phenomena in their various settings or contexts, and its method is often to begin with the question, to what environment or context may this surface feature be related?

It is necessary to emphasise that the word environment does not only mean physical environment. School geographers have sometimes fallen into the error of teaching about man's activities as though these were inevitable developments from a physical background; as though, for example, soil types determine types of farming. The concept of environment is complex, and wherever man is involved, it includes items as diverse as custom and tradition, man's knowledge and perception, social and economic policies, as well as physical conditions.

THE LIMITS OF GEOGRAPHICAL STUDY

De Geer's definition is useful here. First it limits the study to surface distributions, and second, it specifies distributions at the present day. Clearly these are guide-lines, not absolute limits. Many surface distributions are largely determined by sub-surface conditions, at least in detail; the distribution of oil wells is an example. They are also affected by – indeed they largely depend upon – the distributions and movements of the atmosphere and oceans. But, as a general rule, the geographer is concerned with these only in so far as they help to explain what is on the surface. In school, discussions of geological, atmospheric and oceanic phenomena need to be related very firmly to surface conditions, and especially to the conditions for man's life and work. To pursue them in too much depth tends to disintegrate the geography course.

It is likewise unrealistic to limit geographical studies completely to present-day conditions. Many surface forms and distributions can only be understood in their historical contexts. But again, the geographer will normally start with present-day conditions, and refer to the past mainly to explain the present.

Teaching Geog
P. Bailey.
Pub. By DAVID & CHARLES. 1971.

Although it is important to have a working definition of geography, this must never be treated as a final and unalterable statement. Definitions are no more than aids to development. In school, pupils need to be introduced to the widest possible variety of explanations. It is probably true to say that, in recent years, geography has suffered in schools because its boundaries have been too narrowly drawn.

GEOGRAPHY'S CONTRIBUTIONS TO EDUCATION

Next one must ask why and how geography should be taught. The answer depends upon the nature of the learning process itself, about which little is known for certain.

The learning process may be regarded as that by which the growing child orders his experience. The infant, so far as we know, at first perceives his environment as total confusion. Very quickly, however, he begins to learn that there is order in this confusion. He perceives that some things are related to others; that people are different from animals and things; that there are different kinds of people, such as family and non-family; and so on. By the time he goes to school, the normal child has achieved a remarkable feat of classifying his environment.

The process of education in school should build upon the child's own mental ordering. Later it helps him to separate the component parts of his total environment and to understand the causal relationships between them, and increasingly it seeks to give general conceptual form to the particular things he learns. In the first place, therefore, much of the child's education needs to be environmentally based. The subjects of the secondary school curriculum arise in part as distinctive ways of ordering the child's environment.

Geography grows from that part of the child's perception of his place in a world where spatial relationships are important. The special educational contribution of the geographer is to begin with the child's spatial perceptions and to develop, systematise and elaborate them.

The process of spatial ordering normally leads the child to discriminate between various classes of phenomena; to perceive

14

that, on those parts of the earth's surface which he can observe, some things are natural and some are not; that certain objects are related to the supply of food, drink, shelter and clothing which he and everyone else needs; that others are related to the movement of people and things; and that others again are to do with work.

An important concept to be developed from this general environmental differentiation is that of landscape. This term is understood to mean everything that can be seen at a particular place. It includes both natural features and those which are modified or made by man. It includes urban landscapes, often termed townscapes.

The interpretation of landscapes is a very important part of school geography. Every landscape may be thought of as a document which can be read, given the necessary skills. Regional geography sometimes begins with, and will normally include, the description and analysis of regional landscapes. The systematic branches of geography, such as geomorphology, economic and urban geography, can be developed out of studies of total landscapes. Studies of processes of all kinds can begin with an identification of their effects on landscapes in different parts of the world.

Pedagogically it is sound practice to use total landscapes as the starting-point for much geographical work, and especially those landscapes which pupils can study at first-hand. It is always desirable to proceed from what the pupil knows and can observe to what he does not know and can only learn about at second-hand.

From this view of geography as a distinctive way of ordering the pupils' experience, a number of teaching principles may be deduced:

Geographical learning and teaching will often begin with landscape interpretation, at an appropriate level.

Geography courses will be designed to develop the pupils' understanding of spatial order.

Their method will be to lead the pupils to order experience for

15

themselves, not to present them with ready-made structures. In the early years of school, say up to age 13–14, geography will be developed gradually out of general environmental interpretation.

This will mean that geographers will need to co-operate with other subject specialists.

Teaching will normally proceed from the concrete to the abstract. General principles and ideas will be deduced from the study of examples.

As the course develops, there will be a shift in emphasis from observation and description towards theory.

The various systematic branches of the subject will be developed from general landscape studies.

Skills used in geography

Like other subjects, geography uses skills which are more or less special to itself; and it contributes to the development of a range of general skills, which are the preserve of no single subject. These general skills include the effective use of language and the manipulation of numbers, drawing, the capacity for oral self-expression and for logical thought. The geographer shares with his colleagues a responsibility for developing these skills in all his pupils, according to their capacities.

Geography has a special part to play in the development of graphicacy, which Balchin has defined as 'fundamentally the communication of spatial information that cannot be conveyed adequately by verbal or numerical means'. Maps are commonly the most efficient way of communicating spatial ideas and information; in no other subject are they so widely used in schools. Map work demands a wide range of skills, the chief of which are the capacity to relate the ground to the map and vice versa, and to translate spatial information and ideas to and from map form.

Closely related to graphicacy are the skills learned in picture interpretation. These are very important in geography teaching; no other school subject makes such frequent and systematic use of pictures of all kinds. Among the visual aids most often used are colour slides, filmstrips, films, printed pictures of all kinds and air photographs. These aids are only effective when the teacher has taught his pupils how to learn from them. The use of illustration in geography is referred to at appropriate points throughout the book.

Numeracy is involved in the skills acquired through the simple statistical methods which are used by the geographer. Cole and Beynon have demonstrated that these skills can be introduced into the junior school, and they are an integral part of all branches of geographical work at the secondary level. It is reassuring to non-mathematicians to remember that statistics are concerned first with processes of thought, and that the handling of numbers comes afterwards. Reference is made in this book to the use of statistical methods, wherever appropriate, as the tools of modern geography. However, it is important to be clear that there is no such branch of the subject as 'statistical' or 'quantitative' geography.

Field work requires another group of skills. In outline these are the observation, recording and interpretation of surface phenomena and associated processes. For work of this kind a large number of practical techniques has been developed. For the teacher, however, field work also calls for quite different skills, those of field teaching and the planning, organising and managing out-of-doors of ideas, resources, equipment and pupils. Field work is a very important aspect of geographical teaching, and Chapter 9 is devoted to it.

THE EDUCATIONAL IMPORTANCE OF GEOGRAPHY

All school work must aim to illuminate the pupils' understanding of the world beyond school. What lessons of importance, related to the problems of living in the modern world, may pupils learn from geography?

The contribution of geography to the process of education may be summarised in a number of distinctive ideas, all of which are important to the education of world citizens. No other subject specialist undertakes to teach these ideas in a structured way. All of them are derived from the interpretation of distribution phenomena over the surface of the earth.

The ideas are expressed as conclusions, which pupils may be expected to draw for themselves as a result of their geography courses. Some pupils will go only a short way towards drawing these conclusions; others will grasp them thoroughly, develop and continually make new connections between them.

All the ideas are interrelated. They have no one starting point and no particular order of importance. No idea can be said to be easier or harder to understand than any other. Each will be introduced many times; it will be developed at different levels and related to different subject matter. The ideas will not be taught directly. Rather, pupils will be given the evidence from which they can develop the ideas for themselves and they should develop many other ideas in the process.

To state the learning objectives of a course in the form of ideas to be understood leaves the teacher free to choose his own subject matter. At present, the structure of examination syllabuses makes this method of course development somewhat difficult; this need not always be so.

Geography's distinctive ideas

1 The physical world is arranged in broad patterns, about which many general statements can be made.

The world which can be directly observed includes a lithosphere, hydrosphere, biosphere and atmosphere. There are distinctive patterns of land masses and ocean basins, of zones of crustal stability and movement, of physical landscape types and landforms, of climate, soils, vegetation. There is also a world-wide pattern of dominant landscape-fashioning processes; for instance, the balance of processes in a hot desert is quite different from that in the humid tropics.

2 The physical forms of the earth's surface have been brought into existence by long sequences of physical events and processes.

Such events include uplift, mountain building, lateral displacement of continents, vulcanicity, changes of sea level and deposition and denudation under varying climatic conditions. Many landforms are therefore visible evidence for the operation of processes which are no longer at work at that place.

3 A theoretical state of equilibrium exists between physical processes and surface forms, and all forms are continually being changed towards this steady state (which may itself change through time).

In the development of a slope, an angle of rest will be reached, given time, at which erosive and transporting processes are balanced by friction, the holding power of vegetation and other stabilising forces. This steady state would appear to depend mainly upon the climatic conditions at a given place. The development of many physical landscapes may be explained partly in terms of adjustment from one steady state to another. The British landscape, for example, is mainly in a state of post-glacial readjustment.

4 All forms of life, including man, are parts of a global dynamic system, related to the inanimate surface, the atmosphere and the oceans.

The geographer's studies of spatial distributions continually point to the interdependence of all parts of this system.

5 There would appear to be a theoretical state of equilibrium, or 'balance of nature', within this global system, and its localised parts.

The nature of this balance has to be understood, at least in outline, before it can be interfered with safely.

6 Only man, of all living creatures, can affect the natural balance deliberately. He is also the most powerful and fast-acting of all agents of change.

7 Man and the natural world cannot help being related.

Man cannot help affecting the conditions of the natural world, even when he intends to do nothing. He may try to maintain an African game park in its natural state and yet produce a disastrous imbalance between elephant population and natural vegetation, indirectly through his conservation measures.

8 Natural conditions for man's life and work vary over the earth's

The geographer in schools has a responsibility to help to create as far as anyone can, a sympathetic understanding of other people + places, + it is his business to try + breakdown parochial attitudes where surface; these variations depend mainly upon world climatic patterns and relief.

A knowledge of these variations is part of the basic grammar of geography – and of world citizenship. The variations have to be understood if man is to make rational use of his environments.

9 In every area, natural conditions present man with a range of possibilities for ways of living, if that living is to be related mainly or wholly to the local environment; but natural conditions do not dictate how man shall live.

The simplest and poorest communities are the most dependent upon their local areas. Today, many communities achieve some freedom from purely local dependence through trade. The environment of technologically advanced, relatively rich communities may be world-wide.

10 As soon as man modifies the natural landscape, he produces a cultural landscape. Cultural landscapes are the imprints of man's ways of life upon the earth's surface. The imprints range from subtle changes in natural vegetation produced by years of bush clearing and burning to the total surface occupancy of the modern city centre.

11 Cultural landscapes almost always include a succession of human imprints or overlays, which are the products of past developments as well as of present conditions.

The older imprints can be interpreted to reconstruct past geographical conditions. Thus, Iron Age field boundaries may persist in modern East Anglia, pre-Norse administrative boundaries may be modern Orkney parish boundaries, and the street plan of a medieval market town may survive in the centre of a modern industrial city.

12 To change or to ignore the natural environment always involves costs, which may be of many kinds.

To change an environment may be expensive, eg to irrigate pastures so as to produce fresh milk throughout a Californian summer drought. To ignore environmental conditions and processes may lead to destruction, eg soil erosion.

13 The use man makes of any part of the earth's surface can rarely be explained solely in terms of natural conditions.

Man's use of the surface is everywhere governed by his knowledge, and especially by his level of technology, his material resources and his desires. The last may depend very much upon a generally accepted or imposed philosophy of life, or a political system.

14 The knowledge and ignorance, capacity and incapacity, aspirations and fears of influential men and women are often decisive in shaping the geography of an area.

We rarely know who makes the critical decisions in an area, or why they are made. Biography is a neglected aspect of geography, as it is of most branches of humane studies.

15 The relative accessibility of a place is always a powerful control upon man's activities in that place.

At present, new motorways are continually changing the relative accessibility of towns, country areas, national parks. Every alteration in air fares changes the relative accessibility of some part of the earth's surface. A longer-term example is provided by the contrasting development of areas of 'Mediterranean' climate, along different parts of the Mediterranean coast and in central Chile, South Africa and Australia. Many of the variations are the result of differences in accessibility, for whatever reason.

16 Past conditions are always liable to affect present-day geography.

The most obvious examples are perhaps the planning problems of large cities, the reconstruction problems of old-established industrial areas, and the social and economic problems of areas of persistent political difficulty, such as the Middle East and South East Asia.

17 Urban and industrial 'street and supermarket' societies are just as dependent upon the natural world as are rural and non-industrial societies.

It is essential that urban people, who are numerous and influential, understand the dependence of their artificial, indirect world upon the conditions and resources of the natural world, and make their political, economic and other decisions accordingly. City and country are parts of one social and economic system.

18 All settlements, from nomadic camps and single farms to major cities, have functions. They are not primarily objects on the earth's surface.

These functions relate to the size, location and spacing of settlements, and also to their historical, economic and social environments. All settlement functions demand space and have spatial effects. Functions often compete for limited space, eg commerce may replace residence in part of a city, an airport may replace market gardens, roads may replace buildings.

19 Movement, of people, goods, services, information and ideas, is necessary to all forms of human development – cultural, social, industrial, political, technological and so on.

Movements of information and ideas are the most important; in a sense, all other movements follow from these.

20 The barriers to free movement of people, goods, information and ideas are primarily economic, political, social and ideological, rather than physical.

Man-made boundaries such as the 'Iron Curtain' may be harder to cross than mountain ranges. Such boundaries and barriers exist within countries as well as between them.

21 The natural resources of the earth must be used rationally because of the limits to their availability.

Supplies of many basic commodities, such as petroleum, are finite. Other resources, such as soils, need to be carefully conserved if they are not to deteriorate. Even the land itself as a resource of space, has to be used with care, because it also is limited in extent.

Two final points concern the geographer's contribution to world understanding. The points are as much ethical as geographical, but only the geographer need refer to them, at least by implication, as an integral part of his teaching. The first point is that all human groups consist of men, women and children much like ourselves; there is always a need to remind pupils that statistics and general statements ultimately mean people. The second point is that no form of society is more or less 'normal' than any other; normality is not to be equated with what one happens to know at first-hand.

The geographer in schools has a responsibility to help to create, as far as anyone can, a sympathetic understanding of other peoples and places; and it is always his business to try to break down parochial attitudes wherever he finds them.

2 Teaching, Learning and Geography

Throughout this book, teaching and learning are discussed together: it is a pedagogical error to separate them. The teacher must always relate the ideas and knowledge he presents and the methods he uses to the learning capabilities of his pupils. It is all too easy, especially for the beginner, to prepare apparently stimulating material, to give oral lessons that are highly competent, judged by adult standards, or to work through a carefully graded sequence of ideas, and yet so to teach that only a minimal learning effect is achieved.

The capacities of pupils to understand ideas and to engage in abstract reasoning develops continuously. In consequence, an idea which is perfectly understood, even obvious to the teacher or sixth former, may be quite beyond the grasp of an eleven-year-old. However clear the explanation, the young learner literally may not know what his teacher is talking about. A year later, he may understand the same idea immediately.

Unfortunately, we still know comparatively little about the learning process, and much of the relevant research deals with children below secondary school age. A further difficulty is that generalisations about the learning capabilities of a large sample of pupils may not be valid for any one individual of that age. In the main, therefore, the practising teacher still has to learn by experience how to correlate his teaching with his pupils' learning capacities.

For geographers working in middle and secondary schools, three things would seem to follow. First, it is important to recognise that a learning problem exists, and to discuss it with other teachers. Departmental discussions about new courses and improved teaching methods are of little value unless they take account of pupils' responses and performance. The question 'Can they learn it?' is just as important as 'What should we teach?'

Second, the organisation, both departmental and whole-school, should make it possible for each teacher to get to know a limited number of pupils really well. It may be an exaggeration to say that one can only teach pupils well when one knows them well; but it is certainly true to say that, the better one knows them, the more effectively they can be taught. This is partly because the process of knowing includes the perception and diagnosis of their mental development and learning problems.

Third, every teacher often needs to question himself: Are the ideas implicit in this piece of work at the right level of difficulty for this particular teaching group? Does the work require a level of background knowledge and understanding which the pupils do not yet have? Lacking this background, will the work appear either trivial or obscure? Only continual self-evaluation along these lines will ensure that genuine communication takes place between teacher and taught.

THE LEARNING PROCESS

From the point of view of practising teachers, the best-known and most useful theory dealing with the development of intelligence is that evolved by Jean Piaget and his followers. Some of Piaget's experiments with young children are very well known, and can be easily repeated; but his voluminous theoretical writings are expressed in a strongly mathematical mode and are difficult for the layman to read. They are seldom consulted by practising teachers. Some attempts to popularise his ideas have been misleadingly trivial. Readable and easily accessible surveys of Piaget's work may be found in R. M. Beard, *An Outline of Piaget's Developmental Psychology for Students and Teachers* (London, 1969) and in M. A. S. Pulaski, *Understanding Piaget: Introduction to Children's Cognitive Development* (New York and London, 1971).

Piaget suggests that children's mental development may be

divided into five stages or periods. The first two, which he terms the sensori-motor and pre-operational, cover the years from birth to seven, and do not therefore concern secondary school teachers directly. Nevertheless, a knowledge of these early stages sometimes helps to explain the learning difficulties of older pupils. In these early years, the child gradually learns to use language and to think about persons and things which are not immediately present. He perceives relationships singly, and makes judgments on an intuitive and perceptual, rather than a logical basis. At this stage, reasoned explanations by adults are liable to go straight over his head. Make-believe play becomes very important, and here we see the natural beginnings of those simulation games which can capture the interest of pupils so effectively in the secondary school and later.

According to Piaget, at about the age of seven the child begins to perform mental operations upon concrete situations. The whole method and scope of his thinking develop dramatically. He becomes capable of abstract thought provided it is firmly related to his own direct experience. Piaget calls this the period of concrete operations, and many secondary school pupils are at this stage of development, wholly or partly. Therefore the geographer teaching pupils in the seven to eleven age group needs to provide plenty of practical experience and factual examples for his pupils. Theoretical explanations will be kept to a minimum. Field work will be related to the local area, to things which the pupils can see, hear, touch, smell, draw, measure. When discussion leads outwards from the local environment, there will be an emphasis upon factual, down-to-earth case studies of actual people in real places, with many illustrations. There will also be plenty of practical work, such as model-making and the preparation of displays.

From the age of about twelve, Piaget suggests, the young person enters the stage of formal operations. Increasingly he breaks free from the limits of his own direct experience. He begins to make generalisations, to consider hypotheses and to reason about things he has never seen. At this stage, it becomes less necessary for all teaching to proceed from the concrete to the abstract, even though it may still be helpful to do so, especially when unfamiliar ideas and material are being introduced. At the same time the absolute need for abundant illustration diminishes, though of course illustration is still useful.

Piaget has provided a theory about the development of intelligence which has many implications for teaching, at all levels. In particular, it permits the consideration of curriculum design in terms not merely of content but of learning. It is very important to realise that the boundaries between the various development stages as proposed by Piaget are anything but clear-cut, and that they may not apply to any one individual. Many children are capable of abstract reasoning before they are eleven; others find it difficult all the years they are in school. Many sixth formers appear to be partly at the concrete operational stage; moreover, they may oscillate from this to the stage of formal operations according to the type of work they are doing, and in response to external conditions, especially personal relationships with their teachers. Confidence and security clearly help most individuals to reach their highest levels of mental operation.

There are no clearly defined guides about how to teach geography to pupils of a given age. The teacher has first to know his pupils, and then lift them by his teaching to the highest conceptual levels they can reach.

Closely related to Piaget's work is that of Gustav Jahoda, who has examined children's concepts of time and space. His work in the early 1960s showed that, for instance, the concept that towns are located in regions, and that regions are parts of countries, may not be understood by children under eleven; yet most geography teachers would probably assume that such relationships are self-evident. In a well-known experiment the children were given a small black circle to represent a town, a somewhat larger white square to represent a region, and a coloured rectangle, larger again, to represent a country. They were asked to place these shapes in logical relation to one another. The older children had least difficulty in perceiving the 'correct' answer. Few below the age of nine had yet grasped the concepts involved, and almost no children younger than eight had done so.

The moral of such work is for the teacher continually to examine his most basic assumptions, especially when working with younger and less able pupils. What 'obvious' relationship is being assumed? What precisely do his pupils understand from his words, maps, diagrams, illustrations? Whenever possible, he needs to test their understanding, preferably by non-verbal means. This applies even at sixth form and higher levels. For example, almost without thinking, the teacher may draw a Burgess-type concentric representation of a town on the board. He may assume that his pupils know what the rings mean. But before going further, it may be worth asking each member of the class to mark the position of their own school on the diagram as applied to their own town. Many may not be sure. Again, a third-year pupil may have learned where to place a dot on a map to represent his home village; but he may not understand why this is the correct position. Presented with an unfamiliar version of the same map, he may be quite unable to place his dot correctly.

VARIETY IN TEACHING METHOD

It has already been suggested that learning may be regarded as an ordering of experience, but this is not the only way in which pupils learn. If a geography course were designed solely on this basis, with a strong emphasis upon carefully graded progressions, it might fail to hold the interest of those pupils who appear to learn by a series of intuitive leaps. Such pupils may infer what a lesson is about from the teacher's first few words, and spend the rest of the time being bored and possibly disruptive. Provision has to be made for such pupils through individual investigations, 'resource packs', even programmed learning.

Again, some pupils find group work frustrating, and prefer to work on their own. Generally speaking they should be allowed to do so, unless the nature of the work demands group co-operation. Others, especially the highly intelligent, may find resource-based discovery learning insufficiently demanding. They may realise that the teacher could tell them in five minutes what they are expected to spend an entire lesson finding out, and so be justifiably impatient with the whole procedure. The problem is always to make the objectives of discovery learning sufficiently stretching.

Key questions for the teacher are 'how quickly can the pupil learn what I want him to know, and what will he do next?' It is important to remember that discovery methods should accelerate and deepen learning, not slow it down.

To teach as though all one's pupils learned in the same way is a grave mistake. As the teacher comes to know his pupils, he learns how to match his methods to group and individual differences, for at least some of the time. Yet again, a pre-condition of success is for teachers and pupils to get to know each other well.

PROBLEMS OF PERCEPTION

Experience, backed by a limited amount of research, suggests that a major problem in making local studies and field work effective is that pupils and teachers often perceive the same environment in quite different ways.

Faced by the welter of impressions in a busy street or an area of countryside, pupils may find great difficulty in separating the various elements which they can see, hear, smell and touch. Furthermore, their perception of the relationships and relative importance of what they observe may differ considerably from their teacher's. The latter, by his training and greater experience, looks at the scene, selects certain features as significant and rejects others. He assigns different degrees of importance to objects and events. Some items are seen as a foreground to the mental picture, others are pushed into a vague background. The pupils will do none of these things unless they are systematically taught how and why to do them.

Sometimes a chance phrase in a composition, or perhaps a drawing, shows what a pupil perceives. Following a visit to the Tower of London, one twelve-year-old wrote that it was 'next to the ice-cream stall where we stopped'. His sense of foreground and background was significantly different from his teacher's. Again, a town transect can impress itself as an endless succession of hot pavements, rather than a succession of architectural 'age-and-function' zones, while a small boy whose consuming hobby is butterflies and moths may notice only that there are Lime Hawk Moth caterpillars on some of the trees.

29

The development of a geographical perception of the local environment is a slow process. It can only be achieved by a continual analysis of one's own assumptions, and by a patient questioning of the pupils to see what they perceive.

Developing the imagination

It has become increasingly common to ask pupils to study socio-economic problems in their local area and in the world beyond as part of their geography courses. Such studies may easily require a capacity, which the pupils do not have at that stage of development, to imagine people, places and conditions of life outside their immediate experience.

For example, if a young person has lived all of his fourteen years in one of the poorer parts of inner London or Chicago, or on a vast post-1960 housing estate, it is very hard for him to imagine what it is like to live in the country. True, he may have seen television programmes about the countryside, but of themselves these are unlikely to convey a coherent, or even a reasonably complete impression of rural conditions. It is even more difficult to imagine and understand the problems of over-population, under-employment, lack of capital investment and under-nourishment which characterise many rural areas in, say, Latin America and Asia. The imaginative leap is far too great. In consequence, a considerable amount of apparently interesting teaching, backed by elaborate resources, fails to involve the learners at more than a superficial level. The pupils just cannot imagine what life in these far-off places is like.

Geography courses have to be designed to develop pupils' imagination; and it is usually wise to delay the study of highly adult topics such as those mentioned in the preceding paragraph until late in the school course. James Fairgrieve, one of the greatest of geography teachers, insisted that the development of an accurate imagination was a vital purpose of geographical education; it still is.

SUB-CULTURAL BARRIERS TO LEARNING

When curricula and courses are being designed, thought is rarely given to the learning problems likely to be generated by sub-cultural differences between pupils and teachers. Do the pupils share their teachers' culture, values, priorities? What are their parents' culture, values and priorities? A cultural gap between teachers and pupils may well be one of the most serious barriers to effective teaching; and it always affects geography teaching, because the subject deals with topics where culture, attitudes and values are important.

It is difficult for the teacher who has always had a comfortable and adequate home to identify himself with pupils from poor, deprived, overcrowded homes – homes which may not always be poor in money terms, but which are culturally restricted, and perhaps disturbed by family tensions. However interesting his courses may seem to be, however attractively presented, they will almost certainly fail to engage the attention of pupils whose thinking is dominated by home difficulties. Neither the geography department nor the school as a whole is equipped to deal with such problems, but it is important to recognise that such home difficulties exist, and as far as possible to bridge the gap they create. Again, the first step is so to arrange the curriculum that teachers and pupils have the chance to know each other.

Rigid attitudes, preconceived notions and prejudice, on the part of parents, pupils and teachers, can also affect learning. Thus, the teacher in an English industrial town may well find that his ideals about a local, national and world-wide multi-racial community are not shared by many of his pupils or their parents. The latter may fear for their homes and jobs, and may have been influenced by racial propaganda. The problem of communication will be increased if the teacher himself has never lived in a multi-racial locality. It thus becomes difficult to design school work which assumes the inherent value of, say, an African culture, and it becomes very difficult to agree about the nature and objectives of planning problems in the local area.

Effective teaching always has to take account of the standpoint of the learner. Therefore the teacher has to find out what his pupils really believe, what they know and do not know, and what prejudices they hold before he can hope to teach them anything

31

which implies values and demands moral judgments. Failure to establish this communication will mean that much geography teaching, about the local environment, the homeland and the world, will fall on deaf ears.

PROBLEMS OF UNDERSTANDING MAPS

Maps are the distinctive tool of the geographer and the basic documents for much geographical teaching; they present pupils with greater learning problems than is generally realised. This section attempts to summarise some of these problems and to suggest ways in which they may be overcome.

Topographical maps, such as the Ordnance Survey 1:63360, 1:50000 and 1:25000 series, and comparable maps in other countries, are very adult documents. They are highly selective and conventionalised representations of the real world, and their interpretation demands of pupils a considerable feat of imagination and the mastery of difficult conceptual skills. It is helpful to start by defining those characteristics of maps which produce learning difficulties.

Selectivity

The selectivity of map makers is often forgotten. No map shows everything; what it shows depends upon the purpose for which it is intended. This selectivity can be a source of bewilderment to pupils, who may find it difficult, for instance, to understand how plain white paper on the O.S. 1:50000 map can be a representation of the cultivated landscape they see around them.

The idea of selectivity and its relation to the purpose of the map needs to be developed systematically. If the map is meant for motorists, what kind of detail ought to be included, and what left out? What details will hill-walkers or mountain climbers need? What information do engineers planning a new motorway need? What sort of map would a mine surveyor require? Would the geological detail of his map be of any interest to, say, walkers or road-builders? This type of discussion, repeated at different levels, helps to impress on pupils the need for selectivity. The principle of selectivity will, of course, be developed when pupils draw their own maps. Left alone, many pupils will try to include everything.

It is a useful exercise for the teacher to consider what the maps he uses with his pupils literally show. For example, a town on a small-scale map will be shown by a dot. What do the pupils 'see' in this dot? Do they visualise the town in the same way as the teacher – its layout, appearance, growth-stages, functions? Have they any idea at all of what it would look like if they actually went there? The answers are almost certainly in the negative in very many cases. Small-scale maps give an extremely skeletal picture of reality, and their full interpretation requires a wealth of background knowledge which pupils do not have. The teacher may be able to visualise what an American Midwest or a Japanese town is like; he has to teach his pupils to make this interpretation in a deliberate, systematic way.

Map conventions

Map conventions, including conventional signs, also pose problems to pupils. One of the conventions that causes most misunderstanding is that of colour. The younger pupils may have no idea why it is logical to show water surfaces in blue: rivers, lakes, marshes and the sea are not generally blue, except in certain states of the light. It is worth noting in this connection that, as far as we can tell from the literature, the ancient Greeks never thought of the sea as blue; why should our pupils? Again, they may see no reason why main roads should be marked in red, or built-up areas in grey. Roads are usually made of asphalt, towns are a variety of colours, certainly when viewed from street level, and they are almost never grey.

It is necessary to develop the logic behind the use of map colours in a systematic way. If we do not use blue for water, what colour should we use? Do we always need the same colour? Suppose we were to use green for water? Surely, green can be used most logically to represent cultivation and plant cover? However, since most of lowland Britain for example is cultivated and we do not want to print green all over our maps, it might be logical to assume that everyone knows this, and to leave cultivated land white: green could then be reserved for special aspects of natural and cultivated vegetation, eg plantations and woodland. The point needs to be established that the uses of conventional colours are decided by a process of discussion and compromise.

Having established the need for a consistent use of colour on printed maps, so that maps from different parts of the world can be compared, the argument has to be extended to include blackboard, whiteboard and overhead projector maps, and to the maps which pupils draw in their notebooks. On the blackboard, a satisfactory convention is to use blue chalk for all water features – sea, rivers, lakes, marshes, canals; green for lowland, and for all details connected with agriculture and forestry; brown for upland and for relief drawing, also for detail connected with animal husbandry; red for settlement details – towns, villages, single houses, and also for main roads; orange for railways, docks, airfields and all industrial and mining detail; white for most lettering; and yellow for anything requiring emphasis.

Confusion can arise over the use of green for lowland on atlas and wall maps. Because most lowland in Britain and other temperate zone countries is cultivated, there may be an unintended transfer of the idea of cultivation and fertility to lowlands in all parts of the world. The lowland parts of the Sahara are green on standard wall maps, for instance, and so are large areas of central Australia. Care has to be taken to show that, on a relief map, colours represent heights above sea level and nothing else.

Relief and contours

The representation of relief by contours implies a whole series of underlying concepts, and many pupils find contours difficult to read, even when they grasp the principles involved. The teacher, schooled in map-reading over many years, may be able to 'see' the relief of a piece of country from a contour map; his pupils, even in the upper sixth, are unlikely to be able to do so, certainly not without studying the map rather carefully. This is particularly the case in country of subdued relief, where the broad configuration of the surface may be hard to discern. In the lower school, many pupils may not be able to see the direction of even the most obvious slopes, without careful study.

The principles of contouring need to be taught early in the secondary school, and regularly reiterated. The use of solid models on which contours are drawn, and perspective drawings which show, say, an island and pieces of country of various shapes and increasing variety are to be recommended. From about the fifth year, the interpretation of photographs by contour sketches may be found useful.

Similar problems occur when the teacher draws contour sketches on the board. He may for instance sketch the site of a settlement using form lines; can his pupils visualise the form of the ground from his sketches? It can be instructive to draw three contour sketches on the board, and ask pupils to match these with three perspective drawings of the same pieces of country; or to have pupils match a contour sketch with a landscape photograph. The task of matching drawing or photograph with sketch-maps can produce some surprising results.

Scale

Another difficult problem is that of map scale. Piaget and others have investigated the average age by which children can understand the idea of scale, and conclude that few can do so until they are at least eleven, and often fourteen. However, if large-scale plans and maps of familiar areas are introduced early, preferably in conjunction with large air photographs (or even photographs taken from tall buildings) then there is no doubt that much younger children can understand the principles involved.

Another aspect of the problem of scale is being able to visualise distances and heights from map reading. This capacity has to be developed gradually over a period of years, and some pupils never get very far with it. One's appreciation of the scale of a landscape is closely related to one's own first-hand experience. Having climbed Ben Nevis, it is relatively easy to visualise what a 1,000m peak in, say, Appalachia would be like; possibly one could visualise a peak twice that height. But it will almost certainly be impossible to imagine what it would be like to live on the slopes of or climb a mountain as vast as Kilimanjaro, the dimensions of which are outside one's experience.

35

When using the atlas, it is often useful to compare distances in other parts of the world with distances at home. Overhead projector overlays which show one country placed over another, at the same scale, can be helpful. Lake Kariba, superimposed upon an outline of southern England, stretches from London to Bristol. North and South Vietnam, placed over the British Isles, extend from Shetland to the south coast. A line showing how far a school bus can travel in a day, when placed over Canada or Siberia or China, can show how enormous these territories are. The problem here is that younger pupils may have little idea how far a bus can travel in a day, so that comparisons of this kind are of limited use.

The teacher has to contend with difficulties connected with the concept of scale throughout the school. Field work is clearly helpful here. If pupils walk a kilometre along a shingle spit, climb a 1,000m hill, walk up a 1 in 4 or 1 in 7 slope, they will gain experience which helps them to visualise the distances, heights and slopes they see represented on maps and photographs.

The overhead view

Perhaps even more difficult is the convention whereby maps show everything as though from directly overhead. It requires a major feat of imagination for pupils to visualise even the area they know well as seen from above and to represent it conventionally. Piaget and other workers have tried to establish the age by which children can grasp the idea of plan. They found that not until the age of about eight could children visualise what objects would look like from viewpoints other than their own; and not until nine could they co-ordinate different perspectives, ie carry out the mental re-orientations implied in the plan view of a whole landscape.

Model-making can be used as an aid to understanding the overhead view; so can air photographs, pictorial maps and perspective drawings, which show as it were a view of the country from a helicopter. But the most important requirement is for the teacher to realise that pupils do not necessarily grasp the idea of the overhead view automatically; many have to be taught to understand and use it.

3 Developments in Geographical Methodology

Since the 1950s, university geography has undergone a considerable transformation. New approaches to the study of the subject have been adopted and developed, and there has been a significant broadening of subject content. The nature of these changes has not always been clear to and comprehensible by teachers in schools. Those who trained before they occurred do not always grasp their significance, and may be apprehensive about them. Those whose training encompassed the changes sometimes fail to see recent developments in perspective, and are liable to set too high a value upon them.

This chapter deals with two questions: 'In what way does the "new" geography differ from the subject as it existed before about 1953?' and 'What significance have these developments for teachers in schools?' The significance of a number of methodological developments is then explored in detail.

It may be added that the choice of significant aspects of new geography is inevitably a personal matter. As yet there is no general agreement as to which of the recent developments are of major and minor importance. In the meantime, schools have to redesign their geography courses so as to take account of changes in the universities. It is hoped that this chapter, whatever its omissions and defects, will help them to do so.

NEW DEVELOPMENTS IN GEOGRAPHICAL STUDY

It is at least arguable that most aspects of the new geography are logical developments from what had gone before. Certainly the origins of some important ideas are to be found in early twentieth-century, or even in nineteenth-century literature. Examples include Alfred Weber's theory of industrial location, which dates from 1909; E. W. Burgess's concentric model of town development, 1927; and Walter Christaller's first statement of central place theory, 1933. These ideas remained latent until changes in the general academic climate, particularly the widespread adoption of scientific method into virtually every branch of knowledge, drew attention to their potential value.

It may also be argued that, for school geography, the adoption of some of the new ideas from the universities represents a return to the mainstream of geographical development, after a lengthy diversion. The period of diversion was characterised by static regional descriptions and a strong emphasis upon memory work, even at sixth-form level. The stock cupboards of older schools still hold large numbers of textbooks from this period, which are regrettably expensive to replace.

Many of the recent developments in geographical thought are embodied in the list of distinctive ideas already considered (pp 18–23). The major developments may here be identified more precisely. Their widespread dissemination from a relatively small number of universities in Sweden, USA and Britain began about 1965.

There has been a widespread acceptance of the view, held for many years by a relatively small number of geographers, that geography is a scientific discipline and that therefore geographers must use standard methods of scientific enquiry to pursue their studies. Research methods widely adopted include the application of statistical procedures, the use of theoretical models, and the formulation and testing of hypotheses.

The view, held by some geographers in universities and by many in schools, that geography holds a 'special position' as a bridge subject between the arts and sciences, has been largely abandoned. The emphasis is now upon developing geography as a distinctive scientific discipline in its own right.

New methods of research have led an increasing number of geographers to express their data and ideas, where possible, in precise mathematical terms, susceptible to statistical analysis. This has led to an emphasis upon measurement, in all branches of the subject.

There is a search for general statements, principles, even laws, some of which may be used for prediction. This emphasis upon what is of general application supplements, but does not wholly replace, the descriptive and analytical studies of particular cases, characteristic of earlier periods.

In every branch of the subject, there is now a strong emphasis upon the study of processes. Conceptually, geography has moved from a predominantly static towards a dynamic view of the world.

Geomorphologists, for example, are now concerned with studies of physical processes, including attempts to measure the rates of operation of such processes, and with the mechanisms and rates of change in physical landscapes. They endeavour to unravel the complex interactions between physical processes of all kinds and the forms of the land surface. Much biogeography is a study of processes and interactions within natural and man-modified environments. In the field of human geography there is now a strong interest in all aspects of spatial behaviour, in movement patterns and changes in spatial organisation. Thus, urban geographers tend to focus their attention upon socio-economic processes and interactions within, around and between cities. They are likely to regard an office block as a traffic generator and a competitor for scarce urban space, rather than as a building.

Studies of man-and-environment relationships have long been a major concern of geographers. These studies have now been extended to include not only physical, biotic, historical, cultural, social, economic and political environments, but also man's own perceptions of his environments, and his consequent responses.

Geographers have become much more aware of the extreme complication of environmental relationships. This heightened awareness is exemplified by the adoption from biologists of the idea of the ecosystem as a vehicle for study. W. B. Clapham defines ecosystems as 'complex self-sustaining natural systems, of which living organisms are parts . . .' The whole world may be regarded as one ecosystem, and whole-world ecosystem studies have lately engaged the attention of many scientists. Geographers on the whole have concentrated upon more limited ecosystem or community studies, and they have attempted to apply the idea in the socio-economic field. They may look at part of a town as a kind of ecosystem, and assess the impact of planning decisions upon it; or they may try to calculate the multiplier effect, in terms of new jobs and services, of placing an oil terminal in a remote Scottish island community, or a new factory in a developing country.

Some geographers have embraced 'general systems thinking' with enthusiasm, and have attempted to apply it in many branches of the subject. In consequence, terms such as 'input', 'through-put', 'output', 'feed-back' and 'black box' (part of a system one does not understand) have lately appeared in the literature. Some geographers find this terminology no help whatsoever in understanding their subject, and deplore its use, except where technically necessary. The view has been proposed that systems thinking offers a way of integrating physical and human geography into one coherent whole, also of relating geography itself to other disciplines. Both views must be regarded as not yet proven. Nevertheless, systems thinking has undoubtedly exerted an influence upon the thinking and perceptions of geographers, and has helped to emphasise the multi-dimensional nature of all geographical studies.

In virtually every field of knowledge, in both pure and applied science, in medicine and in industry, multi-disciplinary research is now accepted practice, and has proved itself highly productive of new insights. Examples abound of problems being solved by research teams, drawn sometimes from a number of widely different disciplines. Thus, historians are now working with archaeologists, psychologists and sociologists to explain the societies of past times. Studies of the origins and diffusions of peoples have been helped by archaeology and also by palaeo-linguistics; and studies by biologists of minute anatomical variations in small mammals in island environments have been explained in terms of human colonisation. Geographers are involved in an ever-increasing number of joint research projects, most notably in the fields of regional and urban planning, and their distinctive contribution is more widely recognised than ever before.

NEW DEVELOPMENTS IN SCHOOL GEOGRAPHY

The new geography is essentially a way of thinking rather than a body of knowledge; it is a distinctive way of handling geographical data, but it is not itself a body of data. The content of a school course in new geography will still arise, as geography has always done, from the study of the world's physical and cultural landscapes, the forms and processes of the natural world, the locations and distributions of human activities of all kinds, and of man's interactions with his natural and cultural environments.

There are a number of characteristic approaches to teaching geography according to the new concept of the subject:

(1) There will be a strong emphasis upon analysis, logical explanation and reasoning, rather than upon description. Description will still be important, but one of its principal functions will be to supply the factual knowledge upon which reasoning can be based.

This emphasis upon reasoning will be complemented by an abundance of work designed to nourish and inform pupils' imagination.

Studies of dynamic processes, interactions, systems, changes of all kinds will be important throughout the course, and in all branches of the subject.

(2) Resource materials and field work will be used to present pupils with evidence, from which they can draw conclusions for themselves.

New techniques of study, eg the use of statistical methods or geological maps, will be introduced in response to learning needs. For instance, the need to extract the fullest possible information from a table of climatic or population data will lead naturally to the teaching of appropriate, simple statistical techniques, in this case the determination of mean, median and mode. Similarly the geological map will be introduced, if possible, so as to explain observations made in the field, or colour slides of landscapes.

(3) Wherever possible, pupils will be involved in the processes of decision-making, through the use of simulation games, role-play, prepared discussions, debates and other pedagogical techniques.

Studies of particular examples will often be related to general statements, general relationships, principles. Thus, a sample study of a Dutch farm will probably lead to a discussion of farming problems and methods in densely populated, highly industrialised countries with high wage-levels.

Studies of particular cases will also lead to the formulation of theoretical models which, where possible, will then be tested and modified. Established models, such as those of Von Thünen, Christaller, Weber and Burgess, will be compared with real situations through field work, the use of maps, air photographs and up-to-date publications.

(4) Teaching will sometimes be structured around the formulation and testing of hypotheses. Hypothesis-testing at simple levels will be a commonly used mode of thought, introduced into questioning and discussion. In a map-work lesson, for instance, one might ask what general statement can be made about the distribution, size and relationship of settlements on the Ordnance map? Is this statement completely true? How can it be modified to take account of the exceptions?

(5) Pupils will be asked to examine social, economic and political conditions and problems in the areas they study, including their own local areas, and as part of their systematic work. Topics such as world population, famine, under-development, conservation, recreation, the human problems of cities, the consequences of technological change, world power resources and demands are likely to appear on the syllabus. Wherever possible, they will be taught by presenting pupils with evidence on which they can work for themselves.

Geographers will be collaborating with other subject specialists in both the humanities and science fields. There may be linked, even multi-disciplinary, courses which will probably be taught by a team of teachers. Geographers will make clearly defined contributions to such work, and not lose their subject identity in so doing.

Unfortunately, it is only realistic to say that, in many schools, the effects of the new approaches are still minimal. There are several reasons for this.

In order to teach geography by these methods, the geography department requires expensive re-equipment. An abundant, or at least an adequate supply of new books, especially reference books, has to be obtained, together with maps, duplicated materials, audio-visual apparatus, slides, filmstrips, tapes and so on. Geographers must establish their claims for these things at a time of unprecedented curriculum reform, when almost every subject department needs re-equipping. Few schools can afford to make a major investment in more than one or two subjects at once.

A block-timetable is also desirable, giving teaching periods longer than thirty-five minutes. Without adequate equipment and time, even the most able and enterprising teacher may be forced back towards traditional methods. In schools where geography has to be taught in non-specialist rooms, without enough equipment and reference material and often without blackout facilities, introduction of the new approaches can be a slow, frustrating and often a hard-fought process.

This struggle has mainly to be carried out in the schools themselves. Help will come from public examination boards as they develop the new approaches in their syllabuses and question papers; but the speed at which they can do this will always depend upon the schools' capacity to follow; and this is substantially an economic matter.

STATISTICAL METHODS

The most publicised development in geography teaching methods has probably been the introduction of statistical techniques. Teachers who qualified in geography before the use of statistical methods became widespread sometimes view their introduction with alarm, and it may be reassuring to remember how old the use of statistics is.

Thus, the Domesday survey of 1085–6 was essentially a statistical compilation, an attempt to obtain comparable data for specific purposes (taxation in this case) from every parish in England. The returns were not of course analysed, save perhaps in very simple ways, until the present century. Again, the word 'statistics' was invented in eighteenth-century Scotland by Sir John Sinclair of Ulbster, the Caithness landowner and agricultural innovator who, among other remarkable feats, organised a survey of every parish in Scotland, using a questionnaire of 166 items. His enterprise is enshrined in that unique publication, the *Old Statistical Account* of 1791–9.

In modern times, geographers have in fact made a limited use of statistics for many years, in climatic and weather studies, for example. What is new is their adoption into virtually every branch of the subject, and the elaboration of techniques which are analytical rather than descriptive.

It is impossible to include an introduction to statistical methods in this book. The beginner is recommended to read S. Gregory, *Statistical Methods and the Geographer* (London, 1963), and to work through the examples.

What uses should be made of statistical methods in school geography? The answer always depends upon the contribution a particular statistical method can make to the development of a geographical idea with a particular group of pupils. There is no all-purpose answer. Above all, statistical methods will never be used for their own sake, in a course whose purpose is to teach geography, not statistics.

The special contribution of statistical methods at the school level is to clarify and give precise form to geographical ideas and information; they can identify patterns and relationships in tables of figures; they can indicate trends; they can test the reliability of statements, hypotheses, impressions, generalisations; they can indicate the importance of chance factors; and they can make the drawing of comparisons and contrasts more exact and therefore more useful.

Statistics are concerned first and foremost with ideas, rather than with numbers. Mathematical forms and procedures are devised to make the ideas operational and exact. In school, it is essential to introduce the ideas well in advance of the statistical procedures; also to check that, when pupils use procedures, which they may do with great dexterity, they really do grasp the ideas involved. Partial comprehension and routine thinking are fatal to the intelligent use of statistics, at any level.

Many statistical ideas are very simple in principle, and can be introduced very early in the secondary school course. For instance, the idea that the sum of, and relationships between, meteorological variables must be considered when the climate of a place is described can be introduced at the very start of a course in world geography. The best way of introducing statistical ideas is by concrete examples, such as a comparison of overall winter weather conditions in Orkney and the northern Aegean, both close to the 4° C January isotherm. Again, a simple piece of field work may introduce the notion of a bid-rent curve, namely that the cost of buying or renting a house or a flat varies in different parts of a town according to a well-defined and explicable pattern.

The level of statistical calculation attempted with any one group of pupils depends upon the teacher's enthusiasm and skill in the appropriate methods, the pupils' capacity to understand, and the time and equipment available. The importance which geographers attach to statistics varies enormously, and it can be disastrous for a teacher who is good at other methods to get himself trapped in statistics, without knowing quite why. Nevertheless, he does need to understand what statistical techniques offer the geographer.

The pupils' capacity to understand statistical work can only be established by experiment. Many of the less academic pupils find it hard to see beyond the figures to the real world which the figures symbolise; and almost all pupils, especially the most able, find lengthy and repetitive data collection boring, and so learn little from it.

Many statistical methods need a lot of time, which is short in most schools. The decision to use them has to be taken in terms of clear advantages to be gained.

For certain statistical methods, special equipment has to be available. The range of methods may be extended if the teacher has access to a desk calculator; an electronic calculator; a desk-top computer; and a computer terminal. Computer access can sometimes be negotiated with polytechnics and industrial concerns. It is worth emphasising, however, that, whatever equipment is available, the teacher of geography will use statistical techniques

45

appropriate to the geographical problems being studied, not those which the machines may seem to suggest.

In the following sections which describe and illustrate a number of statistical methods, the purpose is to provide starting-points for geography teachers who are unfamiliar with statistics, or who are good statisticians but as yet inexperienced in classroom and field work methods. The interdependence of statistical and other teaching methods is also suggested. While the list is not exhaustive there are probably too many types of techniques for use in a single school.

As a general rule, statistical methods are best introduced by an unselfconscious use of facts and figures in geography lessons, beginning in the junior school, coupled with a simple, systematic training in the use of statistical maps, graphs and diagrams. Statistical methods must never be allowed to become a barrier to learning. This means that the teacher has to know about the problems his pupils are likely to encounter in understanding and using numbers, and deal with these in a systematic way, just as he has to know about pupils' difficulties with words; also, that the difficulty and style of numerical language always have to be adjusted to the capacity and experience of the pupils being taught. It is not enough for the geographer to understand the mathematical procedures he uses; he also needs to know something of the methodology of teaching mathematics.

The geography teacher must have the same kind of knowledge of statistical methods as he has about field work methods. It is unnecessary to keep all the details in one's head, but one has to be familiar with what statistical methods are available, and how they can benefit teaching and learning. As one becomes thoroughly conversant with statistical methods, one uses them quite naturally in the normal course of teaching; and their potential contribution will be neither over-assessed nor undervalued.

Network analysis

This technique allows statements to be made about the characteristics of route systems: their completeness and efficiency; the relative importance, and probable loadings upon various parts of a system; the relative accessibility of places linked; and so on. At the present time, the analysis of route networks, by road, rail, sea and air, is becoming more and more important; this is a time of unprecedented mobility, for people and goods. Network analysis is therefore a necessary part of a course in economic geography. A pioneer school text on the subject of road networks is K. Briggs, *Introducing Transportation Networks* (1972). Naturally its ideas have to be integrated into a course by the individual teacher.

To be more than a kind of abstract geographical geometry, network analysis has to be related to actual problems. It can thus be linked with a simulation exercise, related to map work, and followed up by field work.

For example, the railway network in north-east Norfolk at its greatest extent, just before the closures of the late 1950s and '60s could be compared with the network shown on the latest Ordnance Survey map (Sheet 134 – Norwich, scale 1:00000). Pupils may be given the task of planning a programme of closures, designed in the first place to eliminate sections of line which offer less direct journeys to Norwich, the regional capital, than do bus routes, using main roads. In order to do this, they will first ascertain the relative attractiveness of each section of line to passengers who wish to visit Norwich. Working in groups, they construct a matrix which shows the distance of each station from Norwich, compared with the shortest possible main-road distance. Some stations have a positive, and some a negative advantage. The matrix gives a basis for deciding which lines to close first. At this stage, however, other factors have to be considered: what bus services are at present available (consult the local timetable); should a holiday centre keep a railway; do industries need railways? After each group has reported, giving its reasons, proposals can be compared with the actual programme of line closures, the dates of which are shown in brackets on a map.

In the same part of Britain, network analysis may be used to help explain differences in size of population between the various market towns. A topological map of A and B class roads in the Norwich–Great Yarmouth–Sheringham triangle may be constructed. The accessibility of each town from each of the others,

47

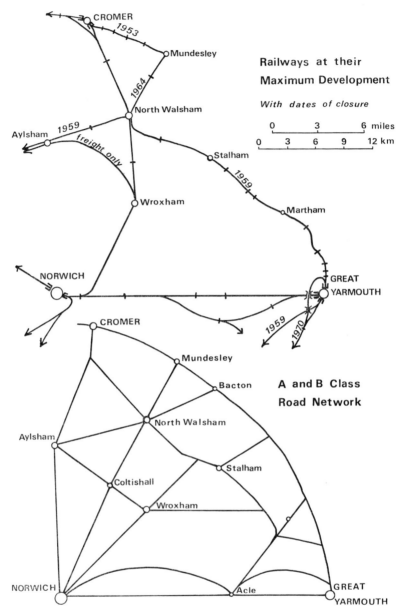

CROMER

Mundesley

1953

1964

North Walsham

Aylsham *1959*

freight only

Stalham

1959

Wroxham

Martham

NORWICH

GREAT YARMOUTH

1959 *1970*

Railways at their Maximum Development

With dates of closure

0		3		6 miles

| 0 | 3 | 6 | 9 | 12 km |

CROMER

Mundesley

Bacton

North Walsham

A and B Class Road Network

Aylsham

Coltishall

Stalham

Wroxham

NORWICH

Acle

GREAT YARMOUTH

Norfolk railway and road networks

expressed as the number of 'edges' one has to travel along when going between them, is next determined, and plotted in matrix form. The degree of accessibility of each town is then placed in rank order, and compared with the ranked table of population figures. Generally there will be a direct relation between the accessibility and size of a town, but there are exceptions, and these make excellent starting points for further work, including field work.

Topological maps

Network analysis often involves the use of topological maps, which show only the relative positions of places and the links between them, exact direction and distance being ignored.

Almost every map drawn on the back of an envelope to show somebody the way has been topological; probably the world's best-known topological map is that of London's Underground. Airlines make frequent use of topological maps of their route systems. In school, such maps can be constructed to show pupils' journeys to school, and parents' journeys to work; to define the characteristics of a regional route and settlement pattern; to analyse bus and rail services – indications of service frequency can be added to the map; or to define the nature of a town's traffic problems. Topological maps can also be drawn of physical features, such as drainage basins, or to show the relationships between landforms.

The transformation of features to topological map form can be instructive. For example, settlements can be mapped according to their travel time apart, at the present time and in the past, by air, land and sea. Old railway timetables can be useful for making such a map. The consequences, in terms of travel time, can be mapped of re-opening the Suez Canal, building a new canal through the Kra Isthmus, or building a new motorway. Travel cost-distances can also be mapped. The countries of Europe or the world can be drawn to a scale related to their populations, or their production and consumption per head of petroleum, or their gross national products. Such constructions are unfortunately time-consuming; often it is enough for the teacher to sketch such a map on the blackboard, as a basis for discussion.

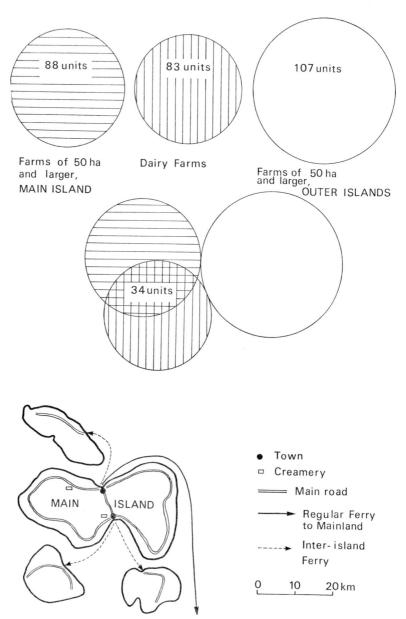

88 units

83 units

107 units

Farms of 50 ha
and larger,
MAIN ISLAND

Dairy Farms

Farms of 50 ha
and larger,
OUTER ISLANDS

34 units

● Town
□ Creamery
═══ Main road
——➤ Regular Ferry
to Mainland
----➤ Inter-island
Ferry

MAIN ISLAND

0   10   20 km

Venn diagram showing the distribution of large farms and dairy farms on the main and outlying islands of a North Atlantic island group, eg Orkney.

Set theory and Venn diagrams

Another useful method of representing geographical relationships is by Venn diagrams. These are really a form of shorthand. They relate to set theory, to which children are normally introduced in their junior schools. The concept of the set is an important one in geography.

An example will illustrate their use. North Atlantic island groups, such as Orkney, Shetland and Faroe, the Aland Islands in the Baltic and other groups, may be divided into a main island, which has regular ferry connections with the mainland, and a number of outer islands, which have less frequent connections with the main island, sometimes interrupted by winter storms. In recent decades, rural depopulation has proceeded most rapidly on the outer islands, where there are many large farms, produced by the amalgamation of abandoned properties with those still inhabited.

On the main island of each group, dairying is possible, to supply the requirements of creameries, which make cheese and other easily transportable milk products for export. Dairy herds have to be large if they are to be economic, so they are only found on the larger farms. There are relatively few large farms on the main island compared with the outer islands, because depopulation has been less serious, and land is more expensive and hard to obtain. There are no dairy herds on the outer islands, because unreliable ferry connections in winter make daily milk deliveries to the creameries impossible.

The relation between farm size, location and possession of dairy herds may be shown in diagrammatic form (p 49).

As with topological maps, it is often quite sufficient for the teacher to sketch a Venn diagram as a basis for discussion, or to have his pupils do this, rather than to spend time drawing it precisely.

Rank correlation

Geographers often find it useful to compare the rank orders of geographical items, as a stage in defining a problem. For example, they may wish to place settlements in rank order according to their

51

population and their numbers of shops, and to see where the two rank orders differ, and why. This kind of comparison can be given precise form by using the Spearman Rank Correlation test, which is described with examples in S. Siegel, *Nonparametric Statistics for the Behavioural Scientist* (London, 1956), 202–13. Two rank orders can be compared at a time; but, when the method is combined with group work, a whole series of pairs can be matched by a class simultaneously, which makes the technique much more useful.

Returning to the convenient example of the Norfolk market towns: these may be ranked for (1) nearness to Norwich; (2) frequency of bus services per week; (3) numbers of A and B class roads radiating from the town; (4) population; (5) numbers and variety of shops – national chain stores, supermarkets, food, clothing and furniture shops, etc; (6) numbers of professional services offered; (7) numbers employed in industry; and so on. Some of this information can be found very quickly from the Yellow Pages Classified Telephone Directory. The number of items considered will depend upon the purpose of a particular lesson.

Spearman Rank Correlation can be combined with group work based on topographical and land-use maps to analyse and compare the characteristics of landscapes in different areas. To return to the example of Norfolk: it has long been traditional to divide that county into a number of 'regions', to which names are attached – the 'Good Sands' region, the North-Eastern Loam region, Broadland. Can these regions be detected by map analysis? Sample grid squares are taken from each supposed region, and relationships between the rank order of a number of items are worked out by the pupils in groups, eg:

1   mean altitude of the highest points in the square
2   difference in altitude between the highest and lowest points
3   numbers of contours crossing the north-south and east-west axes of each square
4   total length of streams shown
5   percentage areas of woodland, parkland, arable, pasture, marsh, waste, built-up area judged by eye

6   number of road intersections
7   number of Celtic/Anglo-Saxon/Scandinavian place names
8   number of primary and secondary settlement names

Comparisons between pairs of variables may show positive correlations between, say, mean altitude and range of altitude; numbers of contours and percentage of woodland and waste; numbers of road intersections and percentage of arable land. Negative correlations may appear for lowland and parks, lowland and settlement and road intersections, and so on. From these comparisons, statements about the characteristics of the alleged regions of the county can be built up. If they are found to exist, one may ask to what extent they are relict features, and this provides a useful introduction to field work at sixth-form level.

Probably the most important point of all, which should be instilled into pupils at every stage in a correlation exercise, is that correlations are not causes, and that, in the real world, causation is always a complex matter.

Product moment correlation

Besides comparing ranked data, it is sometimes useful to find out what degree of correlation exists between two sets of actual data. One may wish to know how likely it is that a change in one set of data is linked with changes in another set; or one may wish to test a hypothesis that two sets of data are, or are not, related. For instance, it may be thought on commonsense grounds that river discharge is directly related to total precipitation over the catchment area; or that coffee yields per unit area will improve and banana yields decrease with an increase in altitude on the slopes of a tropical mountain. Relationships of this nature can be examined by calculating the product moment correlation coefficient of two sets of figures.

This is a fairly laborious test, and is only reliable when proper safeguarding procedures, also laborious, are undertaken. It is first necessary to make sure that the raw data conforms to the normal curve of distribution, and if it does not, to adjust it; this can be done by computer without any difficulty. Second, one has to calculate the statistical significance of the correlation coefficient once obtained, to see whether it means anything. In practice therefore, the technique is unlikely to be used below the sixth form, and then only sparingly. For most purposes, it is enough to introduce the idea of data correlation, and to represent some well-chosen examples graphically. At every stage, it is helpful to illustrate what one is talking about.

Chi square

The study of distributions and their relationships is central to the study of geography, and pupils will be introduced to work of this kind early in their school courses. Map work for instance will often consist of getting pupils to recognise and describe distinctive distributions and of relating one distribution to another.

As far as possible, it is desirable in terms of education, to give this general and mainly descriptive work on distributions a more precise form. In particular, the notion of expressing distributions as percentage frequencies should be developed. Typical questions to be asked are: What is the precise nature of this distribution? Does this pattern of settlements which we think we can detect on the map differ from a random distribution? How certain can we be that these two distributions are related?

Thus, out of a discussion about maps and slides might come the suggestion that, in northern England, settlement density declines at a regular rate with altitude. Is this true? A count of settlements between successive contours in sample grid squares in, say, Cheviot and the Yorkshire Dales may suggest that no clear relationship exists. How then can the strength of the relationship between settlements and altitude be expressed precisely for each area? A discussion of this nature serves to introduce pupils to the chi square test, which allows frequency distributions to be compared, and which therefore has applications in every branch of geography.

The chi square test begins with the null hypothesis. In this case, it would be postulated that altitude does not affect settlement density, and that therefore, in each sample area, the percentage of settlements will be directly related to the area between successive contours. A similar method can be used to study the relation of settlement density to geological outcrops. Chi square can be used to study relationships between two or three sets of frequencies; it can also help to decide whether the frequencies within a sample are likely to be characteristic of the whole population of those items.

Sampling

Pupils need to understand the principles of sampling at an early stage in their geographical education, for two main reasons. First, much geographical information which is presented in the form of general statements is inevitably based upon sampling; second, because only sampling techniques make it possible to make useful statements about large bodies of data, at least in a reasonable time. Among the ideas that should be introduced early are that a sample must be random if it is to be unbiased; that minimum sample size is related to the amount of data being studied; that the reliability of any sample is related to its size, and that bigger always means better; and that, at some stage, the degree of reliability of a sample needs to be tested. Random numbers will be introduced as soon as pupils are able to experiment in sampling techniques.

Sampling is a useful tool for map study. It allows quantitative statements to be made about large amounts of information without the labour of counting or measuring every item. Without sampling, map interpretation has to remain impressionistic.

For instance, sampling may be used to compare the percentage land use of two upland areas, such as Dartmoor and Derbyshire, or two lowlands, such as Norfolk and Cheshire. Such comparisons provide an excellent basis for explanatory studies. In such an exercise, the relative merits of random area, random point and random line sampling will be discussed.

Commercial applications of sampling techniques will be noted at appropriate points in the course, often in the form of a problem. How, for example, can we discover the percentage of useful timber in an area of inaccessible forest in the Canadian Shield? The answer may include discussion of sampling methods based upon air photographs.

Levels of confidence

As part of their thinking about sampling, pupils need to be introduced to the principle of confidence levels, and to the simpler tests for finding out how closely the mean value of a sample approximates to the true mean of a total population. Unfortunately, all such calculations are laborious, and are only worth undertaking when there is a clear geographical objective in view. They might well be appropriate for sixth formers who are gathering data for individual studies at A-level.

THEORETICAL MODELS

A model may be defined as a simplified, schematic representation of some aspect of the real world. Thus a topographical map may be thought of as a model, because it represents the real landscape in simplified and conventional form at a reduced scale. A number of other models have long been familiar to geographers, though the term 'model' was seldom used. For example, W. M. Davis's all-embracing theory of landscape development was a kind of model, which tried to impose order upon the complexities and distracting details of the real world. There were several well-known climatic models, such as Bjerknes's schematic representation of a depression and the 'ideal continent' simplifications found in many elementary textbooks; while Herbertson's scheme of major natural regions was a form of model, at least as important as the Davisian theory of landscape development.

Model-building has lately been developed in many fields related to geography, such as economic forecasting. It has also found favour with ecologists, who in the early 1970s designed models which tried to represent the whole complicated system of relationships which exist between human society and the natural world. These models are essentially mathematical in form, and are expressed finally in the form of graphs. One use made of them has been to predict a general environmental disaster within the next half-century, and to show how this might be avoided.

From the foregoing, it appears that theoretical models are of two main types: those which are descriptive, eg Davis, Herbertson; and those which are predictive, eg the global ecosystem models.

56

In school, descriptive models are far and away the most useful. For example, one may study the development of an industrial city from a rural market town, and work out with the pupils a generalised model of the stages and processes involved. It might be found that, in the present-day townscape, the following components are represented:

1   the relics of a medieval core, consisting of a market place, parish church and possibly a manor house;
2   zones of eighteenth- and early-to-mid-nineteenth-century workshop industry;
3   a discontinuous zone of small factories just outside the central area of the city, mixed with housing;
4   a line of small factories along a canal;
5   railway stations, some disused, of two kinds: those located at the edges of the city when they were built; those built in the city centre;
6   distinctive zones of inter-war and post-1945 municipal and private housing;
7   several former village centres which have been enveloped by the growth of the city; some of these are now suburban shopping centres;
8   an inner ring road and other planning developments.

This descriptive model has several uses. Through working it out, pupils begin to recognise what distinctive areas of the city look like, eg inter-war housing; the model serves as a useful, logical summary of the development of the town, and provides a key to its age and functional zones; and it may be used for comparative purposes when other towns are studied. James Bird's 'Anyport' model, which is an attempt to generalise about the way seaports develop on a world-wide scale, can be used in a similar way as the basis of port studies.

Of the more abstract models, represented by schematic diagrams, the most useful from the schools' point of view are those developed in the socio-economic field and concerned with man's use of space. Most of these models are simple in principle. They may be used descriptively, as shorthand forms of generalisation; or they may be applied in the form of worked exercises on maps and in the field, in which case some straightforward mathematics is necessary. Among the most useful are von Thünen's model of land-use zonation around a town; the town development models of Burgess, Hoyt and Ullman, and some more recent modifications; Christaller's well-known hexagonal model representing the arrangement and hierarchy of settlements on a uniform land surface; and Reilly and Huff's retail distribution models. There are, of course, many others, and the number is growing. The number of simple models so far shown to be useful in schools is, however, very limited.

Von Thünen

Von Thünen, a practical farmer and scholar working in late nineteenth-century Germany, devised a land-use model based on the concept of economic rent. He postulated that farmers normally desire to obtain the maximum return possible from their land, and that this desire, or principle of operation, causes them to do different things in different locations, but mainly according to their distance from market.

Taking the case of an isolated town surrounded by country – south Germany had many such towns at the time – von Thünen suggested that farmers close to the edges of the town would find that they could obtain maximum profit from intensive horticulture and fresh milk production. Nearness to market would enable them to sell their vegetables with minimum waste, while as dairy farmers they would have an advantage over farmers further from town, being able to get their milk to market in good condition. More distant farmers would have to make their milk into butter, because they had no effective means of keeping it fresh, especially in hot weather. Farmers close to town would also fatten livestock brought in from a distance, and supply hay and straw to dairy farms in the town.

Because towns at that time needed wood for fuel, von Thünen suggested that a zone of woodland would be maintained, beyond the zone of intensive horticulture, from which firewood and timber could be transported to the town cheaply by horse and cart. To use this kind of transport over long distances was very expensive. In practice, much timber was moved by water, which was a relatively cheap method, but this was not catered for by the von Thünen model.

Beyond the woodland, von Thünen identified four further zones, in each of which land use was less intensive than the last. The result of this process was to surround the 'ideal' town with six concentric rings of land use.

Although the details have changed, and modern transport, refrigeration, world-wide trading and pricing arrangements and other developments have made von Thünen's isolated town a fiction, his model is still a useful starting-point for land-use studies in the field and from maps. Land-use zones are clearly observable around many towns and conurbations, in many different parts of the world. Questions for the geographer to ask concern the nature of these zones, the reasons why they have come into existence, and how and why they are changing and developing. How and why are zones around one town different from those around another town in the same country? How and why does zonation around British towns differ from that in Canada, or China, or New Zealand?

Von Thünen's was the first of all geographical models. A full discussion of his contribution and its modern implications may be found in W. B. Morgan, 'The doctrine of the rings', *Geography* 58 (1973), 301–12. A worked example which attempts to compare von Thünen's model with actual conditions in County Durham through map analysis may be found in W. V. Tidswell and S. M. Barker, *Geography, A Socio-economic Approach: Quantitative Methods* (London, 1971), 11–12.

Burgess, Hoyt and Ullman

E. W. Burgess proposed in 1927 that, because of the way towns develop (he was thinking of 'western', and especially North American towns), they tend to exhibit five concentric zones, viz:

1   a central business and shopping district;
2   an old-established commercial and small-scale industrial area;

3 a zone of old, low-quality housing;
4 a zone of medium-quality housing;
5 high-class housing.

Even a quick inspection of many towns shows that there is a good deal of truth in this model.

The Burgess model results from a number of social and economic processes, which can be discussed with pupils at a variety of levels, from upper primary school to the sixth form. Aspects of the argument include these: that the most accessible part of a town is its centre, and that therefore shops and services tend to congregate there; that in the nineteenth century (and earlier in Britain), small workshops and factories were built around the original core of the town; and that, immediately outside this zone, low-cost housing was put up for working people, which became substandard by the end of the century. As people became more prosperous, some moved further out of town, helped in their daily journey to work by the developing tram routes. With changing standards, the area of low-cost housing became relatively less desirable, and further migrations took place. In the era of the private motor-car, beginning in the 1930s, large numbers of business and professional people went to live still further out of town, often in large estates of privately owned houses; after about 1960, many went to live in outlying villages. Of course, this simple model seldom closely fits an actual town; the discrepancies are a fruitful basis for analysis and discussion.

Hoyt modified the basic Burgess model in 1939 by suggesting that urban growth was channelled along transport axes and that this produced a series of sectors rather than concentric zones. Ullman (1945) added the idea that many towns have grown around more than one nucleus. Many large European towns, eg Birmingham or Leeds, have incorporated villages in their expansion, and these continue to exist as secondary shopping and business nuclei, with concentric zone and sector development of their own. In fact, most towns include elements of all three models, as well as other modifications.

A combination of field work, map work and air photo interpretation may be used in schools to assess the validity of the Burgess, Hoyt and Ullman models. The interest in such investigations lies in what is actually found and its explanation. It is necessary for the teacher to have a good knowledge of his local area in order to make the most of such studies.

Christaller and Central Place Theory

Christaller, working in the 1930s in a south Germany which was still predominantly rural, was the first to propose a model which explained the spacing, relative sizes and functional relationships of settlements. His work, which has since given rise to an extensive literature, embodies a number of basic ideas, which should be included in a school geography course, eg:

1 Every settlement, of whatever size, requires an area of land to support it;
2 Settlements serve their areas as 'central places', or trade and service centres.

Christaller was thinking in terms of almost self-sufficient village and small-town communities, few of which exist in the technologically advanced countries. Nevertheless his basic idea holds good in principle. In all countries there tends to be a minimum economic area for a farm, and therefore farm buildings tend to be spaced out across the countryside in a somewhat regular way; also the spacing of villages still in some measure depends upon the distances which it is convenient for country people to travel to buy their day-to-day requirements from village shops.
3 On a level and otherwise uniform land surface, with population evenly distributed, and with the movement of people and goods equally possible in every direction, settlements will be regularly spaced. Each village will be supported by and serve its own small area of countryside, each market town will serve a number of villages, each major town a number of market towns; and so on.

All these service areas will be circular, having their central place at the centre. The circular shape makes the central place equally accessible from all parts of its area. However, when circles are drawn in over the whole of a piece of country, spaces are left in

61

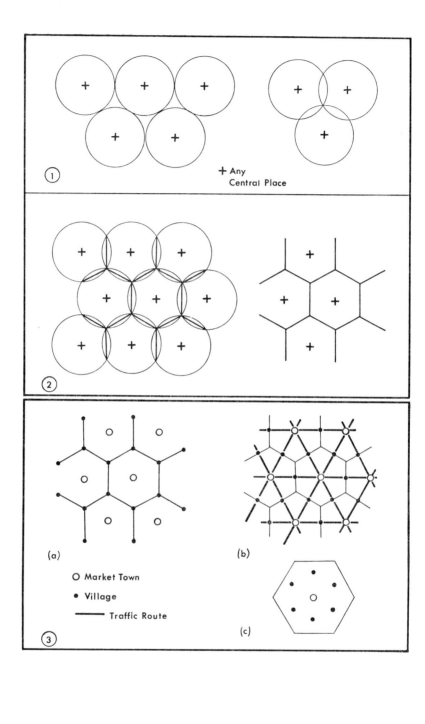

① + Any Central Place

②

③ (a)

(b)

(c)

O Market Town
● Village
—— Traffic Route

between, apparently unserved by any central place. This does not happen in practice, and a more satisfactory representation of reality is obtained by making all the circles overlap. If we then join up all the intersection points of the circles by straight lines, a hexagonal lattice is produced.

The spacing and size of central places, and therefore of the hexagons, will depend upon the density and wealth of the population. Clearly, a sparse and relatively poor population will need fewer and smaller central places than a prosperous population with a high density; also, a highly mobile population, eg a car-owning or a nomadic pastoralist society, will need fewer central places per unit area than one which is less mobile, eg an agricultural society which depends for movement upon walking, bicycles and local buses.

4 Every settlement has functions, which are related to its size.

5 Within a given socio-economic system, every settlement has those functions which it is large enough to support. There will be population thresholds below which, for instance, supermarkets will cease to be profitable and dentists will not have enough patients.

Christaller's hexagons. A uniform land surface, with rural population evenly distributed and movement equally easy in any direction are assumed.

1 Every settlement requires an area of land to support it, and it serves this area as a 'central place'. The most efficient shape for this service area is the circle, with the central place in the middle. Circles will not 'pack' together; spaces are left, apparently served by no central places. This is impossible in reality, so that it is more accurate to let the circles overlap.

2 If all points at which circles intersect are joined by straight lines, a hexagonal pattern of service areas is produced.

3 (a) Where the first consideration is nearness to markets, the most efficient arrangement of villages is at the points of the hexagons. Each village is then equidistant from three market towns. (b) Where the first consideration is to make traffic flows as direct as possible, the most efficient arrangement of villages is to place them on direct lines between two market towns. (c) For administrative purposes, it is most efficient to make all six villages related to each hexagon tributary to only one market town.

The concept that the functions of settlements vary with their size may be illustrated by considering what services are likely to be provided by a village and a major city in Britain and by the capital, London. The country village is likely to have one shop, which sells bread and newspapers, both of which are distributed daily from the nearest town. It will probably hold small stocks of a wide variety of foodstuffs, frozen and tinned, which the proprietor knows from experience that his customers will buy. He will also sell sweets, household items such as soap and other cleaning materials, and some gardening and 'do-it-yourself' items. He will rarely give discounts or cut-price 'offers', because these depend upon a much bigger annual turnover than he is likely to have.

In contrast, a major town of, say, 300,000–500,000 people will have supermarkets and department stores, where many discounts and special offers may be had. These are made possible by bulk purchases and rapid turnover, often in a multiple chain of shops. There will be a wide range of specialist shops, eg furniture, clothing, footwear; one or two bookshops, which require a large population to support them, because relatively few people buy books; and some luxury and semi-luxury shops, such as camera dealers (who may be combined with chemists or opticians, except in the largest towns), radio and television retailers and television rental dealers. There will be several car showrooms. A number of government departments will have regional offices in the town, and there will be a selection of banks, insurance, architects, house agents and legal offices. In addition to its own administrative offices, the municipal authority will almost certainly support a museum, central library with a reference section, a theatre and concert hall. There may be a regional hospital, a polytechnic and possibly a university.

London, at the summit of the settlement hierarchy, has many additional functions. These include parliament; the national headquarters of government departments; the embassies and consulates of foreign powers; the national offices of multi-national corporations, eg oil, chemicals, mining; and the head offices of a majority of all commercial and many industrial firms in Britain.

64

Plate 1 *Town panoramas and old maps are useful aids to town studies.*
(above) *Newcastle upon Tyne 1745 by Samuel and Nathaniel Buck;*
(below) *Thomas Hinderwell's map of Scarborough, 1798.*

REFERENCES.
1 Independent Chapel.
2 Baptist Do.
3 Quakers Meeting House.
4 Methodists Do.
5 News Room.
6 Theatre.
7 Donners Assembly Rooms.
8 Free Masons Lodge.
9 Post Office. on Palace Hill
10 Custom House.
11 Gaol.
12 Old Pier.
13 Locker House.
14 New part of Old Pier.
15 New Pier.
16 North Battery.
17 South - Steel Battery.
18 Cross.

A PLAN of
SCARBOROUGH.
Scale of Chains.

Plate 2 (above) *Composite sketch on the blackboard, summarising landscape components, used in conjunction with slides in a study of the south-west peninsula with a third form;* (below) *analysis of a colour slide, Malvern Hills.*

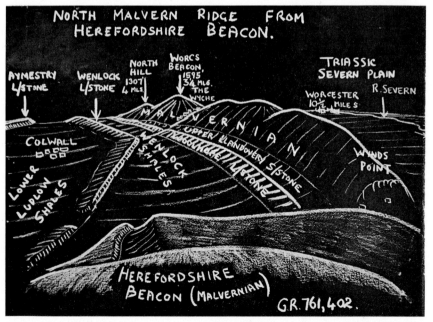

London's shops include some of the country's largest department stores, which sell goods imported from all parts of the world, and a range of specialist shops unparalleled elsewhere. Some of these sell luxury and ultra-luxury items, eg fashion houses, art and antique shops. The city supports symphony orchestras, opera and ballet companies, theatres, cinemas. It has one of the oldest and largest universities in Europe, and equally prestigious medical schools and hospitals, where fundamental research is carried out. Its museums, libraries and art galleries are of international repute.

Christaller's ideas have been elaborated and modified by later workers, notably by Lösch (1954), who redesigned the original model to take account of economic processes and pointed to the probability that 'city-rich' and 'city-poor' sectors would develop in any given region. For a fuller account of central place and related theory, the reader is recommended to consult J. A. Everson and B. P. Fitzgerald, *Settlement Patterns* (London, 1969), 101-11; and R. J. Chorley and P. Haggett (eds), *Socio-economic Models in Geography* (London, 1967), 309-29.

Central Place Theory in school geography

Christaller's ideas and their derivatives can be used in schools in various ways.

There is nothing difficult or profound about central place ideas. They are useful because they help to impose simplicity and order upon a large number of extremely varied and complex items, and they are a guide to questions to be asked about patterns of settlement, as the following suggestions show.

Does the theoretical pattern of hexagons fit the actual spacing and sizes of settlements in a given area, and if not, why not? The distances apart of chosen sets of settlements, villages and market towns for example, may be measured from an Ordnance Survey or similar map, and average distances apart calculated. A hexagonal lattice is then drawn on tracing paper, showing the ideal arrangement of settlements at this spacing. When the lattice is placed over the actual map, correspondence and discrepancy between the model and reality can be identified. Can these differences be explained? It may be possible to establish that discrepancies have been caused by such factors as variations in relief, slope steepness, rock and soil types, availability of water; by the way in which transport networks have evolved; by patterns of land ownership; by the presence and absence of minerals; and by factors which cannot at first even be guessed at. These may turn out to include the locational decisions made by individual entrepreneurs and by accidents of history. Field work may be needed to arrive at an explanation. Clearly, the depth of analysis attempted will depend upon the age of the class being taught, the time available and other circumstances.

Many related questions may be developed out of Central Place ideas, such as: What causes the size of populations of comparable settlements in a hierarchy (eg market centres) to vary widely?

With the aid of the *Automobile Association Handbook* or some other readily available source of population figures, the population of each settlement in an area may be determined. Variations in the sizes of, for example, villages and market towns may emerge. How may these be explained? It may be discovered that some villages have estates of new houses, most of which are inhabited by people who travel daily to work in the town. Other villages may not have any new housing estates, and this may result from deliberate planning strategy. Certain market towns may have attracted industries, while others have not done so. The reasons for these differences may include the availability of mains sewerage at one town and its absence at another, access to trunk roads or railways, or the unpredictable factor of personal choice.

Again, why do the radii or the shape of service areas around central places of a given order of size vary? And, why are there variations in the range of services provided by central places of a given order of size? These questions are likely to arise out of field work and from the study of the classified advertisement pages in telephone directories. Thus, one village may be found to have almost no service area whatsoever, whereas another village of comparable size has a well-developed service function. Or market town A may be found to have a much narrower range of shops and professional services than market town B, though both have about the same numbers of inhabitants.

Variations may be found to depend upon relative distance from a major central place, eg a regional city. Minor central places close to large cities tend to have fewer functions than the Christaller model would suggest; in a car-owning community, they may even have no shops at all, because no village shop can compete at close range with urban supermarkets. Only when increasing distance and therefore costs of travel begin to cancel out the latter's price reductions does the village shop become viable.

Conversely, some relatively small centres far from major central places may be found to have exceptionally large numbers of functions. Examples include Lerwick in Shetland. Kirkwall in Orkney, Thorshavn in Faroe, small towns (pop. 6,000–8,000) which serve island communities remote from major centres – Aberdeen in the first two cases, Copenhagen in the third. A number of isolated cities in predominantly rural surroundings exhibit similar tendencies, eg Inverness, Norwich, Nairobi.

Reilly and Huff

A number of models have been devised to delimit the spheres of influence of towns, as measured through retail distribution. Towns may be said to exert a 'gravitational' pull as market centres upon their surrounding areas, and upon other towns. In general, the power of attraction of a town is proportional to the size of its population; within a single socio-economic system, the relative attraction exerted by a number of towns will depend upon the population of each, and their distance apart.

Where there are two neighbouring towns A and B, there must be a point somewhere between them at which the pull of B begins to exceed that of A: people living farther from A than this point will do their shopping at B. How is the position of this break-point determined? A formula devised by Reilly allows this to be done quite simply:

$$\text{Distance of break-point from town B, where B is smaller than A} = \frac{\text{Distance A–B}}{1 + \sqrt{\dfrac{\text{Population A}}{\text{Population B}}}}$$

Having calculated the theoretical position of the break-point, it can be instructive to take the pupils into the field to find out whether the break-point exists in fact. This can be done by asking villagers in which town they do their shopping. If no clear break-point is found, or it proves to be nearer either to A or B than one expects, then an explanation for this discrepancy should be sought.

A further step can be to delimit the theoretical spheres of influence of a number of towns in a region, by calculating the break-points between them. The resulting map can be compared with reality by, for example, determining the actual circulation area for a town newspaper (information on this may be obtained from the advertisements pages), or interviewing the managers of a number of important shops in each town as to the areas they serve, in terms of customers' home locations.

Similar field investigations can be used to confirm or disprove the slightly more complicated Reilly and Huff formulas, which allow us to determine (1) the proportions of retail trade which two centres may expect to attract from a third; and (2) the probability of a resident in town A doing his shopping in that town, rather than in nearby towns which offer a wider range of shops. A discussion of the use of these two formulas, which involve the time-consuming accumulation of data from directories, bus and rail timetables and maps, may be found in Tidswell and Barker, op cit, 46–7.

Simple models have many applications in school geography, at all levels from the junior school upwards, but it is very important to relate this approach very firmly to reality. It is dangerously easy to over-simplify, to suggest a system of relationships which is so tidy and schematic that it becomes untrue. At every level of teaching we need to stress the complicated nature of explanation in geography.

THE STUDY OF PERCEIVED GEOGRAPHY
Perception studies try to discover how the decisions and actions of individuals and groups are affected by the ways in which they 'see' their environment. Sometimes the results of such studies can

be drawn as mental maps, which show how an environment appears to the person or group being studied. This form of enquiry is still at a relatively early stage of development, and may well prove to be at least as important as the quantitative revolution. Already it has implications for teaching geography in schools.

The importance of considering not only the facts but also people's perceptions of those facts has long been recognised by marketing and advertising experts and propagandists. The advertiser knows that customer behaviour is seldom wholly rational. The customer decides to buy because he has accepted certain facts; there may very well be other relevant facts which he does not know about or decides to ignore. His decision to accept certain facts and ignore or reject others may depend upon his philosophy of life or a set of values or prejudices which are held by the group or sub-culture to which he belongs – or would like to belong.

In short, each individual and group makes decisions and acts within a behavioural environment, the environment in which they believe they live. This important point is often omitted from geographical explanations, which all too easily assume that people respond directly to their phenomenal environment; that is, that they know and can handle all the facts of their situation in a strictly rational way.

The importance of the behavioural environment may be illustrated by considering how a farmer uses his land. His decisions will depend somewhat upon climatic and soil conditions, but they will also depend upon other factors: his knowledge, understanding and assessment of market opportunities – not just those opportunities in themselves; his capital assets and debts, and his skill and confidence in handling these; the availability of various kinds of service and farm subsidy, and his perception of the opportunities these offer; his location, eg within the sphere of influence of a frozen vegetable factory, his acceptance of the opportunities thus offered, and his willingness to make changes in his methods; his knowledge of examples of good farming practice – not just the existence of such examples; his general and technical education – education can be thought of as a filter between the farmer and his environment; if his technical education is inadequate, he may not be able to use the advice and opportunities available; his attitude to risk. All these items and others form part of the behavioural environment in which the farmer lives and works. Explanations of his actions which ignore such items will always be more or less inadequate.

Perception studies are clearly important when industrial location and regional development are being considered. Attempts by the British government to attract new industries to the North-East face the problem that many southerners have never visited northern England and visualise it in ignorance and to its detriment as a wilderness of gloomy mill-towns. Official publicity has therefore shown a tendency to concentrate upon the nearness of the proposed industrial areas to areas of great scenic beauty, such as the Lake District and Hadrian's Wall; these in fact are just as untypical of the northern region as mill-towns. A similarly selective picture has been given by Australian government literature intended to attract immigrants. There are many more examples from all parts of the world.

In many cases, it may be assumed that explanations of industrial location have to take account of the perceptions of influential men and also of their wives. Such information is difficult to obtain. It is to be hoped that many more case-studies of industrial locations which include a biographical element will appear during the next decade.

The Australian seaport capitals

Some interesting examples of the effects of the knowledge and perceptions of influential men upon the location of cities have been given by Professor James Bird in his studies of the Australian seaport capitals. In these cases, the events happened quite recently and were well documented, and – unlike many sources on industry – the information is accessible for study. Moreover, except in the case of Melbourne, the initial settlement location was selected by one individual.

Brisbane, for example, now has its central business district hemmed in by a meander of the Brisbane river. Because of this,

70

there are many bridges and much rush-hour traffic congestion. These difficulties may be attributed ultimately to the founding of the city in 1824 as an offshoot colony for second offenders from Sydney.

John Oxley, then Surveyor-General of New South Wales, was instructed to find a site from which escape to the interior would be difficult. Perhaps he did not obey his orders fully, realising that the future of Australia was more than that of a convict colony. At all events, despite his instructions to the contrary, he placed the new settlement where *access* to the interior was easy, and he seems to have been aware of this fact. He did, however, choose a site from which immediate *escape* was difficult, inside a bend of the river, and this is now the constricted business centre of Brisbane.

The location of Adelaide was decided by Francis Light in 1836, and his field notes and maps, all of which survive, record his observations and reasoning in detail. In this instance, the government in Sydney had instructed Colonel Light to find a site which gave access to the interior through the Mount Lofty ranges. Light believed there was a natural routeway inland from the site he selected, but in fact there is not. Thus the city of Adelaide was founded partly in response to perceived locational advantages which did not exist. Nevertheless the settlement stayed where it was. Governor Hindmarsh asked permission from the British government to relocate it on the coast, but this was refused on grounds of cost, estimated at £200,000 – an immense sum in present-day values. Light's initial decision proved to be irreversible.

One is reminded here of the attempt to move Sydney, which also proved abortive. Only two months after the initial settlement at Farm Cove in 1788, Governor Arthur Phillip realised that a site at Parramatta, on level ground at the head of Port Jackson, would be much more convenient, and he asked permission to move the settlement there. This also was refused on grounds of difficulty and cost. So Sydney grew on the south shore of Port Jackson, which soon became a major obstacle to land communications northwards.

Many decisions about location must have been based upon incomplete information, or upon misconceptions about the layout of a piece of country. One suspects that similarly uninformed decisions are being taken today, by industrialists, economists, planners, government agencies and so on; and also by pupils' parents when they plan their holidays or move their homes from one part of the country, or even of the same town, to another. The study of perceived geography is fascinating and important, and it begins in school.

Perception studies in schools

It can be highly instructive to the teacher to map his pupils' perceptions of their local area. Almost always, a surprisingly restricted and selective perception will be revealed, even among older pupils, and the pattern may be affected by the pupils' socio-economic class and other factors. The information thus obtained can be helpful to the teacher for a number of reasons. Teachers often refer to local examples when discussing far-away places and systematic themes, believing that by so doing they are giving added reality and interest to their lessons; but this may not be so. Many pupils may not know the local examples referred to. Again, it is easy to assume that local studies will build upon the pupils' first-hand knowledge; this also may be incorrect. They may know almost nothing about their local areas as a whole, and have thought very little about what they have perceived.

For example: the central business district of the local town may be mentioned: do the pupils know which part of the town the teacher means? Some may seldom or never go to that part of town. If they do, they may not perceive it as a 'district', with a definite area and boundaries; they may know only certain shops, a cinema or two, a discotheque, the ice-rink, football ground and other places of amusement. The need to introduce the local environment in a systematic way, and to work on it subsequently through maps, illustrations and field exercises, is thus made clear. It can be instructive, for example, to ask pupils to identify slides of different parts of their own town, and to map the results; to do this for successive age-groups, and different ethnic groups in multi-racial towns; and to map those parts of a town pupils say they visit regularly, and the routes they use.

More generally, explanations of geographical phenomena will take account, where possible, of the existence and power of behavioural environments. Physical conditions alone, such as relief features, soil quality, the distance from one place to another, are probably never adequate to explain man's use of any part of the earth's surface. Of themselves they do not explain the location of settlements, either small or large, the location and development of manufacturing industries, or the alignment, development and present use of transport routes, and they should never be taught as though they did.

SIMULATION GAMES

Another significant development of the 1960s was the introduction of simulation gaming into all levels of geographical teaching, from the university downwards. These games require students or pupils, suitably briefed, to act out roles in a developing situation and to make decisions.

Simulation games have their ultimate origins in adult games such as chess, which call for powers of analysis and synthesis, an ability to think ahead from an existing situation, to anticipate the probable actions of opponents and foresee the consequences of alternatives, and to evaluate the pros and cons of alternative courses of action one might take. Their more immediate ancestry includes war games and business games. War games were developed to train German officers in tactical decision-making before the 1914–18 war. They have since been widely adopted and applied to the study of decisions of all kinds, including strategic decisions at the highest level. It is said for example that the Japanese general staff played out an elaborate military-economic war game before deciding to attack Pearl Harbour, and that this showed that the long-term consequences of such an attack would be victory for the United States and its allies. Presumably they had good reasons for ignoring this prediction.

Business games developed rapidly following the widespread

introduction of computers. In the so-called office game – there are many varieties – business executives are placed in separate booths. Each represents a company whose start-of-play specifications are known in detail to its 'director'. A stream of information is then fed to the executives, about market conditions, wage demands, technological developments, capital availability and cost, decisions by competitors, changes in the law, chance factors, and so on. Each executive makes decisions for his company, the consequences of which are worked out in relation to everyone else's decisions by the computer, for the short-, medium- and long-term. Some companies make fortunes, others go out of business. Participants find this game a powerful teaching tool.

An early geographical game, perhaps the best-known, was *Railway Pioneers*, developed by Rex Walford, and published in his book *Games in Geography* (1969), 64–76. In this game, groups of pupils act as boards of directors of railway companies who are building westwards from Chicago in the nineteenth century. They play on a map of the United States, which is divided into squares; a building cost is allocated to each square, depending upon its relief. Major rivers are marked, and crossings have to be costed. Chance cards feed in additional information, about natural disasters, relations with the Indians, financial crises, cattle booms, government policies and regulations, and give a cost to each, for each company. The cost can depend upon the stage of building reached, capital assets and decisions already made. A dice is thrown by each 'board' in turn, and its score translated into moves on the map. Chance cards must be picked up after every round. The game helps to teach pupils the general geography of the western United States, and introduces them to some factors in the choice and development of transport routes.

The educational effectiveness of this or any other game depends on three things. First, it must be related to the rest of the geography course – games played in isolation can be of little value. Second, the lessons learned from the game need to be made explicit. Third, the game must be realistic. *Railway Pioneers* is good in this respect because it is based upon actual events in railway history. There is a very real danger that games will deal with imaginary situations, of no educational worth. Games which have been devised and used successfully in schools explore various kinds of problems.

Man-and-environment games

The most frequently used are variants of the farming game, which can be adapted for use anywhere, at many different age-levels.

Groups of pupils represent individual farmers, all with farms of the same size. Each 'farmer' (ie the group) must decide what crops to grow, and in what proportions, in an unpredictable climatic situation represented by throws of the dice or chance cards. He has a range of possible crops; the yield of each varies with different climatic conditions. Thus, crop A does well in a warm, wet year, crop B needs cool, wet conditions, and crop C will be more profitable than either should the year be hot and dry, but may fail completely if it is wet. Over a period of, say, five years (five rounds), each farmer attempts to make the highest possible profit per unit area. Success and failure are measured by farm balance sheets. Market conditions, changes in transport costs and other factors can be introduced into this game as extra variables.

Man-and-environment choice games have been based upon the way of life of social and ethnic groups. A good example is the *Karamojong Grazing Game*, devised by Norman Whiting. The Karamojong are a pastoral group living in Uganda. Each player represents a herder whose aim is to increase his herd. The game is played out on a map of Karamojong territory, and the players plan grazing routes based on their knowledge of local environmental conditions. The game thus has a skill element, but chance factors are also introduced; for instance, a herder may lose cattle through drought or disease, or through attacks by predators or cattle-raiders. The effects of over-grazing are simulated by restrictions on the re-occupation of an area, and aspects of social behaviour are introduced, eg a family has to pay ten cattle as bride-price on the marriage of a son. There are few rules, but if the need for more is felt these can be devised by each group of players. The definition of rules serves to focus the players' attention on the reality that the game is representing.

Search games

These introduce pupils to the processes by which resources, whose exact location is unknown, are found. A well-known example is Rex Walford's *North Sea Gas*. Groups of pupils represent exploration companies with certain capital assets. Their basic information is a map of the North Sea divided into concessionary squares, and a gravity map of the same area. First the companies bid for drilling concessions, then they have to decide how best to proceed. They may, for instance, buy or hire a rig. Three types are available, with different capabilities and at different costs. Within their concession areas, they must select squares in which to drill – only the umpire knows which squares contain gas. When drilling starts, chance cards are introduced to simulate weather hazards. Gas is struck, and the umpire tells the company the value of its find. The next decision is whether to lay a pipeline to bring this gas to a shore terminal, or to sink further capital in fresh drilling, in the hopes that a more profitable find will be made. The aim of each company is to make the highest profits over a given number of drilling periods (rounds).

Best-location games

These require pupils to find the optimum location for a specified industrial or commercial enterprise, such as a steel works. A good example is *Location of the Metfab Company* in the American High School Geography Project.

In games of this type, pupils usually begin with a map which shows where raw materials and markets are located, and the available transport routes, by river, canal, rail, road. If import and export are involved, the location of a port may be shown. The costs per unit distance of moving each raw material and finished product by each transport method are given. Costs of improving transport facilities may be requested if necessary. The task is to work out a location for the enterprise which achieves minimum cost at the market for the finished product.

76

A variant of this game is to consider best-locations at several different times, eg a steel works in Britain in 1890, 1930 and 1975, and within different socio-economic systems, eg a Soviet Russian and a North American capitalist environment as with Metfab.

Development games

These games deal with the mechanisms and problems of regional development. Teams of pupils are given information about the existing situation in a region, untapped resources, costs of development and capital availability and costs. They are asked to work out a rational plan of development over a number of years. As they proceed, they find that decisions already made begin to constrain later decisions.

A straightforward example is the *Kuwait Development Game*, devised by Jack Hodgkins. The oil resources of Kuwait may run out within a short period. Meanwhile, oil revenues yield an enormous income. Pupils are given the problem of investing this income in capital works so that, when the oil is exhausted, Kuwait will be an industrially and commercially developed area. They work with a gridded map of Kuwait, and can find out the costs of roads, port works, industrial plant, hospitals, schools, hotels and so on from reference materials. Suggestions are costed and mapped. The game is not competitive, but the plans worked out by different groups in a class can be discussed with profit.

At the university level, J. P. Cole has devised a massively documented development exercise for Peru. Students receive a 60-page briefing. Peru is then divided into twenty planning regions, and the development of each of these, and of the country as a whole, has to be planned up to the year 2000.

Town building games

These are closely related to development games. An early example is *Portsville*, part of the American High School Geography Project. Pupils work in groups to model a typical North American town, starting from the initial pioneer settlement and adding buildings of various types, railways, a central business district which continually wants to expand, new roads, suburbs, and so on. A handbook describes the town at successive periods, and says what has to be added.

Portsville is a distinctively North American town, but the idea can be worked out for any part of the world. A British example is *The Growth of an English Industrial Town*, in R. Dalton *et al*, *Simulation Games in Geography* (1972). Town development games can be used to consider problems of urban re-planning, the probable development of a Burgess-type concentric town in the 1970s, the location and design of new towns, and so on. Very simple applications, such as how to develop a village so that the new inhabitants feel part of the community, take little time and can be extremely valuable.

Games about routes and journeys

Many games have been devised which are based upon network analysis. They deal with such concepts as relative accessibility, the connectivity of networks, route efficiency, the 'friction' of distance, urban hierarchies and their relation to route frequencies.

Examples have been developed which study topics such as the effects of building a new bridge or motorway upon the relative accessibility of towns; planning delivery routes, eg for travelling shops in a rural area, for a team of doctors and nurses serving a sparsely populated region, or for a national supermarket chain which distributes items from one or two centres; planning export routes, using different means of transport for different routes and different goods; planning bus routes in town or country; and working out minimum-distance shopping routes through a town centre, so introducing ideas about optimum location.

Diffusion games

These are not so much games as demonstrations of the operation of chance in the development of distributions, especially those which involve man.

For a number of years, geographers, along with archaeologists, market research specialists, historians, management consultants, biologists, epidemiologists, geneticists and other workers have been greatly interested in problems of origin and dispersal. There has been much debate about such questions as to where man originated on the earth, where he first learned to cultivate crops and domesticate animals, where various human groups originated, eg the Finns, Amerindians, Australian Aborigines, Basques, how the Polynesians peopled the Pacific islands, and by what mechanism El Tor cholera spread from Celebes to Russia and Spain in the decade 1961–71.

On a highly practical level, there has been much concern with studies of the diffusion of innovations, and barriers to diffusion. In a world where many people are poor, technology is still primitive over wide areas, and population is increasing, we urgently need to know how best to disseminate ideas about, say, improved agricultural and irrigation techniques, population control, hygiene and diet through large populations; how to diffuse educational ideas through school systems; how to redesign business and government organisations so that they become more receptive to change. None of these problems is specifically geographical but, because all diffusions include a spatial component, geographers are legitimately concerned with them. The intrinsic, practical importance of diffusion processes suggests that they should certainly be referred to in school courses.

Much of the work done on diffusion in school will be descriptive; examples of diffusion processes and problems will be introduced and discussed by teachers with their pupils. However, something of the 'feel' of diffusion problems may be brought home to older pupils by the use of simulation games.

Theoretical models on which diffusion games are based derive mainly from the work of Torsten Hägerstrand in Sweden. Much of his early work was descriptive, like that of geographers, eg Carl Sauer, who preceded him; but, after about 1967, he began to stress the regularity and order of diffusion processes, and suggested that they might be represented by operational models, from which eventually predictions might be made. This line of thought led Hägerstrand to apply Monte Carlo simulation techniques to represent the spread of an innovation from a point of origin. Monte Carlo simulation is a method of showing how diffusion might occur through the operation of agreed rules and constraints, combined with chance. A fully worked out example, applied to the development of the city of Adelaide, may be found in C. A. Forster, 'Monte Carlo Simulation as a teaching aid in urban geography', *Geography*, 58 (1973), 13–28.

The following example shows how a simple diffusion simulation may be designed to demonstrate the problems which arise when large numbers of townspeople decide that they would prefer to live in the country and travel to work each day by private and public transport.

A large-scale map of the area, eg the Ordnance Survey 1:63360 or 1:50000 map, will first be used to identify areas likely to attract people from the town. The level of discussion will depend upon the age-level and the amount of time available. It may be developed to include work with slides, house agents' advertisements, population figures, details of shops and other facilities in the villages, the location of doctors' surgeries, bus and rail routes and frequencies, and so on.

Questions likely to be raised are: what do people expect to achieve by moving their homes out of the town? Will they tend to favour existing villages, or wish to build isolated homes away from villages? What might be the advantages and disadvantages of each type of location, and for which groups of people? Will private builders prefer to build estates of houses, probably attached to villages, or single homes? Is there likely to be a price differential between the two, and if so why? Will access to main roads be important? How far will people be able to travel to work in the town each day? Is their journey to work to be measured most realistically in distance or in travelling time? Will the existence of public transport be a locating factor, especially for one-car families? What public and private services already exist in the area, eg doctors, shops, travelling shop networks, milk deliveries, and will these be able to cope with increased population? This discussion will continue until a clear picture has been built up of the probable requirements of families who wish to move out from the town and the effects of such a movement. This will be recorded, in note and map form, on tape or by other means.

The pupils next work singly or in pairs. Playing the part of a

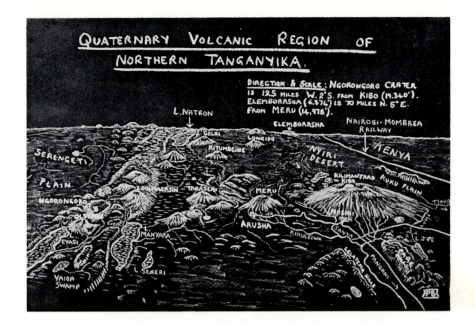

Plate 3 *Panoramas drawn from maps bring out essential features which many pupils find it difficult to 'see' from the relief on the map.* (above) *Northern Tanzania;* (below) *the physical site of Newcastle upon Tyne.*

Plate 4 *Sequential blackboard drawings can illustrate the physical processes of glaciation and post-glacial change in an upland area.*

family, each selects what they regard as the ideal site for their new home. Some may decide to try to move into the country, some may prefer the suburbs, others may decide to move as close as possible to the town centre. Their choices will be marked on the map. This constitutes Round 1. The process will be repeated, with the pupils representing new waves of home-seeking families who soon find that they have to take account of homes already established when making their choices. The questions likely to arise concern the allowable density of housing per unit area and the means and justification for preventing large numbers of people congregating at the most attractive rural spots, and so spoiling them – in the opinion of some people – for everybody.

At about Round 4, a 'firm' of speculative builders may be formed by a group of pupils; the firm will select a village for large-scale expansion. The pros and cons of allowing them to do this will then be discussed, and the need for a general planning strategy brought out. The teacher will point out that mains water and sewerage plant are unable to cope with the increased numbers, and that expensive new improvements will have to be financed out of the rates. In successive rounds, further attempts will be made to expand villages and to build estates on the edges of the city.

The simulation may be continued and elaborated as appropriate. It may be useful to discuss the problems likely to be produced by a severe winter, by a sharp rise in petrol prices and by the virtual extinction of country bus services.

This discussion illustrates the necessity for a thorough 'debriefing' of pupils after all simulation games. In this case, the teacher might go on to discuss the planning strategy actually decided upon for this area of country, and to examine its justification. In countries where planning responsibility rests ultimately with the people's elected representatives, it would seem important to involve school pupils in the discussion of planning procedures. However, a final word of warning is necessary.

In order to be manageable in schools, simulation games have to be relatively simple, but they always represent a reality which is extremely complex. This simplification can be socially dangerous when simulations deal with questions, such as urban planning, which have social and political implications. Unless they are handled by a teacher who is thoroughly informed about the social, financial, technological and other aspects of the problems being studied – and this is very difficult to achieve – such exercises tend to convey misunderstandings and prejudices rather than the truth.

Thus, a study of urban motorway construction solely in terms of improved accessibility to the central business area of a city may easily amount to social and economic nonsense. In order to introduce pupils to the full range of decisions which have to be made, such a study must consider the socially divisive effects of re-locating 'inner ring' communities in distant parts of the city and demolishing their houses. The displaced people may view the consequences of the planners' decisions as a species of official vandalism which they are powerless to prevent, and it will not be altogether surprising if their children then indulge in vandalism in school and elsewhere. It may be impossible to quantify social 'costs' of this kind, but one feels that society ignores them at its peril.

It is always necessary to avoid facile simplifications, whatever one's teaching method; but it is especially important to do so when using simulation games, because they can strongly involve the emotions of the pupils.

4 Running the Geography Department

It used to be common in secondary schools, in Britain and elsewhere, for geography to be taught by one specialist teacher, possibly helped by non-specialists in the lower forms. The geographer planned, taught and examined his courses, and made his annual requisitions, with little reference to anyone save the head of the school, who evaluated his performance mainly through public examination results.

Small schools and one-teacher geography departments still exist, but they increasingly tend to find themselves parts of linked systems of schools, eg middle and upper schools, or schools for 11 to 16-year-olds followed by sixth-form college. Because they are parts of a system, they have to develop professional links with the other parts of that system, at whole-school and departmental level. Failure to do this impairs the efficiency of all the schools and departments in the system. Thus, even in small schools, the day of the isolated specialist teacher may be said to have ended.

In many areas, comprehensive reorganisation has produced very large schools, of 1,000 to 2,000 pupils and sometimes larger, with a hundred or more staff – staff numbers depend mainly on the size of the sixth form. These large schools may be in specially designed buildings, but more often they make use of old buildings, sometimes on multiple sites. In large schools, the former geography specialist is replaced by the geography department, a team of teachers led by a head of department who holds a recognised place in the administrative structure of the school. He is not only a teacher but an organiser and manager of staff, pupils and resources, and has tasks to perform which were unknown in small schools.

If the head of department is to perform these tasks effectively, he himself, his head of school and his junior colleagues all need to recognise their relationships and duties clearly.

The head of department has to build his team into an effective teaching unit. The head of school has to allow him sufficient non-teaching time to carry out the managerial tasks this involves. Junior members of the department have to learn to accept tasks delegated to them, to work as a team, and above all, to communicate with each other about what they and their pupils are doing.

The new British comprehensive schools are non-selective in pupil entry. Their aim is to provide a worthwhile education for all their pupils, with every kind of background, ability and life expectation. Increasingly they also try to teach pupils of all abilities together for part of the time, instead of separating them into streams, bands or sets, based on ability. These developments imply wide variations in curriculum content and process within the one school, and they create formidable problems of organisation and management which must be solved before the school can fulfil its teaching function effectively.

In this new situation, one which is still unfamiliar to a great many teachers, the head of department and his team have organisational and managerial tasks to perform in five areas: staff deployment, coupled with staff development; pupil deployment; teaching organisation; resource procurement and deployment; monitoring pupils' performance.

STAFF DEPLOYMENT AND DEVELOPMENT

In small schools, it was and sometimes still is the practice for the head to deploy the whole staff through the timetable. This is unsatisfactory in a large school, because the head cannot possibly know the potential of every staff member. Certainly he cannot know their potentials as specialists. Heads therefore, tend now to agree broad matters of policy with their senior staffs, and then ask departments to undertake the tasks of detailed deployment themselves. Each department is given an allocation of time, space, staff and pupils, and asked to make its own timetable within the general school framework. The method is not confined to large schools, but it is most clearly necessary there.

Staff deployment within a department tends to be a delicate matter, and it is necessary to decide what one's objectives are. Any department of more than one person must include teachers with varying degrees of subject competence, varied teaching experience, and a wide range of professional strengths and weaknesses, in class-control and adaptability, for example. Perhaps the most important objective in deployment is to make the best possible use of staff knowledge, experience and skills.

The teaching strengths of individuals have to be matched with the various teaching situations found in the school. It is a truism that every teacher teaches best in his own best ways; but the head of department may well find that some of his own and his colleagues' 'best ways' are not appropriate to certain groups of pupils with whom they have to deal. Therefore he will have to find ways of extending their repertoires of 'best' methods. A second, most important objective is therefore to increase the professional range of each departmental member.

A third objective is to facilitate the continuous exchange of ideas and information within the department, about geography, about developments in pedagogy and the practical matters of day-to-day teaching. The head of department has to ensure that such exchanges can and do take place and that they involve all members. An increasing number of schools arrange departmental meetings fortnightly or monthly, and incorporate them in their timetables. Departmental meetings are particularly important where members teach in widely separated buildings and rarely meet in the course of their work.

A common problem in geography departments is how to introduce older members to the ideas and approaches of post-1960 geography teaching. A complementary problem is how to help junior members, trained in the new approaches, to relate these to their pupils' capabilities and to re-appraise what is valuable in the older approaches in the light of their more recent experience. The ideal arrangement is to bring about a two-way exchange of ideas and information, about 'new' geography on the

85

one hand and real-life pupils on the other. The head of department is responsible for seeing that this happens.

Building the departmental team

To an increasing extent, heads of departments are now being asked to help in appointing new staff to their departments. A school head will normally ask his head of department to specify the kind of person he needs to strengthen his departmental team, and he may also arrange, in consultation with the governors, for the head of department to be present at the appointment interview. In such a case, it is necessary for the head of department, in consultation with his colleagues, to draw up a job specification for the desirable candidate. In a growing and evolving school, this specification will indicate how the job will probably develop in the future. The specification needs to be sent to all members of the appointing panel.

It is still somewhat unusual for job specifications to be drawn up in schools, except in a very general way, though it is fairly standard practice in industry. In fact, it is possible to set down the attributes of the person required, and even to mark each applicant for each attribute on a five-point scale. The following points may be found helpful in drawing up a job specification; the weight given to each item will depend on the school.

1 Details of the teaching to be done: teaching organisation, eg sets, mixed-ability classes. Teaching methods to be used, eg resource-based learning. Ages and characteristics of the pupils. Objectives and content of courses. Time allocations.
2 Desirable qualifications. Is a brilliant academic needed, able to stretch a sixth form aiming towards university entrance; or is a good all-rounder needed, with a general, rather than a specialist degree, a non-graduate rather than a graduate?
3 Is specialist competence within the field of geography required, eg in biogeography, statistical methods?
4 Desirable teaching experience: is it necessary to recruit someone with experience in non-selective schools, with mixed-ability classes or immigrants?

5   Competence in class-control, and capacity for forming good relationships with colleagues and pupils: every department will have its views on these matters.
6   Familiarity and sympathy with the conditions, problems and objectives of the kind of school and department to which application is being made.
7   Desirable contributions to the school outside the classroom, eg outdoor activities.
8   The appointing committee's attention might be called to marks of special distinction in applicants, eg publications, courses attended since initial training.

PUPIL DEPLOYMENT

The way in which pupils are deployed always affects the ways in which they are taught. Thus, the skills required to teach homogeneous groups are substantially different from those needed to manage mixed-ability groups. The department has therefore to consider its deployment policy in relation to proposed and feasible teaching methods.

Schools can deploy their pupils in several different ways, and it is important for the subject specialist to know about these, and to consider the relative advantages and disadvantages of each, in the setting of his own particular school.

It used to be common to stream pupils according to their ability. This is still widely done, even in schools which are termed comprehensive. Pupils are, however, seldom if ever streamed according to their ability in geography; the usual criteria are mathematics and English, possibly some kind of intelligence test, and junior school head's reports. A stream may very well turn out to be a mixed-ability group as far as geography is concerned. Nevertheless, streaming is likely to have an effect, in that it tends to be self-fulfilling. The performance of a pupil may agree closely with what is expected of the stream he is in.

To avoid this self-fulfilling tendency of streaming, many schools adopt various forms of setting. For example, a grammar school may deploy all its pupils in alphabetically arranged 'populations' for work in most subjects; and then group them into sets for certain subjects, based on ability in those subjects. Such sets normally include mathematics, modern languages and science, but rarely include geography. In consequence, geography and other unsetted subjects may be regarded as of low status, by pupils and staff. When this kind of arrangement is combined with certain kinds of option system, in which pupils have to choose certain combinations of subjects for advanced work, the geography department may find itself attracting mainly the less able pupils. It will need to combat this tendency by excellent teaching, and by informing pupils about career openings for sixth-form geographers.

Partly because of this unintentional devaluation of certain subjects by partial setting, some schools form sets for almost all subjects, including geography. This produces much pupil movement about the school between lessons, and usually means that nearly all teaching is done in general-purpose classrooms, with specialist rooms – such as geography rooms – being reduced to a minimum. It also tends to prevent the formation of closely knit groups of pupils, because the composition of every set is different; yet the closely knit group with whom a teacher has excellent relationships is the most effective teaching group. All methods of grouping have their consequences for the geography department and for the whole school.

The present trend, however, is away from groupings altogether and towards the formation of mixed-ability classes. Within such a class, each pupil follows a programme of work which is adapted to his particular needs. The teacher now becomes a class leader, a tutor to individuals and small groups, a planner of learning situations, a deployer of resources, a final arbiter in matters of discipline, noise and movement, sometimes a link between the class and the world outside school.

Mixed-ability teaching is, without doubt, the highest form of the teacher's art, and is extremely difficult to do well with the size of class normally found in secondary schools. A department which intends to adopt mixed-ability organisation needs to consider most carefully what this involves. The staff concerned must have a very thorough and flexible grasp of their subject and of ways of teaching it; they must be prepared to devote almost unlimited time to resource preparation, especially in the first run-through of the course; and they must spend time mastering the organising and managing skills needed to establish and then develop learning situations. The question of resources always has to be studied with particular care, because, unless resources are adequate in quantity and appropriate in form, mixed-ability work cannot succeed. Enthusiasm for the method, though laudable, is not enough; capital investment is also necessary.

It is always necessary for a department to cost the implications of major innovations in its courses and methods of work. This costing takes the form of a detailed analysis of the amount of preparation time and what resources each new course will require, and how these demands will affect the department's existing programme in the school. It is helpful to work out the total work-load for each member of the department in a number of specimen weeks. This kind of detailed costing is unfamiliar to teachers, but it has to be done if a department is to make a balanced contribution within the school, and introduce innovations without overloading its members.

TEACHING ORGANISATION

The diversity of pupils in a comprehensive school at once poses the questions of what kinds of courses should be provided, and how should they be taught.

For many years, geography teaching in secondary schools has been powerfully affected by public examination requirements. This is still the case in the new comprehensive schools, which feel impelled by parental, pupil and other pressures to show that they are at least as good at academic work as their selective predecessors. In consequence they sometimes overstress examination performance in their first few years of existence, and subject departments feel themselves constrained in all aspects of their work, not only in their examination classes.

One of the undesirable effects of public examinations has been to prevent geographers from thinking out, from first principles, the educational reasons for teaching their subject. An extraordinary uniformity of courses and methods has been the result. Faced with the syllabuses of the Ordinary and Advanced levels of the General Certificate examination, the average geography teacher, and especially the newcomer to the profession, is so fully occupied in trying to cover the ground prescribed as to have little time for fundamental thought about the justification of what he is doing. But in the comprehensive school, this fundamental thinking simply has to be done. Many pupils – perhaps half – are so clearly unsuited to courses based upon any kind of public examination, as at present constituted, that quite different kinds of courses have to be devised. Questions of the kind raised in Chapter 1 have to be answered in the context of that particular school: What has geography to offer the less able pupils? How can it be taught to those who read and write only with great labour, and whose span of concentration is only a few minutes? Failure to think through these questions usually results in watered-down examination courses being offered to non-examination pupils, with discouraging results for all concerned.

It may be decided that, for many pupils all the time and for some pupils some of the time, geography will be linked with other subjects. When joint courses are offered, it is necessary for geographers to think out the distinctive conceptual contributions of their subject, and to relate these to the contributions of other specialists. The only satisfactory basis for a worthwhile 'integrated' course is co-operative work by specialists.

Where large schools are divided into several more or less autonomous parts, eg lower, middle and upper school, or where several schools are grouped into a linked system, the objectives of teaching geography at each stage have to be defined. This requires consultation. Without it, pupils may come up from the lower school inadequately prepared for their examination work; or the lower school may feel itself unduly constrained by ill-defined examination demands from above. The repetition of almost identical field work in successive years is another obvious hazard.

First year courses in non-selective schools have to be diagnostic. The capabilities of each pupil have to be assessed by subject departments, so that appropriate kinds of learning experience can be provided later on. Clearly, the course taught during this diagnostic period must be the same for all pupils, and its content and method need to be thought out with especial care. Ideally, it will develop from work already done in junior schools, and it will lay foundations for more systematic work later. Above all, it should stretch the pupils in a variety of learning activities and skills.

RESOURCE PROCUREMENT AND DEPLOYMENT

It is convenient to distinguish between two kinds of resources: internal and external. The latter include various kinds of help obtainable from commercial firms, libraries, museums, record offices, embassies and national travel information offices, travel agencies, teachers' centres, banks, regional planning boards, and so forth.

As teaching moves away from oral exposition towards group and individual learning, resources become more and more important. Books are still the most valuable resource of all, and reading is still arguably the most important skill our pupils need to learn at school. Access to a well-stocked school library is therefore a most important requirement. Unhappily there is a tradition in some schools of using the library as a teaching room. Geographers are likely to suffer particularly from such arrangements, because of their very heavy demands for reference material. Geography room libraries suffer the disadvantage of being inaccessible, except to the class using the room at the time; they are no substitute for a large, accessible central library.

A crucial management problem is how to make resources and equipment available yet secure. To solve it, many schools are developing centralised resources centres, under the control of a full-time director, who is also a qualified teacher and librarian. Such centres contain books, pamphlets, photo-copied materials, tapes, filmstrips, slides, all properly indexed, together with apparatus for their use, eg hand-viewers, tape recorders with ear-phones. Where a lot of audio-visual apparatus is used there may be a technical assistant to support the director of the centre. Under these circumstances, the geography department has to decide what items should be kept within it for regular use and what material should be stored in the central resources area. As a general rule, the movement of delicate and heavy apparatus, such as a slide- or overhead projector, should be kept to a minimum.

Within the department itself there are three principles of resource use. First, resources needed for each part of every course have to be worked out in detail well in advance; second, there has to be a long-term plan for procurement and resource preparation; third, resources have to be deployed systematically.

Part of the departmental costing operation already mentioned consists in identifying the resources needed at each stage of each course. It is helpful to plot the requirements of each course week by week on a flow chart; this will show at once where conflicting demands are likely to occur and the programme can be adjusted accordingly. The flow chart will carry such information as the latest dates by which key items have to be procured; the latest dates by which one member must finish with a certain set of books so that another member may have them; dates on which outside speakers, films and the school lecture theatre have been booked; and so on. The chart is useful for other administrative purposes: as a reminder to members of meetings and examination dates, dates and times of useful broadcasts, and so on. By revising the chart as term proceeds members can keep in touch with departmental work as a whole.

An important task of the head of department is to make requisitions. Normally, items have to be ordered under a number of standard headings: books, stationery and materials, apparatus and equipment – the exact headings vary between different education authorities. The head of department must know what items are included under each heading. For example, it is likely that wall maps will be classed as equipment, while Ordnance Survey maps will be regarded as stationery, and therefore expendable. Money earmarked for use under one heading cannot be transferred to another, nor can money granted for one year be carried forward into the next. Invoices received by the education authority after the end of the financial year are charged against next year's requisitions; hence it is advisable to order items as early in the year as possible.

Long-term planning is necessary if full value is to be gained

STAFF	MONDAY	TUESDAY	WED'DAY	THURSDAY	FRIDAY
		Faculty mtg *4.15 Rm 7*	*Geog Soc 1.20* *(Film Matter-* *horn)*	*Students meet* *KR 10am*	
KR			OHP *Periods* *2 and 4*	ATLAS *Set 2*	HIGH VAN-TAGE STUDY *(if fine) pm* COACH
PJF	*Film – Tribe* *that Hides* *from Man* *Yr 1 periods* *1, 3, 4*			LAKE DIS-TRICT MAP *Set 1* *5th GCE*	
DJG		*Film, Yr 1* *periods 1, 2, 5*		RESOURCE PACK 3B *for 3rd yrs* *periods 6 and 7*	
MB	LOCAL STUDY (if fine) *Yr 4 all pm* *GCE sets* *KR and* *student help*		*Film, 6th* *Form-* POST!		
BMH					*6th Form* *Simulation* *Exercise* *Development* *of the* *Camargue-* ALL WELCOME

Fair copy of a departmental organisation chart for one week, 8-form entry comprehensive school. Each staff member enters only those requirements which are exceptional or crucial to the success of his/her teaching. Routine requirements are not entered. Members know each other's timetables in broad outline, and which years and classes each one teaches. Information is written on cards, which are attached to the chart with plastic adhesive.

from departmental funds, which are always limited. Given a clear policy for the procurement of expensive items over a five-year period, a department can build up its resources quite rapidly. Piecemeal requisition year by year is always a mistake.

In a large department, it is sometimes difficult to achieve complete requisition. Cases occur of departments forgetting to order enough projector bulbs to last the year – some authorities only allow requisitions to be made on certain dates, say twice a year; or of underestimating for film hire, so that an important part of a course, based on a film, has to be abandoned. It is helpful to have one member of the department responsible for checking the adequacy of spare-part and 'software' requisitions, eg duplicating paper, stencils, sound tapes, and recording their use throughout the year.

Resource preparation, such as the making of audio-visual aids, is a major departmental task. All resource-based teaching relies for its success upon the appropriateness of the resources used; this means that teachers themselves have to prepare a great many resources, because the published items are rarely just what are required.

The aim of resource-based teaching is to give pupils starting-points in a network of resources, from which they can advance at different speeds towards common goals. One effective way of doing this is to prepare worksheets, which contain a certain amount of basic information and lead pupils forward to specific references in books, to maps, duplicated extracts, articles in magazines, mounted and labelled pictures, tapes, filmstrip pictures, slides and so on. To be effective, worksheets have to be written with specific groups of pupils in mind, and they have to be continually revised to incorporate new ideas and information.

The number of worksheets prepared in a large department in a year can be very large and storage becomes a problem. This is probably best done by boxing them in class sets and treating them as books. A departmental album of all available sheets acts as an index.

Partly because of the reading difficulties of many pupils, it is necessary to build up a departmental resource bank which appeals to pupils in other than literary ways, and a fair proportion of the departmental budget has to be devoted to this purpose. Illustrations are especially important for all kinds of pupils taking geography and a collection of labelled pictures mounted on card is a most valuable resource. Pictures can be stored most conveniently in a filing cabinet. The preparation and use of other types of teaching materials will be discussed fully in Chapter 8.

The larger the department, the more individualised and resource-based its teaching becomes, the more closely the work of its members interlocks, the more necessary it is to reduce the handling of major resources and apparatus to a system to which all members adhere. The flow chart, whose uses in planning have already been noted, can be used to record the week-by-week use of resources and apparatus. It is helpful for all members to note on this chart what items they are using or are about to use; also items that they had been forecast to use, but do not now require. The *immediate* reporting of faulty apparatus is also essential.

The purpose of systematic deployment is to make maximum use of the resources available. Without a clear-cut system there will be under-use because members will never be sure where anything is.

MONITORING PUPILS' PERFORMANCE

This is not a matter for the geography department alone, but it is so important that it seems necessary to mention it briefly. However the school is organised, and whatever its teaching methods, it must always be the teacher's responsibility to know how each pupil is progressing. Clearly, where large numbers of pupils are being taught by teams of teachers, this becomes difficult. Various forms of communication and record-card system are to be found in the schools. Some centralise their record-keeping procedures in houses or other forms of pastoral unit, but departments usually have an important part to play in gathering the necessary information, and they may indeed have a primary responsibility for record-keeping.

As a general rule, record systems have to be simple if they are to work, and it is therefore necessary, both at the departmental and whole-school levels, to decide what items of information about pupils' performance are really important, and then concentrate on obtaining these. The temptation to elaborate the information-gathering process is to be firmly resisted.

It seems sensible that the school record system should enable the following basic information to be known:

Was the pupil present or absent at a given time?
What work was he set, on what dates, by which member of staff?
Was this work done to an acceptable standard?

If not, what action was taken, and with what result?

Has the pupil any special learning problems, eg poor reading, frequent absences; is he a recent transferee from another school, perhaps another country?

Is he being a 'problem' to his teachers, and what is being done about this?

The attendance record of every pupil is contained in the school registers. The additional and more personal information listed above will be noted by individual teachers. In a large department, or in a teamwork situation, it is very important that this information be exchanged regularly, so that an overall picture of the pupil's performance is built up. Discussions about individual and group progress will normally occur at departmental, team and/or faculty meetings. Such discussions will, of course, deal both with geographical and more general matters.

It is important that members of a department plan in advance what work they will set, especially homework; what its quantity will be, and by what dates they will expect to receive it. It can be helpful to show this information, in outline, on the departmental flow chart. Variations from the original outline will also be recorded in cases where other members of staff need to know about them.

In their role as personal tutors, teachers will also observe the amount and timing of work each pupil in their charge is required to do in, say, a week or a month. From time to time, it will be necessary to consider the matter of set work at the whole-school level, and geographers, along with other subject specialists, may then be asked to justify the nature and quantity of work they set, and to decide their priorities if the total amount has to be reduced.

Teachers sometimes think of record-keeping as a time-consuming chore. However, as schools become larger and more complex, and teachers begin to work in teams which straddle subject boundaries, it is necessary to replace the memory of the individual teacher by an information system. This is especially the case in a period of high staff mobility like the present. Only with proper records is it possible to achieve a continuity of learning experience for the pupils.

5 Planning the Programme

When the contributions of geography to education have been defined, at least in an interim fashion, in the context of a particular school, and the administrative framework within which the geography department has to work has been analysed, work can begin on planning the teaching programme.

This planning operation falls into four stages. First, the syllabus has to be written. Essentially this is a specification of what the pupils should know and be able to do at the end of the course. Second, a course plan has to be drawn up; sometimes this is termed a teaching syllabus. This describes the ways by which the desired destination, identified in the syllabus, will be reached. A third stage is to break down the course plan into a series of teaching units. The fourth stage is to plan individual lessons.

THE SYLLABUS
Purposes and objectives

As a first step, the educational purposes and objectives of the geography course as a whole have to be set out. These purposes and objectives will be related to the purposes and objectives of the school as a whole.

Purposes and objectives – that is, long-term and short-term, easily measurable or observable goals – will be of two kinds: those which are specifically geographical, and those which are more generally educational. To write a syllabus purely in subject terms is always a mistake; teaching one's subject is only a part of the work of a teacher. For example, in many schools, and with certain groups of pupils, a first consideration will be to encourage pupils to express themselves orally, and to develop a reasonable level of literacy; the work in geography will be designed to help these things to happen. Sometimes, parts of a course will be specially designed to teach pupils to work on their own; this will determine what teaching methods are used, also the content and form of the syllabus. Again, in some schools, the socialisation of pupils may be considered particularly urgent, and departmental work will be designed to foster close and secure staff–pupil relationships and opportunities for different kinds of practical, co-operative work.

The geographical purposes and objectives of the course will be expressed in terms of the ideas, knowledge and skills that pupils will acquire. It is hoped that the discussion of the theme Why teach geography at all? in Chapter 1 may help teachers to define their purposes and objectives in their own particular situations.

Syllabus preamble

It is always useful to set out the purposes of a course in the form of a syllabus preamble. This document has three important functions, in the school as a whole and within the department.

First, the preamble is a statement to the head, the rest of the staff and possibly the pupils of what geography is all about, and what its distinctive contributions are to the work of the school. This statement is often badly needed: regrettably, many heads and teachers still think that geography is a species of low-level guide-book subject, lacking in intellectual rigour.

Second, the syllabus preamble is important whenever geographers collaborate with other specialists in team teaching and joint courses. Such courses are fashionable, and providing they have a well thought out theoretical basis, they would appear to be a necessary part of the curriculum for pupils of all abilities. They are, however, complementary to, not substitutes for, geography courses. It helps all concerned if the geographers, along with other contributing specialists, set out in principle what they have to contribute to the joint course.

A third function of the syllabus preamble is to keep the objectives of the various geography courses clearly in view. This is important, for, once term starts, teachers are usually so busy with day-to-day tasks that they may lose sight of longer-term objectives. The preamble also helps to maintain continuity of approach between different members of staff, and it is useful to non-geographers who may be drafted in to do some teaching in the department. It can help to reduce the disruptive effects of staff turnover. If the preamble contains references to teaching methods, it reminds staff to vary their methods sometimes. It is all too easy, in the midst of a long and trying term, to fall back upon one or two standard methods of teaching, and a list of possible variations, readily available, can be useful.

The following suggests a possible form for a syllabus preamble:

I The purposes of teaching geography in this school are:
1 to arouse and train pupils' perception of and interest in those features of the earth's surface broadly termed geographical; that is to say, those concerned with places, distributions and areal differentiations, spatial relationships and man-environment systems;
2 to teach pupils to observe and interpret natural and cultural (man-modified) landscapes at home and abroad;
3 to show pupils ways of observing, classifying, relating and measuring (as appropriate) the phenomena of the earth's surface, and of relating these phenomena to their various contexts – physical, biotic, economic, social, technological, political, historical, etc;
4 to establish the concept that, in the landscape, objects are always the products of events and processes; and, that all phenomena of the landscape, physical and human, are in a state either of dynamic change or dynamic maintenance;
5 to study the local area and home region, in the field and with large-scale maps and reference materials, to demonstrate general geographical principles and to give pupils points of reference for world-wide studies;
6 to extend this local work into a study of the homeland, viewed in its world context;
7 to show how systematic studies arise from general studies of total landscapes;

8 to study world geography, that is to say the local, distribution, areal differentiation and interactions of surface phenomena on a world-wide scale;

9 to demonstrate relationships between spatial and other kinds of phenomena, eg historical, technological, cultural; having regard to Mackinder's dictum that 'geography is a standing protest against the disintegration of culture'.

II Points of practical detail requiring constant attention are:

1 in each year of the course, and with each group of pupils, a balance will be maintained between the gathering of facts, the development of thinking in various forms, and the enrichment of the imagination;

2 a balance will also be maintained between the various parts of the subject. However, with certain non-specialist, non-academic and remedial groups, most work will be related very directly to the theme of urban living, and based on local examples;

3 the first three years of the course (ages 11–14) will be strongly man-centred, and will be based upon descriptive and simple analysis of man-environment systems in various parts of the world;

4 a good English style will always be required. Credit will be given for neatness, correct spelling and punctuation, clarity of writing, keeping to the point;

5 pupils will be required to draw and think about clear, simple, purposeful sketch-maps. An agreed uniform style of mapping will be used by staff and required from pupils;

6 audio-visual aids will be used as appropriate. Their primary function is to transform learned fact into shared experience;

7 statistical data, eg climatic information, will be plotted in ways which will facilitate the comparison of sets of figures;

8 the globe, world map and atlas will be continually used, to stress the point that ultimately all geography is world geography;

9 teaching methods will be varied, but not unnecessarily so. As far as practicable, each part of the course will be taught by the most effective method available.

THE COURSE PLAN

In a small and homogeneous school, there may be only one course, which is followed by all pupils; but in a large comprehensive school, several quite distinct courses will have to be planned in order to implement the syllabus. These courses will be of various lengths. Some will run from the first to the fifth (examination) year. Others will be designed for pupils who take no public examination. Others again will be completed at intermediate terminal points, dictated perhaps by pupils' choices of subjects within an option system. In every case, it is necessary to be clear about who the course is being planned for, what its objectives are, how long it is to be. Ideally, every course mounted by a department will make good geographical sense within itself, whatever its length, and this is possible only if courses are thought out in terms of ideas and skills and not merely of content.

It seems attractive to suppose that, with a great deal of hard work and patient experiment, it would be possible to break down the conceptual structures and ideas of geography into a sequence of steps of graded difficulty, and then to relate these steps to precisely defined stages in pupils' mental development. In fact, this is very difficult to do, may well be impossible, and the wisdom of trying to do it at all may be doubted. There are two main reasons for this.

First there is the obvious difficulty of arranging the very diverse ideas of geography into any kind of order of difficulty. However, the ideas associated with a specific topic within one of the branches of the subject might be so arranged. For example, it is clearly possible to arrange ideas contained in a step-by-step explanation of the formation of a moraine in a logical order (not necessarily *one* order), and to do this at several levels of difficulty. But it would seem to be impossible to arrange ideas about moraines and industrial location on a single continuum of difficulty.

Second comes the even greater difficulty of defining precisely what kinds of ideas and concepts can be grasped by pupils at certain ages. It has been the experience of practising teachers for many years that almost any geographical fact or idea can be introduced at virtually any stage in the school course, provided

101

only that it is treated in an appropriate way; and on this very point, Jerome Bruner wrote in *The Process of Education* (1960) that 'the foundation of any subject can be taught to anybody at any age in some intellectually honest form'. There is a third objection to the notion of a course designed to match precisely defined stages in mental growth, namely that it would severely restrict the freedom of teachers to teach and of pupils to learn, in their own ways and at their own best speed. Both would be made subject to a tyranny of average performance.

The abundant evidence for the self-fulfilling tendency of streaming warns us of the danger of categorising pupils on any theoretical basis, whether of ability (however measured) or of age. There is indeed some evidence to suggest that children up to the age of about twelve years have much more difficulty with abstract reasoning than they do a year or so later. For this reason, it has been suggested that geography for these younger pupils should emphasise fact and minimise explanation. This appears to be unnecessarily restrictive. A sound factual foundation is clearly important, but facts are learned most effectively when they are applied and used. Many children can reason perfectly well long before they are twelve and, providing that the teacher continually checks that his explanations are being understood, there is absolutely no reason why he should not introduce reasoning into his teaching. Also, it is surely legitimate to establish the point right from the start that geography is about reasons, not just about facts.

Instead of trying to develop better ways of categorising pupils, or of dividing up geography into more and more exact stages of difficulty, it is necessary to improve teaching organisation and methods so that each pupil can advance at his maximum speed and fulfil his individual promise. Above all, ways have to be found of making it possible for teachers to get to know their pupils well. These are primary objectives in course planning.

There is no single right way to plan a course, but the following outline may be helpful. It is first necessary to obtain the information which is basic to realistic planning, in terms of the potentialities and requirements of the teacher and the pupils. Then decisions are needed as to the best design for the course in order to achieve the desired purposes.

Analysing the planning context

First it is necessary to analyse as fully as possible the teaching situation with which one is presented. This procedure is very important for students and new members of staff; it helps to cut down the initial period of trial and error during which teacher and class are adjusting to one another, a period in which, if one is unlucky, problems of control can arise.

For each teaching group, it is necessary to have the following information:

1   Number and ages of pupils: how many items of equipment, copies of books, worksheets, etc, will always be needed?
2   Class structure: are pupils unstreamed, and if so, do they span the full range of ability? Are remedial pupils included or extracted? Are they setted, broad-banded or streamed?
3   Basic skills: what competence have pupils in writing, reading, calculation, oral work, note-taking from speech, map work, use of references, listening?
4   Are they accustomed to group or independent work? If they are grouped already, how is this done, and who is in which group?
5   How much space is available? Is group work feasible?
6   What equipment and resources are available?
7   What basic equipment do the pupils possess, eg pencils, note-books, files, drawing equipment, log tables? What basic equipment is normally provided by the teacher, and where is this kept?
8   What geography have they studied so far?
9   How many teachers have they had so far in the geography course?
10 How much time is available, per week and per term, bearing in mind the inevitable interruptions and deductions?
11 Does the class present a disciplinary problem? If so, what kinds of work are most effective in controlling this problem? This information can be crucial for a student or young teacher.

Next, a decision has to be made about the course plan. There is no theoretically right or wrong way of putting a course together, for a particular age-range or ability level. The decision will be made after assessing what is necessary and feasible in a particular school, and it may take account of the teacher's own preferences.

Four standard methods of course planning have developed over a very long period of geography teaching in schools: regional, systematic, topic-based or thematic, and ideas- or concept-based. However, because all geography courses must be designed to develop certain ideas and a distinctive way of thinking about the world environment, these distinctions may be regarded as outmoded; all courses will be ideas- or concept-based, however their factual material is arranged.

Regional courses. These use the study of areas or regions, however defined, as a framework for developing geographical ideas and skills. Because of the old-fashioned descriptive connotations of the word 'regional', these courses may better be described as studies of regional systems and regional interactions. Description still plays a part in such teaching, but not the dominant part.

Systematic courses. Geographical ideas, skills and subject matter are now grouped under a series of systematic headings, eg landforms and landscape-forming processes, climatology, biogeography, agricultural systems, industrial systems, urban systems – the terminology will be adjusted to the level being taught. Systematic topics may be taught either in series, ie one after the other, or in parallel, the topics being developed together throughout the course. Regional examples may be used to underpin the systematic work, and to relate the various topics.

Topic-based or thematic courses. Geographical ideas and materials are here structured around topics or themes, eg simple societies in the modern world; farming in the tropics; farming in the industrial countries; old-established industrial areas; new towns; and so on. In theory, it is possible to build up a picture of world geography and to develop the distinctively geographical modes of thought by working through a network of topics of this kind. One popular way of doing this is to study each topic concentrically, beginning with local examples and working outwards to the national, continental and world scales. Regional examples are introduced from time to time, so that at the end of the course, the pupil has achieved world coverage.

Ideas-based or concept-based courses. Abstract geographical ideas are selected as the starting-points, and subject matter is chosen to demonstrate these ideas. Each idea or concept may be related first to the local area, then developed at larger scales. In a town school, the first ideas to be examined will probably come from local work in urban geography. Examples might include studies of the location and association of urban functions, the spatial requirements of these functions, competition between functions, movements of people and vehicles, aspects of transport networks, settlement hierarchies in the home region, and so on. In a rural area, the work may begin with a study of the farm of that area as parts of a man-environment ecosystem – local, regional, national, world-wide.

Selection of courses

All four methods of course design are attractive and logical. On what grounds, therefore, may a choice be made? Clearly, the age of the pupils is of some importance, though this has often been exaggerated. In practice, one tries out ideas all through the school until they prove successful. In some years, pupils seem to grasp ideas earlier than usual. Some individuals grasp them immediately, others never grasp them at all. There are no hard and fast rules about when certain ideas must be introduced. This would appear to argue in favour of courses which are as flexibly structured as possible, in other words, region-based courses. The teacher uses the region to develop geographical ways of thinking with his pupils.

In Chapter 1 it was suggested that a cardinal principle of teaching is to begin with what the pupils know. From this point of view, region-based and ideas-based courses would seem to have a clear advantage over those which are topic-based or systematic. Both begin with the local area, which the pupil already knows something about and can study at first-hand. The region-based course relates its subsequent development to such basic documents as the globe, world map and atlas; these show the world to be made up of continents and oceans, which presumably are legitimate subjects for study. Ideas-based courses tend to move away from the local area in a much more abstract and theoretical way, and younger pupils particularly, because of their lack of background knowledge, may not grasp the reasoning behind such courses, even when they do the exercises perfectly well.

A second cardinal principle is to develop one's courses to parallel the way in which pupils learn. Learning has been defined, too simply yet usefully, as a process of mental ordering. A course which helps the pupil to order phenomena is therefore preferable to one which presents him with a pre-structured view of the world. Systematic and topic-based courses would appear to suffer from a basic defect, in that they begin with the teacher's view of the world, not the pupil's. Again, region-based and ideas-based courses, which begin with the local area, would seem more satisfactory in principle.

Conceptually pre-structured courses have a further disadvantage. Most important advances in knowledge have come through the perception or discovery of links and relationships which were previously unsuspected. It is at least arguable that a course which begins by telling the pupil how the world is arranged is a hindrance to original thought. In a world where change is part of the established order, the promotion of original, independent thought in all pupils capable of it must surely be one of the teacher's highest priorities.

Regional courses in schools are sometimes based on the major world regions (essentially climatic) devised by A. J. Herbertson and his followers. Such courses may also suffer from the defect of pre-structuring reality for the pupil. Recognition of the characteristics of major regions is a useful stage in the pupil's growing awareness of the world, but it is best if he discovers their existence – and also the difficulty of defining them – from evidence presented.

Ideas-based courses are a new development in schools, and

theoretically they are most attractive, especially to enthusiasts for the 'quantification-and-models' style of teaching. They are, however, difficult to teach well, for three main reasons. First, to be really convincing, they must be taught by someone with very detailed local knowledge. Unless such a course is founded upon a wealth of local examples it can be highly abstract. The ideas need to arise in the pupils' minds from concrete examples. Second, because of this emphasis upon local work, the teacher has to produce most of his material himself; he therefore needs good reprographic facilities and much time. Third, although ideas-based courses have been shown to suit able pupils, it remains to be proved that they can hold the attention of the less able, and in particular those pupils who find abstract reasoning, generalisation and theorising almost entirely beyond them. For this reason, the adoption of ideas-based courses in all parts of a comprehensive school needs to be approached with caution.

Another important principle of course design is that it should allow room for repetition. Ideas have to be presented again and again, in different contexts and at different levels of abstraction. Once again, the simply designed course is to be preferred, because it gives the teacher room to re-state ideas as he finds necessary. A simple succession of region-based studies may give him the greatest freedom of all.

It is always important to consider whether or not a proposed course will convey a world view to pupils. Admittedly, many pupils seem incapable of grasping a world view, except in the most rudimentary way, but this does not absolve the geographer from doing all in his power to foster such a view. Unfortunately, the development of field work, case studies and environmental work in recent years has made some geographers forget the world view. Courses which overemphasise the study of local geography and particular cases to the exclusion of general, world-wide studies must be deemed unsatisfactory. At the same time, world geography has to be related to pupils' direct experience.

Geography is the only subject in the curriculum which by its nature tells pupils what places and peoples are like. This surely is essential information for the informed citizen, the conveying of which is an important objective of any course in geography. Region-based courses, or at least, courses which include substantial elements of regional description and analysis, probably do this most effectively.

Finally, from the purely administrative point of view, a simply designed course is always to be preferred to one whose parts interlock in a complicated way. The more complicated the course, the more necessary it is to time its component parts accurately, and this at once restricts the teacher's freedom. Good teaching is a two-way activity, in which teacher and pupils exchange ideas. It cannot be timed exactly. Therefore any course plan which tries to set out a period-by-period forecast of work is likely to be a bad course educationally.

A good geography course will be based upon a wealth of ideas; it will present its ideas and factual information in imaginative and varied ways, at appropriate levels of difficulty; it will be interesting to teach, mainly because it will make very full use of staff interests and expertise; it will continually be scrutinised with a view to improvement, and this scrutiny will include a feed-back of comments from the pupils; and it will achieve maximum possible freedom from the various constraints imposed by the school. Pupils who have followed this course will have a vivid and accurate idea of what it would be like to live through a Moscow winter or the wet monsoon in India, as well as a knowledge of urban models and the characteristics of 'Anyport'.

TEACHING UNITS

The next stage of programme planning is to break down the course into its component parts, which may be termed teaching units. Each unit makes a clearly defined contribution to the course structure.

Teaching units need to be planned with more attention to practical classroom detail than is necessary at the course planning stage. The amount of detail depends upon the teaching methods which it is proposed to use, and the way in which pupils are grouped. For example, if most of the teaching is to consist of oral lessons given to homogeneous groups, detailed teaching preparation will be left to the final stage of lesson preparation; but if the teaching is to be individualised and resource-based, then most of the detailed preparation will need to be done at the unit planning stage.

A teaching unit may be planned for the whole class, for part of a class, or even for individuals. In the second and third cases, more than one unit will be in use simultaneously, and the teacher's task will be extensively managerial. His success in controlling a complicated situation and making it profitable to all his pupils will depend upon his capacity for detailed planning and his adaptability to an ever-changing situation. The absolute need for intensive, detailed planning cannot be overemphasised.

A planning outline for a teaching unit will include notes on the following: objectives – what the pupils will learn from this unit, as distinct from the course as a whole; the relation between this and other units; pupil organisation and teaching methods to be used; resources and apparatus needed, for teacher and for pupils; a forecast of the work, in outline, leaving ample opportunity for modification as need arises.

It is essential to determine the teaching objectives of each unit, otherwise no definable progression may take place. Objectives are of three kinds: those concerned with geographical ideas and subject matter, eg to introduce the idea of connectivity in transport networks; those concerned with geographical skills, eg in map work, to match a list of conventional signs with pictures of the things represented; and those which are generally educational, eg to give pupils practice in using the school library index to find information.

Often it is helpful to crystallise the particular contribution of a teaching unit to the course by giving it a title, such as *Glacial Landforms and Processes; Settlement Schemes on the former 'White Highlands' of Kenya;* or *The Location of a Pulp and Paper Mill: Fort William.*

The relation between a teaching unit and the rest of the course needs to be stated as precisely as possible. Links, like objectives, will normally be of three kinds: geographical ideas and content; geographical skills; and general educational processes. For example, the unit *Glacial Landforms and Processes*, taught to a fourth-year GCE class, might develop the idea that landforms are produced by processes, in this case glacial, and follow work on landform recognition and classification. The unit on *Kenya*, taught to a first-year sixth form, might be part of a programme of work dealing with economic development in tropical countries. Both units might include work with reference materials, designed to train the pupils to work independently and to formulate general statements from a study of particular cases.

PLANNING THE LESSONS

The final stage in the planning process consists of breaking down the ideas and content of the teaching unit into a number of lessons.

Lesson preparation is concerned with two things: (1) what the pupils will learn, and (2) how they will learn it. A lesson has to be planned first and foremost from the learner's point of view. Even in relatively formal lessons with a lot of teacher activity, the role of the teacher is essentially an enabling one. He has to decide what he wants his pupils to learn, and then devise a teaching strategy which will enable them to learn it.

The contribution of a lesson to the unit of work of which it forms a part is often made explicit by giving it a title. When the lesson begins, it is usually a good idea to announce this title, or at least to say what the lesson is about.

Every lesson has to be related to what has gone before and what is to follow. Generally speaking, a lesson will either introduce new ideas and materials, or it will continue work already started, and it is as well to be clear which kind of lesson it is. From time to time, lessons may be given which do not relate directly to what has gone before; topical interest lessons may fall into this category. Even so, the lesson will need to be related in general terms to earlier work.

In principle there are two kinds of lesson, the teaching or oral lesson, and the learning management lesson. Most lessons are combinations of the two, and both are subject to almost infinite variation in detail.

In the teaching or oral lesson, exposition by the teacher is the dominant activity, and the pupils' work derives mainly from this.

In the learning management lesson, the teacher designs a variety of learning situations, provides materials from which the pupils learn, and then manages the pupils' use of what is provided. He may inject sessions of exposition or instruction in skills, either to the whole class or to groups and individuals.

Neither kind of lesson can be said to be better or worse than the other, but certain kinds of lesson may suit the circumstances of a particular class better than another. For example, it is difficult to give lessons based upon lengthy exposition to mixed-ability classes, because the levels of understanding and span of concentration of the pupils varies so widely. Conversely, a laboured use of resource-based teaching, in which an able sixth form spend half an hour finding out what the teacher could tell them in ten minutes, may legitimately irritate the pupils rather than instruct them. The art of teaching lies in matching one's teaching methods to the capacities and needs of the class.

TEACHING OR ORAL LESSONS

This type of lesson may be described under four headings: context; objectives; organisation and methods; and development stages. Each of the headings will be discussed in turn.

Context

The first step is to determine where the lesson fits into the course; what aspects of the work already done will be further developed; whether there will be a deliberate revision of previous work; whether the lesson is the beginning, the middle or the end of a sequence; and what is to follow.

Objectives

The objectives of the particular lesson then have to be defined: What is this lesson intended to achieve? Statements of objectives should be realistic and limited. Common mistakes are to propose aims which are so general as to be meaningless; to propose too many objectives; and to write out geographical content as though it were the teaching objective. The statement of objectives will always refer to the pupils' learning, implicitly or explicitly.

Organisation and methods

The arrangement of pupils in the class will next be discussed: how they will be taught, whether as a class or in groups, and if the latter, in what groups. Will they work individually? What resources and apparatus will be used? Will the pupils go to the school library or resources centre, and will the librarian or resources director need to be briefed in advance? How will the progress of individual pupils be observed, and their difficulties dealt with?

Development stages

This part of the lesson plan describes what will happen at each stage. The first step is to identify the major teaching stages; usually there is a change of activity at the beginning of each stage. A simple progression might be:

1 Teacher's exposition – seven to ten minutes.
2 Class to divide into five pre-arranged groups and to work through five related exercises, based on the exposition. Teacher to give individual help as required, but to make a special point of seeing how pupils X, Y and Z are getting on. Time: about twenty-five minutes.
3 Short consolidation by question and answer, each of the five groups being required to say what they have found out – allow ten minutes.
4 Set homework and clear up – begin three minutes before the lesson is due to end.

The success of a lesson like this depends on at least three things. First, the teacher's exposition must be clear and logical, and he must take steps as the exposition proceeds to find out whether he is being understood. His use of vocabulary and sentence construction must suit his pupils' age and background experience. To save time, he will have foreseen difficulties in the explanation, and be ready to deal with them economically. He may illustrate his lesson if this seems to help.

Second, the work set to the pupils must be within their range, and teach them something new. Pupils may be required to use

Plate 5   Models made by classes of middle-school pupils. (above) A fjord-head settlement in Norway; (left) a nineteenth-century Pennine leadmining and smelting site.

Plate 6 *Sequential flannelgraph sketching: stages in building up a picture of a Chagga smallholding on Kilimanjaro, described on pages 173–5.*

reference materials, and the instructions for this must be clear and concise; the teacher will need to read, or at least scan, the reference materials his pupils will use before he sets his exercises or writes his worksheets.

Third, consolidation by questioning has to be carefully planned, otherwise some pupils will never know what others have found out. Questioning is a method of teaching. The teacher decides what points he wishes to elicit from his pupils, and he uses his questions not only to find out whether or not they know the answers, but to lead them to the right answers. Clear, purposeful and relevant questioning is a hard skill to master, and it requires first of all that a teacher has the objectives of his lesson clearly defined.

The teaching or oral lesson is the one most like the university or college lecture, and there is a danger that student teachers and beginners, fresh from undergraduate courses, may adopt this as their favourite, perhaps their only method of teaching. In fact, this type of lesson is mainly suitable for use with homogeneous classes with a considerable capacity to understand and use the spoken and written word. Oral expositions to the less literary-minded have to be short and very much to the point.

LEARNING MANAGEMENT LESSONS

In this second type of lesson, the emphasis shifts from exposition by the teacher towards the planning of work programmes and the assembly and preparation of learning materials. The teacher assumes a predominantly managerial role. He plans the overall programme, acts as director of studies, consultant, encourager and – where necessary – disciplinarian. From time to time he may call together groups of pupils, question them to find out what they have understood, and teach them orally. Throughout, he keeps a running check on each pupil's progress.

For planning purposes, it is convenient to sub-divide learning management lessons into whole-class, contributing group and multi-activity lessons. The progression is one of increasing managerial difficulty for the teacher. In practice, a given lesson may include elements of more than one kind and possibly the oral lesson as well.

Whole-class lessons

This kind of lesson can be used with classes which are roughly homogeneous in ability. Pupils spend most of their time working through written exercises or examples, which may, for example, be literary or statistical in form. The work may arise out of oral exposition in an earlier lesson, or be based on the class textbook, sets of reference books, maps, photographs, duplicated materials or worksheets, possibly specimens. The whole class does the same work, though, if reference items are limited in number, they may divide into groups and cover the various sections in turn.

A planning outline for such a lesson may look somewhat as follows:

1 Lesson title, with a concise statement of what the work is about.
2 Context – relation of this lesson to past and future work.
3 A list of the exercises to be done, with the teaching objectives of each. This definition of objectives is important, otherwise written exercises can degenerate into mechanical copying.
4 A forecast of the teacher's probable contributions to the lesson. Points of expected difficulty need to be identified, also teaching points requiring emphasis.
5 If a discussion or question-and-answer session is planned, its objectives will be identified.

Written exercise lessons require the pupils to have reasonably good levels of literacy and numeracy. They must have been systematically trained to work on their own and to use reference materials. This kind of lesson seldom works well with pupils who find it hard to grasp oral or written instructions, and who find writing more than a short sentence an intolerable labour.

Contributing group lessons

Pupils work in groups and perhaps individually, but all contribute to a whole-class activity. For example, a first-year class may divide into groups to study aspects of Australian geography. One group may concentrate on farming, another on developments in the tropical north, another on mining and industries, another on cities, and so on. Each prepares a display, and comments on it to the whole class. Further up the school, a class may divide into groups to work out Spearman rank correlation coefficients for different pairs of related variables. Group organisation may also be used for practical work, making a class model, for example. Different groups will make the various components of the model and put them all together at the end. An elaborate model, eg of a regional landscape, can be made very quickly by this method.

Clearly, at this stage, the division of work into separate lessons of period length may cease to be practicable. The planning outline will make clear how much time is to be allocated to the work, and will include the following points:

1   Lesson title and statement of teaching objectives; time allowed.
2   Context – its place in the course programme.
3   A description of the activities which will take place. How work will be divided up, what will be the tasks of pupils working in each division; and how their contributions will be brought together for the whole class.
4   A note on special provision for fast and slow workers.
5   Detailed specification of resources, materials and apparatus required, eg worksheets, blue-prints, model-making materials, maps, illustrations, base-boards for simulation games, dice, calculating machines, etc, with details of the deployment of all items.
6   A note on the teacher's probable contributions – whether there will be an initial briefing, and what points will be made in it; what teaching points have to be made as the work proceeds, whether there will be a concluding questioning or discussion session, and if so, what points will be made; what arrangements are necessary for clearing up.

Multi-activity lessons

In this kind of lesson, several different units of work will be in use simultaneously, by groups and individuals; and the parts may not contribute to the whole. Some work may be literary in form,

115

some mathematical, some practical; while at one and the same time, pupils from the one class may be working in the classroom, in the library and resources centre, in a workshop or even outside school altogether. This method of organisation is necessary if genuinely mixed-ability classes are to be taught effectively.

The teacher has to plan all this work, and find or – more likely – prepare teaching materials for groups and individuals, which will involve him in many hours of work before the lesson begins. Once it has begun, he must know what every pupil is doing and where everyone is. He will make himself available as that most useful of all resources, the person who knows what to do next. From time to time, he will bring pupils together, probably in ability groups, and teach them. He will decide what levels of noise and movement are appropriate, and make sure these are adhered to. He will watch individual progress, and take remedial action where required. Above all, the teacher will encourage, stimulate, ask questions and lead the pupils forward at their own best speeds.

Multi-activity teaching is a continuous process, not normally divisible into separate 'lessons'. The main planning effort consists in producing a series of teaching modules, each really a lesson in itself, for the various groups and individuals in the class. An absolute condition for success in this method is an abundance of appropriate resources; and very high priority will be given to training pupils to use these resources.

The planning outline for a unit of multi-activity work may look somewhat as follows:

1   Theme or themes of the work. Statement of objectives, defined for groups and individual pupils.
2   Context – the relation of this work to overall programmes for groups and individuals.
3   Class organisation: how will the pupils be arranged; which pupils will work through which modules?
4   An outline of the learning progression of each module.
5   A detailed analysis of resources and apparatus required.
6   Teacher's probable contributions: is a whole-class briefing needed? Will groups and individuals have to be briefed? Will

116

any special skills have to be taught as the work proceeds? What teaching points will be made to groups and individuals, and how will this be done? Will the whole class be brought together for common experiences, exchanges of ideas and information, visits? How will the performance of individual pupils be monitored?

LESSON PLANNING IN A TEAM-TEACHING SITUATION

It has become increasingly common, in middle schools and in the lower parts of the secondary schools, for subjects to be linked together and taught by teams of teachers. Geography is almost always included in a subject grouping of this kind.

A team-taught course is commonly divided into a series of teaching units, each of which may be introduced by a lead lesson. This lesson may be given to a very large number of pupils, perhaps to a whole ability band or even, in a small school, to an entire year group. It may be given in a lecture hall, or to normal classes by means of closed-circuit television. All teachers taking part in the scheme attend the opening or 'lead' lesson. It will have been prepared very carefully, following discussion between all the co-operating subject specialists, and will probably include starting-points for work in several subjects.

The opening lesson is followed by resource-based work. Pupils progress through a network of learning experiences and activities, designed by the team members. Extra teachers may be brought in to take specialist work with some or all of the pupils.

The planning of both the opening lesson and follow-up work requires detailed co-operation between the specialists concerned. This will be effective only in so far as each identifies what teaching objectives he has at each stage. Topics then have to be selected which allow these objectives to be attained. It is helpful to plot the teaching objectives proposed by each specialist against the topics in matrix form; this helps to show where links can be made, and where there is unnecessary repetition, also where there is an imbalance in the range of mental processes being developed.

117

APPRAISAL

A final word needs to be said about appraisal. How does the teacher know how effective his teaching is? In addition to the regular assessment of pupils' work through the marking of written exercises, occasional tests, problem-solving sessions, listening to verbal reports and discussion, oral questioning and so on, it is useful for regular appraisal notes to be written as soon as each important piece of work has been completed, be it lesson, teaching unit or a year's course. The teacher should continually ask himself what really happened as a result of the work planned. Did all the pupils, or some pupils, or about three pupils, learn what was taught? In this mixed-ability class, did every pupil have something worthwhile to do? Why did this piece of work go so obviously well, while that was a carefully prepared disaster? Only by the systematic and realistic scrutiny of pupil performance and reaction can teaching, course planning and syllabus design be improved.

6 Examination and Assessment

A discussion of the tasks involved in running a geography department and planning its courses inevitably leads to the subject of
examination and assessment. Indeed, so all-pervading are the
effects of public examinations in schools that they must be
considered the most powerful of all constraints on the teaching
of geography at the present time, in Britain and most other
countries.

PUBLIC EXAMINATIONS

Public examination bodies in Britain prescribe syllabuses, and
then leave the individual teacher to plan his own courses. In some
countries, examination bodies also prescribe courses, which may
be set out in great detail and supported by a list of required textbooks.

Even when the syllabus only is prescribed, examination requirements do constrain course design and also teaching methods in a
number of powerful ways. Thus, whenever a department is providing both examination and non-examination courses, it is almost
bound to concentrate its major effort on the examination work,
because the whole future of the pupils involved in it depends
upon their being well taught. Also, the reputation of the school
itself, and of the geography department within the school, depends
perhaps to an unfair degree upon its examination results. Again,
when there is a possibility of transferring pupils from non-
examination into examination classes, the courses taught to the
former must take account of possible examination requirements,
otherwise transfer becomes almost impossible. And, in tiered
systems of schools, the examination requirements of the upper
tier have to be taken into account in the lower tier, to a degree

119

depending upon the age of transfer from one tier to the other.

The influence of public examinations lies in part in their choice of content, which may not correspond with the individual teacher's perceptions of what is important and what his pupils can do. For example, he may very well wish to teach the geography of Europe under political and economic headings. It is arguable that membership or otherwise of groupings such as EEC and COMECON is the most influential of all controls upon the economic and social geography of the states involved. Yet these groupings may be ignored by examination boards. As recently as 1972, the Joint Matriculation Board in Britain asked its Advanced level candidates to study either West Germany, Denmark, Norway and Sweden, or France and Benelux, or Italy, Austria and Switzerland, groupings almost without significance in contemporary Europe.

Examination boards also influence course design and teaching methods by the form of their questions. Some boards seem to think that breadth of coverage is of first importance; arguably it is. They therefore set questions which compel all candidates to study the whole field prescribed. Such questions tend to be strongly factual, requiring a good memory above all else. Boards who regard the grasp of geographical concepts as a first priority set quite different kinds of questions, which require candidates to reason and to present logical arguments, or perhaps propose and examine the tenability of a hypothesis. They may allow him a fair measure of freedom to select factual material for himself. Covering the whole ground then becomes less important when designing the course.

Public examinations affect teachers in other ways. Thus, many pupils take geography mainly because they must gain a certain number of passes, not because of any particular interest in the subject. In these circumstances, they may react unfavourably to work which is not directly geared to passing the examination. The problem is at its worst in some of the developing countries, where a pupil may reach secondary school as the result of great efforts and sacrifices on the part of his whole extended family. It then becomes almost literally a matter of life and death to pass the examinations, and pressure on teachers to stick closely to the syllabus can be very strong.

This problem can be eased by excellent teaching, given time and patience, but it can be most discouraging to the teacher. Often it results in excessively formal and stereotyped work. The only permanent solution is to change the methods of examination, and to emphasise understanding rather than learned fact.

THE BRITISH EXAMINATION SYSTEM

In Britain, public examinations at school level are mainly the responsibility of eight General Certificate of Education (GCE) Boards, which are controlled by universities; and fourteen regional Certificate of Secondary Education (CSE) Boards, which are manned and controlled by teachers in schools. The GCE boards were established in 1950, while the CSE dates only from 1965. Although the boards are autonomous, their syllabuses are broadly similar, though with some notable exceptions. The present trend is towards greater variety of approach as the general movement towards examination reform gathers momentum.

The General Certificate of Education

This examination is intended for the upper 20 per cent of the ability range, and is taken at Ordinary level at about age sixteen, and Advanced level at about eighteen.

The requirements of O level geography syllabuses of the eight boards are very like those of the School Certificate boards which preceded them. They include competence in simple map work, often linked with picture interpretation; a knowledge of the British Isles, and of at least one major region, usually the whole or part of a continent; and a knowledge of world geography, usually based on a world map. This last includes aspects of physical and human geography, and of the location and distribution of important places and phenomena.

Recently, there has been some divergence from this traditional pattern. There is an increased emphasis upon knowledge and understanding of general themes, often on the world scale, such as world agriculture and industry, world population,

121

world human and economic development and world problems.

Syllabuses at A level are also similar to one another, though here also diversification is occurring. All boards require competence in the use of large-scale maps of various kinds, eg topographical, land use, weather maps; but there seems to be a movement to integrate map work into the body of the syllabus. Candidates are required to have a broad knowledge of world physical and human geography; and most boards set a region or large area, such as North America, Africa south of the Sahara, the Middle East or the USSR, for special study. Increasingly these regions are regarded as arenas for the study of systematic themes.

An understanding of simple statistical methods is being required by more and more examining boards, and will probably be required by all as these methods are accepted into the main stream of geographical teaching. The syllabus of the Cambridge Board emphasises practical work, including simple survey methods, no doubt following the tradition established by Frank Debenham, the first professor of geography in that university. The London and Welsh Boards do likewise. There is a growing emphasis upon field work, but this is not yet compulsory for all candidates.

The style of questions set by the various boards varies to some extent, presumably in accordance with the personal characteristics of board members, but a number of general trends may be recognised. Thus, there is now much less emphasis upon questions of fact than there was even a decade ago; both at O and A levels, candidates are now asked to reason rather than merely to recall information. There is an increasing trend towards the setting of questions based on given data, in map or statistical form, the candidates being asked to explain the meaning of the data and draw their own conclusions. More questions are being set which allow candidates to illustrate their argument by reference to examples of their own choice: this means in practice that greater freedom is being given to teachers to select material within the general syllabus framework. Again, questions are becoming more systematic and thematic, even in the so-called regional papers, so that today candidates are rarely, if ever, asked to write 'a balanced and logical account' of an area of the earth's surface. Rather will they be asked questions about settlement, population, mineral resources and economic development, to be answered with reference to the set region. There has been an increase in the number of questions about towns as functional entities; and the number of questions which require a grasp of statistical methods is steadily growing. The latter are likely to increase in popularity with all boards as soon as suitable books become available for use in schools. Many of the early books in this field have been written at far too advanced a standard.

Most boards give credit for the inclusion of relevant sketch-maps in candidates' answers in all papers; but there is a minority of geographers who regret this, believing sketch-maps to perpetuate the geographical tradition of approximation. More and more boards now provide printed maps, including all-purpose world outlines, for the use of candidates, so that the element of approximation is being reduced. Some boards also allow candidates to take an approved atlas into the examination room.

The Certificate of Secondary Education

This examination arose out of mounting concern in the late 1950s about the unsuitability of GCE papers for pupils below the top 20 per cent of the total ability range. After much discussion this concern took practical shape with the setting up of the fourteen CSE Regional Boards in 1965.

The new examination was designed to cater for the upper 60-80 per cent of the total ability range of pupils at age fifteen, then the national school leaving age. In practice, the examination has been taken by an increasing number of pupils below this range, and there is no doubt that many pupils now take the CSE examination who are quite unable to cope with its demands.

The CSE examination may be taken in three 'modes'. Under Mode One regulations, the regional board, which consists of teachers drawn from the region's schools, supported by a small number of paid officials, draws up a syllabus and decides and operates its own examination arrangements. Mode Two allows an individual school, or a group of schools, to draw up its own syllabus, which is approved and examined by the regional board.

Mode Three also allows a school, or a group of schools, to draw up a syllabus; but in this case the entire examination procedure is also operated by the school or schools themselves. The regional board exercises a general supervision of the arrangements, and in particular ensures that the work of individual schools is of comparable standard.

Mode Three is the least traditional form of CSE examination, and its form may be illustrated with reference to an example, that of the East Midlands Regional Board, based in Nottingham. In this case, the examination is in three parts: course work, for which 25 per cent of the total marks are allotted, paper 1 (one and a half hours – 45 per cent) and paper 2 (one hour – 30 per cent). Under the course work requirement, the candidate has to produce either a project (possibly a landscape model which he has made himself, with accompanying notes), a field-work file or a notebook compiled over four terms. He is then examined orally on this work by an external moderator, usually a geographer from another school in the group.

Paper 1 is set on Ordnance Survey map work (scales 1:25000 and 1:50000), on the East Midlands region, and on a selection of regions and topics within the British Isles. Paper 2 deals with world geography, and is divided into seven sections, from which the candidate selects three. In 1972 the sections were: world map, on which items of information had to be entered; meteorology, weather and climate; landforms and processes – earth movements, coastal features and the work of ice; the main climatic types and the products associated with them – equatorial rain forest, savanna and steppe; world problems – European international boundaries, food and population problems in Monsoon Asia, major disasters; world topics – petroleum and natural gas in the Sahara and Persian Gulf; irrigation in Australia and Pakistan; softwoods in Scandinavia; and regional studies – north-east USA or part of the USSR or the Benelux countries.

Papers are set by a Chief Examiner, with assistance from a panel of teachers representing all schools in the group. The panel marks the completed scripts, and meets a moderator appointed by the Regional Board in order to compare standards and make necessary adjustments. The scripts are divided into five grades, below which is an ungraded category, and each is commented upon. Grade 4 is taken as the average sixteen-year-old's score. There is then consideration of special characteristics in certain candidates' performance which might appear to merit the award of Grade 1 – the final result is not completely arithmetical.

Both GCE and CSE examinations involve geography departments in very considerable administrative arrangements, but Mode Three CSE is the most demanding of all. Syllabuses have to be thought out, presented to the Regional Board, justified, probably revised and re-presented before approval is gained. The form of the examination has to be decided, and the arduous process undertaken of analysing what needs to be examined and how to examine it. Question papers may have to be set – not all Mode Three schools work in groups and appoint a Chief Examiner; these will have to be presented and argued for with the Regional Board. Folders and field-work files have to be marked and their standards moderated externally, often by a geographer from a neighbouring school, who will probably conduct an oral examination with each candidate. Scripts have to be marked, and once again submitted to the often lengthy procedure of a moderating meeting with a moderator appointed by the Regional Board. The whole procedure has to begin in May, so that CSE and GCE examinations do not overlap; many candidates take both examinations, though this was never intended originally. In consequence, no new teaching can be done with examination forms after Easter, and the fifth year of school is effectively reduced to two terms.

Examinations based in the schools and conducted by teachers are undoubtedly an excellent idea educationally, but they create many administrative problems which did not exist before. It is hardly surprising that, by 1972, only about 200 Mode Three geography courses were in operation in the whole of Great Britain; and any further extension of a teacher-based system of public examinations seems to be impracticable within present staff: pupil ratios. Teachers simply have not time to do the necessary extra work.

DEVELOPMENTS IN EXAMINATION PROCEDURES

It may be useful to conclude this chapter by referring to some of the current and possible future developments in examination procedures and techniques which are likely to be of practical importance to geographers.

First may be noted the increasing concern of examination boards with the educational purposes of their syllabuses. Until very recently, geography examination syllabuses were almost always couched in terms of subject content; now, the underlying educational philosophy of the examination is sometimes stated quite explicitly, and the ideas and skills, which it is intended that the pupil will grasp as a result of following a prescribed syllabus, are defined.

An example of such a syllabus is that of the New South Wales Secondary Schools' Board syllabus for the Ordinary Course for forms II, III and IV. In an opening preamble, this states: 'The essential core of a course in geography set for study in schools is the relationship between man and his environment. This relationship is expressed in the landscape (that is, the visible features of the surface of the earth), which result from the changes and adaptations of the natural environment by man in his efforts to satisfy his needs.' The aims of the syllabus are then defined as:

A To establish an understanding of
 i distinctive landscape types;
 ii dominant characteristics of these landscape types . . .;
 iii the interrelationship of man and his environment;
 iv Australia and its place in the world.
B To develop skills in
 i observation, recording and presentation of records;
 ii reading and interpreting maps and photographs; map-making;
 iii the use of geographical vocabulary in speaking and writing;
 iv the use of reference material;
 v applying information to the solution of problems.

The syllabus introduction goes on to suggest seven methods of promoting pupils' interest, eg study of the local area, as the starting-point for wider studies; inductive methods; deductive methods; the introduction of some landscapes *in toto* before analysing their various components, on the grounds that pupils perceive the whole landscape first; use of active methods, indoors and outdoors; discussion of the geographical background to current events; and developing the use of maps.

One may wish to disagree with some of the points made in this syllabus – it was indeed extensively revised in 1973–4 – but the idea of setting out the purposes of the course which is to be examined is wholly laudable.

Closely associated with the move away from content-based syllabuses towards those which may be termed learning-based is an attempt to define the various mental processes tested by examination questions. Examinations have always tested pupils' knowledge, but this has inevitably been equated with memory, to some degree; and it is possible to remember and reproduce what one has learned without understanding it. But there are other aspects of learning which have not been examined systematically until recently, mainly because no suitably defined theory of educational objectives existed.

The work of Benjamin S. Bloom and his followers has provided a basis for the more precise definition of examination procedures. Professor Bloom, in his *Taxonomy of Educational Objectives, Handbook I* (1956), classifies educational objectives under six heads: knowledge, comprehension application, analysis, synthesis and evaluation.

A number of theoretical and practical objections have been levelled at Bloom's scheme. For example, it is notoriously difficult to test pupils' comprehension and be certain that one is not mainly testing their ability to memorise reasons. Nevertheless, the general value of Bloom's work can hardly be doubted. Partly through his influence, the design of examination questions and papers is becoming much more systematic, and the precise purposes of questions are being defined more closely than ever before.

The need for examinations to test the whole range of mental processes was noted by P. E. Roe in an important article in *Geography* in 1971. He drew attention to the method of scoring each question on a proposed examination paper under each of

Bloom's six headings. This allows the balance of the paper to be assessed in quite precise terms. Further, the consequences of question choices, in terms of the mental processes being tested, can be seen at a glance. It is clearly undesirable that a candidate should be able to choose questions in such a way that he only has to use his memory, for example; or that he should escape the need for sound factual knowledge by choosing only those questions which involve reasoning from given data.

There is a continual search for alternatives to the traditional essay question. Geographers have for years set questions which depart from the essay form – map and photo interpretation questions, for example, and questions based upon map and statistical data. More fundamental has been the development of objective and completion tests, beginning in the late 1960s. It seems likely that all public examinations in geography will include questions of this kind within a few years.

Objective and completion questions are easy to mark but hard to set. The candidate is given a question and several possible answers, from which he has to select the correct one; or a statement, which has to be completed correctly. The main pitfalls of this method of testing, which every teacher needs to know, include:

1. suggesting less than five answers, so that the possibility of being right by chance is significant;
2. including silly items among the possible answers, of no possible educational value;
3. using words which mislead candidates, eg technical terms which they do not know, even though they may understand the answer to the question if put in simple English;
4. setting chains of related questions, in which success depends upon getting the first answer right;
5. asking for one correct answer when, as the best candidates know, there is more than one.

The last point is particularly disturbing. One of the purposes of teaching geography is to promote independent thought, and few worthwhile geographical questions can be set to pupils in the

128

Plate 7 *Starting-points for regional geography: landscape phenomena in context.* (above) *Shannon Airport industrial estate, Ireland, referred to on pages 210–12;* (below) *Hurst, a Yorkshire leadmining site abandoned in 1894 because of overseas competition and technological changes.*

Plate 8 *City in transition: Minneapolis. Changes in the fabric and function of cities are a major concern of the geographer.*

upper age levels of secondary school which have right-or-wrong answers. For this reason, many teachers are of the opinion that objective tests will be mainly confined to the lower parts of schools. Enthusiasts for the method insist that this need not be so, and that it is possible to design objective tests which examine the full range of mental processes included in school courses up to the sixth form. A full discussion of objective tests may be found in H. G. MacIntosh and R. B. Morrison, *Objective Testing* (London, 1969), and E. J. Furst, *Constructing Evaluation Instruments* (2nd ed, New York and London, 1964).

The problem of pupils taking both GCE and CSE has been noted. It seems likely that a new common examination at sixteen will shortly be introduced, whose papers and other procedures will test the whole range of examinable pupils. It remains to be seen how wide an ability range can be catered for by a single examination, however ingeniously designed. An even bigger question is what will happen to those pupils who cannot do anything worthwhile in the new examination. Will they be forced into examination courses by pressure from employers, parents, schools?

It is envisaged that the questions on each geography paper of the new single examination will be arranged in order of increasing difficulty. Questions are likely to be of two main kinds. Some will be structured questions developed in three stages. Stage one will test the pupils' knowledge of simple facts. Stage two will require simple, mainly descriptive narrative related to those facts. Stage three, the interpretative stage, will explore deeper levels of understanding, and leave room for the able pupil to show his paces. A second type of question will consist of a structured essay, in which the question itself is supported by a list of points to which the pupil is asked to refer in his answer. These points will also be arranged in an order requiring progressively deeper levels of understanding. For example, the type of open-ended essay question long favoured by examiners, ' "Coastal location is the most important consideration in the re-development of the British iron and steel industry." Discuss.' may be used as the basis for structured questions exploring all levels of understanding.

There is much interest in certain parts of the educational field in an even more fundamental advance in examination procedure. It is thought possible to identify and examine a core of ideas and skills which are common to several related subjects; and then to identify and examine those aspects of subjects which are unique, including factual content. If this procedure could be implemented, the examination at Advanced level might conceivably consist of a number of core papers and several special subject papers which would be relatively short. Such a development would greatly ease the pressure upon subject syllabuses, which seems to increase year by year. The need for geographers to define their distinctive contributions to the total body of knowledge is again very clear.

7 Geography Room Design and Equipment

Ideally, geography should always be taught in a room specially designed for the purpose. In practice, it often has to be taught in classrooms which are furnished with no special equipment and are intended for general teaching purposes. Most secondary schools now have at least one specialist geography room; large comprehensive schools may indeed have several; but the geography staff normally have to teach far more classes than can be accommodated in these rooms. A discussion of the ideal conditions for teaching geography must therefore be in some measure theoretical. Nevertheless, it is well worth considering from first principles how a purpose-built geography room should be designed and equipped.

The achievement of the proper functions of a special geography room demands that certain requirements be fulfilled, in terms of the physical disposition of pupils' accommodation, the variety and type of teaching methods which will be used, and the storage of teaching equipment. The room should be so arranged and furnished that it will allow the teacher to conduct classes, equally conveniently, on a whole-class basis by oral methods, or on a group or individual learning basis. The transformation from whole class to group or individual work must be possible with a minimum of movement of pupils and furniture.

To permit a wide range of teaching methods to be used, there are several important furnishing and design requirements to meet the following specifications:

The detailed study of projected pictures from filmstrips by the whole class together.

131

The detailed study of projected pictures by small groups or individuals without disturbing the rest of the class.

The use of at least two items of audio-visual apparatus simultaneously, eg a slide projector and a tape-recorder.

Flat surfaces for practical work.

Adequate space for free circulation of pupils when consulting reference materials.

Adequate blackboard provision both for day-to-day use and for the storage of more elaborate maps and diagrams.

Unobstructed wall space covered with pin-boarding for display work.

Mains water supply and a sink.

Adequate storage facilities for a substantial amount and variety of teaching material in addition to actual equipment: wall maps, topographical maps, wall-charts and large posters, mounted and labelled pictures, duplicated reference materials and worksheets, filmstrips and accompanying notes, slides and notes, magnetic tapes and cassettes, film loops, sets of magazines (eg *Geography*, the *Geographical Magazine*), books (class sets and half-sets, reference books), apparatus held in the geography department, stationery, pencils, model-making materials, and other consumables if held departmentally.

Carefully planned location and number of power sockets, to allow the combined use of two items of audio-visual apparatus, as well as pupils' individual or group use of electrical apparatus.

It will be clear from the foregoing that decisions about pupil deployment and teaching methods have to be taken before those on geography room layout and equipment. Also that the size of a geography room in relation to average class-size will affect the ways in which pupils can be arranged, and therefore teaching methods. Even in new schools, the size and layout of geography rooms is usually a compromise between the ideal and the possible.

FURNITURE AND ROOM LAYOUT

The first requirement in the geography room is furniture appropriate to the tasks which pupils are expected to do. Much of their work is with maps (the Ordnance Survey 1:63360 standard sheet is 70×85cm), so that ample provision of flat working surfaces is essential. Tables are always to be preferred to desks. They should be of a type which can be butted together to form continuous working surfaces. Certain types of stackable tables cannot be fitted together in this way because their legs splay outwards. Unfortunately, in a crowded room, traditional desks may be installed because they occupy less space than tables; and in long-established schools, desks may have been inherited from many years ago and be difficult to replace.

The physical arrangement of tables and chairs will be varied to suit the proposed teaching methods. If a teacher decides to teach most of his classes as units, using mainly oral methods, then the seating plan must ensure that all the pupils can see him and the visual aids he uses. They should be able to take notes in comfort while facing the front of the room. Two seating plans would appear to meet these requirements: the pupils may sit in rows facing the front, which is the most traditional of all classroom arrangements, or they may sit around the outside of a semicircle or rectangle of tables in what might be termed a 'boardroom' arrangement. They would be able to face the front of the room by half-turning to the right or left as the case may be, but should still be able to write comfortably. The boardroom arrangement is much superior to the traditional rows when class discussion takes place, because the pupils can then face the persons to whom they are speaking.

As soon as the emphasis shifts from oral teaching towards resource-based learning, and the teacher begins to develop the functions of 'manager and consultant', the need for a whole-class grouping disappears. A workshop layout is required, which allows pupils to work in small groups and singly, and to move from their seats to consult resources kept in different parts of the room. The teacher still needs to be able to see the whole of his class, and he may still address them together from time to time; but his prime concern will now be that he can circulate easily through the class. This movement must take place without disturbance, which means that there must be plenty of space. If the room is too small, so that those who move continually disturb those who are working in their seats, a workshop layout will not work properly.

Ideally, the seating plan will allow each pupil unobstructed access to a circulating space around the sides of the room, along which all reference materials are arranged. A useful device, if it can be managed, is to make movement in this space one-way.

Working groups can be formed in many ways. In some classes, the arrangement is random, possibly alphabetical; or it may be designed as a teaching and perhaps a disciplinary device, certain pupils being placed with others and certain separations being made; or it may be based on pupil choice, perhaps ascertained through a sociometric test; or it may take the form of ability setting within the class. Each teacher will decide what method of grouping best suits his pupils and his own level of teaching skill.

In summary, the distribution of seating and of working surfaces (whether tables or desks) should desirably be flexible to meet two basic teaching methods, and the room must be large enough in relation to expected class sizes to permit both easy movement of furniture and mobility of pupils and teacher.

EQUIPMENT AND RELATED FACILITIES
Blackout

If classes are to be taught as whole units, even though infrequently, total blackout facilities are necessary. Only total blackout makes possible the projection of pictures which are bright and sharp enough to be studied in detail by the whole class. If pictures are not bright and sharp, they will only be looked at, not studied, and their teaching value will be reduced. Total blackout is particularly important for colour slides, which are physically much denser than black-and-white slides.

Total blackout can be achieved by lined curtains in black material, or by black roller blinds. If possible, blinds should run in slots fitted at both sides of each window, thus excluding stray light at their edges. The various forms of venetian blind favoured by school architects do not produce an adequate blackout and the geographer often has to be very emphatic about his requirements in this matter.

When a room is blacked out for more than about a quarter of an hour, ventilation becomes a problem. If possible, the geography room should be fitted with extractor fans, so that lessons can proceed uninterrupted by the opening and closing of curtains and windows.

The projected picture should be as large as possible; it can never be too large for detailed study. The teacher, about to plan the layout of his geography room, should sit at the back of the room, project a good slide for teaching purposes, and note how large the projected image has to be for all its teaching points to be seen clearly. The best position for the projection screen can thus be selected, though the locations of other items of equipment in the room have to be taken into account.

Slide and filmstrip projectors

The slide and filmstrip projector is normally one instrument, with interchangeable attachments for the two kinds of projected material. However, some slide projectors with automatic slide-magazine units cannot be used for showing filmstrips. Many education authorities obtain all their projectors from one manufacturer. If the geographer wants another make of projector he may have to put his case to the authority, *via* the head, explaining clearly why it is essential to use it.

Most projectors can be fitted with lenses of different focal lengths. Long-focus lenses throw a picture at long range, and are necessary in large rooms and lecture theatres; short-focus lenses throw a large picture at short range, and are useful in small rooms. When ordering a projector, it is necessary to specify what focal length of lens is required. The size of picture each lens will project at a given range is contained in the manufacturers' specifications. At this stage, therefore, it is necessary to decide where the projector and screen will be placed.

In order to comment on the projected pictures, and point out specific details in them, the teacher must be able to stand beside the screen during projection. He may have to walk between projector and screen every time he changes a slide, but this is inconvenient in a darkened room filled with pupils and furniture. A better arrangement is to use an automatic slide-change and focusing attachment, which is held in the hand and coupled to the projector by a length of cable. Automatic projectors have slide magazines, which are convenient for making up teaching sets of slides before a lesson. In a large lecture theatre where the screen is out of reach, an arrow torch may be used to point out detail. This is a long-barreled torch fitted with a projection lens, which throws a brightly illuminated arrow on to the screen. The importance of pointing out precisely what aspects of a picture the pupils are required to look at cannot be emphasised too strongly.

The slide and filmstrip projector will not always be used with the whole class. If some of the teaching is to be resource-based, or if there is to be an element of auto-instruction in the programme, then pupils will probably want to work with projected pictures in small groups and singly. There is an increasing use of projectors for slides and filmstrips by individuals and small groups, either in conjunction with duplicated notes, instructions and question sheets or with cassette tape-recorders in the form of tape-slide sequences. It may be possible by judicious use of furniture, screens and blinds, to produce a shaded area at the back of the room where pictures can be projected at close range, ie by a projector fitted with a short-focus lens.

The projector can also be used to project maps, diagrams and perhaps photographs on to sheets of plain paper for copying, both by teacher and pupils. Excellent display work can be produced in this way. Similarly, outline maps and diagrams can be projected on to a blackboard and traced off.

From the foregoing it is implicit that the projector will have to be moved quite often. Projectors, and their bulbs, are delicate and expensive; therefore a purpose-built trolley, on which the projector can be moved into its various positions, is to be recommended. The trolley may be suitably fitted to hold the projector itself, lenses, a spare bulb, filmstrip and slide attachments if appropriate, an extension lead, spare fuses for plugs, slide magazines or boxes, and filmstrips.

From time to time it can be useful to show two pictures simultaneously, for comparative studies. For example, pictures of the

136

same landscape or townscape, taken at different times, can be most effectively studied together. Physiographic changes along a coast, produced by a major storm or occurring over a ten-year period, may be demonstrated convincingly by pairs of slides.

Overhead projectors

The overhead projector (OHP) is so called because it throws a projected image vertically upwards; the vertical beam of light is then deflected by a glass prism on to a screen. Ideally, the screen should be so situated or angled that the projected beam of light falls upon it directly at right-angles. If a vertical screen is used, as is often the case, then the OHP image will be somewhat distorted, though not intolerably so. The instrument can be used to project writing or drawing of approximately page size, prepared on acetate sheet, so that the whole class can see it.

There are two main ways of using the overhead projector. Prepared items can be projected, eg writing, maps and diagrams, figures; or it can be used as a horizontal writing and drawing surface, on which the teacher writes and sketches as the lesson develops. In the second case the OHP is fitted with an acetate roll. Special crayons or fibre-tipped pens are used to write on the acetate. Most projectors are hot and dazzling to work with for more than a few minutes, and prepared acetates are therefore to be recommended. These may be produced photographically from line drawings in Indian ink or black fibre-tip pen, from newspaper extracts, diagrams and maps in books and journals, typescript, sheets produced on an ink duplicator, indeed any clear document which is uncoloured. Prepared acetates are permanent; they can be annotated during a lesson and cleaned afterwards without damage. Acetates of a non-permanent kind can be prepared in full colour by the use of crayons and fibre-tipped pens. It is also possible to buy prepared acetates, eg maps, which can, of course, be annotated and then cleaned.

The overhead projector can be used to good effect in conjunction with the slide or filmstrip projector. To give examples: a slide may be projected, and its salient points picked out with the help of a line drawing of the same scene, shown on the OHP; contour maps, sketches and slides of physical features can be shown together; the OHP may be used to summarise the teaching points extracted from a series of slides; a series of maps showing stages in town growth may be matched with slides showing what each successive growth-stage looks like, from the air and from street level. Another possibility is to put up statistical information on the OHP screen, and to illustrate it with slides on a second screen, eg statistics about the increasing size of power stations or oil tankers can be illustrated with actual examples.

The overhead projector is a heavy instrument, which must be moved about on a trolley. After a few minutes operation, the bulb filament is practically molten, and the slightest jolt will fuse it. A projector should always be allowed to cool before it is moved.

Projection screens

Projection screens may be fixed or portable, and are of two types, white and ground glass. The old-fashioned silver screen is now a rarity. A plain white screen has the great advantage of being almost completely non-directional – the projected picture appears very nearly as bright when viewed from the side as it does from the front. The ground-glass screen, whose surface consists of tiny granules of glass, reflects a much more brilliant picture than the white screen, provided it is viewed from in front. It is highly directional, and picture brilliance falls off very quickly when viewed from the side; at an angle of 45° the intensity of illumination is reduced by about one-half. This type of screen should therefore only be used when classes are small enough to sit near the line of projection.

Clearly, if two forms of projector are to be used in conjunction it is desirable to have two screens available. Where space is limited one of them may be a portable one.

One further point should be taken into consideration: the positioning of projection screens. It can be very convenient to use the slide projector in conjunction with the blackboard; and certain types of pull-down screens, if fitted above the blackboard, make this impossible. The method of combined use may be illustrated by an example. A blackboard drawing is prepared, showing the characteristics of a glaciated mountain area in Norway. Slides to show examples of each of the landforms represented are then projected and related to the drawing. This helps to make the point that all glacial features in an area are related to one another. The blackboard drawing can be illuminated by the projector light at appropriate points. Pupils can be supplied with a duplicated copy of the blackboard drawing, for annotation during the lesson.

Tape-recorders

There is a bewildering variety of tape-recorders on the market; choice has to be made according to the tasks for which one wants to use the instrument. In a school geography department, there are four main uses:

Playing prepared tapes, to a whole class, to groups or to individuals.
Recording broadcasts for later use and perhaps for editing.
Recording from direct speech in school.
Recording interviews in the field.

Two types of recorder are required to cover these tasks. One will be mains-operated and capable of producing high-quality sound, suitable for use with a whole class. This will be a heavy instrument, best kept in one place. The second type will be portable and battery-operated. Both types will need microphone attachments, which may have to be requisitioned separately.

Prepared tapes are usually marketed in small sealed canisters called cassettes, which can only be played on certain types of recorders specially designed to receive them. Tapes prepared in school which are likely to be used many times may be transferred to cassettes for safe keeping; this makes accidental erasure almost impossible, and helps indexing.

Hand viewers

These instruments enlarge slides up to a size of about 6×9cm. Viewers may be either mains- or battery-operated; some models can be adapted for either. The size of picture they produce is too small for fine detail to be seen easily; further, because only one pupil at a time can use a viewer, it is difficult to arrange for the discussion of picture content, as is possible when a slide projector is used. However, if three or four viewers can be obtained, it is possible to devise units of work for small groups of pupils, two or three to a viewer, including the study of slides, use of duplicated notes and questions, and perhaps a cassette tape-recording.

Episcopes

Sometimes it is useful to be able to show the page of a book or a picture postcard or some other small visual aid to the whole class at once. This can be done with an episcope, which throws an image of the object on the screen. Unfortunately, episcopes work well only in total blackout. Even then, they throw a dim picture on the screen. If possible, a slide or an OHP acetate should always be made of the item to be projected.

Back-projection screens

These allow slides or filmstrips to be projected in daylight, though not in direct sunlight. The projector has to be fitted with a short-focus lens. Projection takes place into a light-tight cabinet, and the picture is reflected from a mirror on to the back of a ground-glass screen. Back-projection screens produce rather a small picture, usually about 40×60cm in size, which are strongly directional. The apparatus is useful with small classes of about twenty pupils, or with small groups.

In circumstances which make blackout impossible, the back-projection screen can be essential equipment. In tropical countries, for example, classrooms often have a light and ventilation space between the top of the wall and the roof, in place of windows. Neither curtains nor blinds can be fitted in such rooms. The back-projection screen is then the only feasible method of showing slides or filmstrips. Of course, an electricity supply is required, and this can present problems, especially in schools away from the main towns. A school is often reluctant to start up its generator during the day for the sake of one lesson. Even when faced by these difficulties, geographers should try sometimes to use projected pictures because of their great teaching value.

Ciné-loop projectors

These instruments, which resemble small television sets, project a two-to-four minute run of ciné film on to a ground-glass screen by back-projection. Loop projectors were first developed for use in athletics training, because they allow the movements of an expert performer to be studied in detail over and over again. A number of loops have been produced for geography teaching, and are useful to illustrate physical processes, especially if they make use of time lapse photography. Some loops which make effective use of animated diagrams are also helpful. It should be noted that projectors and loops are made in two sizes, Standard 8 and Super 8, and these are non-compatible.

Ciné projectors

From time to time in the geography course, it will be useful to show films, either to a single class or to several classes together. This may be done in the geography room, or in a school projection theatre.

Projection in the geography room usually offers the best conditions for working on, as opposed to merely watching, film. However, a good many films are sources of general background impressions rather than of detailed information, and do not warrant close study. If a choice is available, the place where a particular film is shown will depend on the reasons for showing it.

Film projectors are made in two sizes, 8mm and 16mm. Both can project both silent and sound films. Like the ciné-loop projectors, 8mm film projectors are of two types, Standard 8 and Super 8, the two being non-compatible.

The main purpose of the 8mm projector is to show films made in school; very few commercial films are obtainable in this small size. A geography department will therefore only be interested in an 8mm projector when it has access to, and knows how to use, an 8mm ciné camera, and intends to make its own teaching films.

Most schools have at least one 16mm sound projector, which is usually stored centrally. This means that there has to be a proper reservation system for its use. Films for this type of projector can either be purchased (they are extremely expensive); hired from commercially run film libraries; or borrowed for the cost of postage only from municipal film libraries, teachers' centres, the news and information or tourist offices of many foreign embassies and consulates, public corporations and many commercial firms. Some of the most effective teaching films are produced by the last two.

DISPLAY SPACE AND METHODS

The geography room needs to have as much display space as possible. Walls used for display should be covered with pin-boarding, preferably from floor to ceiling. The pin-board should not be framed, and it may be necessary for the geographer to specify this, because many school architects confuse display space with notice boards.

In many new schools, so much glass is used in construction that it is difficult to obtain enough display space. It is, however, possible to cover windows on the corridor side of a room with pin-boarding. This has two positive advantages: it cuts out the distraction produced by movement along the corridor during lessons, and it helps to provide blackout.

Display space can be used for a variety of purposes. It can carry exhibitions of maps, pictures, diagrams, facts and figures, on which groups of pupils will be required to work, probably using some form of worksheet or list of questions. It can be used to show posters and large photographs for background 'atmosphere' – no specific work may be done on these items, but they are useful nonetheless. Pupils' work can be displayed, usually when information about group work has to be exchanged among the whole class. Follow-up work from field courses, school visits and other pieces of pupil investigation can be shown, and perhaps worked upon. Lastly, semi-permanent displays, of interest to several classes, may be mounted. Maps of the local area, at various scales, and air photographs, fall into this category.

Maps and pictures which are displayed frequently should, if possible, be edged with adhesive tape. This will prevent drawing-pin holes at the corners developing into tears. Pictures cut from newspapers and journals should be mounted with cow gum or other colourless adhesive on manila card, and covered with plastic film if they are to be kept for any length of time. Adhesive tapes of the transparent variety should never be used on maps or pictures which are to be kept permanently. Most varieties perish and fall off, leaving unsightly stains. Masking tape, as used by draughtsmen, is to be recommended. A plastic adhesive resembling soft putty is also useful, for sticking pictures to stiff card temporarily, or for attaching materials to wall surfaces without causing damage.

Traditionally, geography rooms have been fitted with glass-fronted cabinets for the display of specimens. Before the geographer decides to ask for cabinets of this kind, he would be well advised to consider what functions they will serve with the pupils. Generally speaking, specimens are only useful in geography lessons when they are being handled by pupils. When not in use they are best kept in store.

TEACHING AIDS
Wall maps
Wall maps are important, both for background display and for specific teaching, often in conjunction with the atlas. They are produced in roller form or as flat maps dissected into rectangular sections, which fold up for storage. In both cases, the actual map is mounted on a linen base and its surface is varnished.

Some firms also produce wall maps in paper-sheet form. The sheets can be mounted and fitted with rollers after purchase. This procedure can also be used with Ordnance Survey or Geological Survey sheets, and it is especially useful for displaying several sheets, joined together to form a single map.

Roller maps may be hung from a map rail suspended from the ceiling, or they may be raised into position on a portable map elevator, which resembles a projection screen tripod. From time to time it is useful to be able to display two wall maps simultaneously for purposes of comparison. However, because space is usually limited, there is much to be said for having one fixed and one portable map display unit. Dissected wall maps usually have metal eye-holes at the corners, and can therefore be pinned to any convenient display space.

Wall maps may be obtained in a wide variety and from many manufacturers. Selection can only be made by deciding the uses of each map. Perhaps the most important function of wall maps is to help develop pupils' awareness of major world patterns and distributions, and the structural frameworks of continents and major relief regions. A selection of world distribution maps would appear to be a first priority. Arguably the most important world map of all is that which shows the distribution of population.

Reviews of wall maps may be read from time to time in the pages of *Geography* and *Teaching Geography*. Advice about them may be obtained from the Geographical Association in Britain and from comparable organisations in other countries. Publishers' exhibitions, such as that organised annually by the Geographical Association, are also helpful in selecting suitable maps.

Topographical maps

The geography room should have a collection of topographical maps at various scales, of the home country and – if possible – of other countries. The teaching purposes of each map will be decided before it is purchased. However, the ideal school map collection would probably include the following:

1 Class sets of maps of the local area, at the various scales available, for use in and out of school.
2 Class sets of other particularly useful map sheets, eg those of the Ordnance Survey 1:63360 sheets which have been described in the Geographical Association's *British Landscapes Through Maps* series. There may be class sets to cover field work areas visited by the school.
3 Class sets of map extracts published by examination boards, selected because of the wealth of detail contained in a small area of country.
4 Single sheets of home and overseas maps, to accompany specific sections of the courses taught.
5 Copies of old editions of local Ordnance Survey or comparable overseas maps, where these exist. Old-established schools sometimes have a veritable treasure-trove of old editions in

their geography rooms. Geographers in new schools have to scour second-hand bookshops. Complete coverage of England and Wales is provided by the David and Charles reprint of the first edition of the Ordnance Survey 1:63360 map.

6 Land use maps: it is desirable to have class sets of the local inter-war (Dudley Stamp) 1:63360 land utilisation map, and the post-war 1:25000 land use map.

7 Geological maps: small-scale sheets covering the whole country, and local sheets on a larger scale, if available, are useful. A class set of the local area may be necessary; much depends upon the type of course taught and the characteristics of the local area. Geological maps of field work areas are desirable.

8 Small-scale maps and special maps, published by national survey departments: sheets of the Ordnance Survey 'National Planning' maps are useful, eg those showing precipitation, types of farming, population density, inter-censal population change, various basic industrial distributions; sheets of such publications as the *Atlas of Kenya;* historical maps, eg Roman Britain, Hadrian's Wall, Offa's Dyke; special map overlays showing gravity anomalies in the local region.

9 Town plans: a class set of the home town is desirable. Examples of town plans from all parts of the world should be collected.

Globes

It is essential to have at least one globe in the geography room. The most useful globes are those with political colouring, and those with a blackboard surface which can be used for demonstrations, eg in mathematical geography. It is useful if the blackboard globe is over-printed with a world outline and circles of latitude and longitude. The politically coloured globe allows pupils to see the true relative sizes and positions of countries, and bearing in mind that nation-states are probably the most significant geographical sub-divisions of the world, this information is important.

Ideally, the blackboard-surface globe will be suspended from a special beam in the ceiling, which allows it to be raised and lowered. The installation of such a beam normally means that the ceiling of the geography room has to be strengthened, an operation best carried out when the school is being built. If a beam cannot be provided a pedestal globe will be found almost equally satisfactory.

Model-making facilities

If class, group and individual model-making is to be attempted, there must be adequate flat working surfaces in the geography room. In many cases, this can only be provided by pushing tables together, but if at all possible, there should be a wide shelf at table height along one side of the room, where partly completed models can be kept.

Mains water supply and a sink are very useful in many kinds of model-making. Water is needed for mixing such materials as papier mâché, plastic filler, poster paints and adhesive paste, and it is also needed at the clearing-up stage. A towel unit should be provided.

Stream and wave tanks

Mains water supply is also necessary if there is to be a stream tank, wave tank or any other kind of geomorphological working model in the geography room. A tank suitable for demonstrating river features in miniature will be at least three metres long, two metres broad and half-a-metre deep. It will be partly filled with a mixture of sand and fine mud, and will therefore be very heavy; brick piers may have to be built specially to support it. Water is introduced at one end by a fine spray, and drainage development on a sloping 'land' surface observed and measured. Phenomena such as the headward recession of waterfalls, the deepening and widening of a river valley, meander migration and delta formation can be demonstrated very effectively. A wave tank, to demonstrate the action of waves of different sizes and directions on a shoreline will if anything be bigger and heavier. Waves are normally produced by a paddle situated at one end of a long narrow tank.

Before deciding to install such a piece of apparatus, it is vital to consider whether the use of space for it is fully justified. What will it be used for, how often will it be used, and when will it be used? – it is difficult to fit the study of a prolonged experiment into the school timetable.

Blackboards

A discussion of this most versatile and simple teaching aid has been left to the end. It is sometimes said by educational experts in the technologically advanced countries that blackboards have been made obsolete by the new audio-visual aids, but this is not so. The blackboard is probably the most adaptable teaching aid of all. It is independent of electricity supplies. It can be written on, maps and sketches can be drawn on it, it can be used for calculation. It is useful both for minute-by-minute jottings and carefully prepared summaries, which teach pupils something about layout, as well as geography.

Blackboards in geography rooms need to be large enough to hold both lesson-by-lesson and semi-permanent work. The best arrangement is probably to fit a large roller blackboard on one wall. This will normally have four panels, one of which can be a white projection screen. Another panel may be squared for scale drawings and plotting statistics. In addition, it is useful to have a portable blackboard, which can be brought out from the store when required, sometimes with a drawing prepared.

In those parts of the world where projectors cannot be used, because there is no blackout, no mains electricity, no spare parts and very little money, the blackboard and a box of coloured chalks are the teacher's main visual aids. Not surprisingly, teachers and teacher-training institutions in these countries take their blackboard work very seriously indeed.

Whiteboards are also available, and are favoured by some education authorities in preference to blackboards. Special fibre-tipped pens are needed to write on them, and they can only be cleaned by using a patent spirit. Experience suggests that whiteboards are better suited to writing than drawing, and they are therefore best used in conjunction with blackboards. They have three practical disadvantages: the white surface is easily defaced, and in many schools this happens very quickly; unless each teacher is issued with a set of special pens, the boards soon cease to be used – sets of pens left in classrooms tend to disappear; and it is difficult to clean the boards effectively, even with the special spirit, so that they soon become discoloured.

STORAGE

Geography departments have special storage requirements, which have to be made clear to architects and education authorities when geography rooms are being designed. Two kinds of storage space are necessary, first for items in current use by teachers and pupils, and second for items temporarily out of use. The latter are best kept in a store room. If possible, a geography department will have a preparation room, where a hand duplicator and teachers' reference materials can be kept.

Most of the materials to be stored require proper arrangements for their maintenance and care:

Wall maps are best stacked upright in a rack specially made for the purpose, or suspended from hooks in the store room ceiling. Some fixed blackboards allow limited storage space for maps at the rear.

Topographical maps will normally be stored flat in a map chest. When ordering this item of furniture, it is important to ensure that the drawers are large enough to allow map sheets of standard size to lie flat; also that drawers are shallow. If more than about thirty sheets are kept in one drawer, their weight becomes excessive, they are difficult to handle and sheets at the bottom of the stack become torn. The map collection must be indexed if it is to be used to capacity, and a loose-leaf file or card index will serve this purpose. It can be convenient to build up an index classified under areas and under teaching units.

Posters, wall-charts and large pictures are most conveniently stored in drawers; indexing is desirable.

Pictures cut from magazines need to be mounted on manila card if they are to survive. They can be stored in a filing cabinet, and the collection needs to be indexed.

Pupils' work has to be stored sometimes, particularly the unfinished results of group projects. It is often convenient to reserve a drawer in the map chest for this.

Duplicated materials, worksheets and similar items can be kept in class sets in strong cardboard boxes, which can be shelved like books.

Bookshelving is needed in or near the geography room for (1) class sets and half-sets and other collections of books, eg for particular teaching units; (2) reference books and pamphlets, which pupils will consult; and (3) atlases. In some schools, atlases are issued to pupils for the year, which releases storage space; but more often, they have to be issued and collected each lesson. The storage problem varies very much from place to place. Unfortunately, there are schools where the issue of atlases for the year would render them unusable after a week. Storage also has to be provided for books not in current use; these are kept in a store room, away from the dust and possible damage of the classroom.

Filmstrips are sold in circular canisters, accompanied by a booklet of teaching notes. The canisters can be kept in drawers – specially designed cabinets are obtainable – or in push-in frames fixed to a wall. Booklets are best kept under direct staff supervision, and a signing-out system is to be recommended.

Slides are obtainable in sets and singly, from commercial producers. More and more teachers' centres now produce slide sets, often of their local region, as do study groups of teachers, working under university, college or Geographical Association auspices. Many teachers make their own teaching slides, and techniques for doing this are described in the next chapter.

The storage and cataloguing of slides always presents a problem. They are best kept in slide boxes, which should all be of one size. The lightweight boxes made by Boots the Chemists in Britain are especially recommended. They hold 100 glass-mounted or up to 300 cardboard-mounted slides, have an indexing space on the lid, and can be stored as books.

Slides can also be arranged and stored in teaching sequences, and for this, plastic envelopes are useful; these usually hold six, twelve or eighteen slides, and may have a space for notes. Such sequences of pictures can be related to worksheets and used for auto-instruction, by groups and individual pupils.

Overhead projector acetates can be mounted in stiff card and stored in an ordinary filing cabinet. Alternatively, unmounted acetates can be interleaved with plain paper and filed on shelves in folders or envelopes.

Magnetic tapes and cassettes are sold in boxes, most of which have a space for labelling. It is important to enter the numbers on the revolution counter of the tape-recorder at which each recorded item starts and finishes, also to note how long each item takes to play, so that it can be fitted accurately into a lesson plan. It is usually convenient to store tapes on a special shelf, possibly grouped according to the courses or teaching units to which they refer.

Film loops are also supplied in canisters, which can be stored as books.

Cataloguing is the key to the full use of resources. It is also useful to keep a loose-leaf file, in which each member of the department notes ideas about the use of resources with the various teaching units, and identifies resources needed next year.

METEOROLOGICAL INSTRUMENTS

The writer is sceptical about the value, and certainly the practicality, of taking regular weather observations at a school weather station. The timetable of most schools, and the numbers of pupils involved, make this very difficult, and there are many more important things to do with one's limited time.

However, it is clearly desirable that pupils learn to observe the weather; that they learn to use the standard weather instruments; to relate observations, sometimes, to broadcast weather summaries; to start to quantify some of their impressions about temperatures, wind speeds, humidity, precipitation; and to understand the combinations of meteorological conditions which produce certain effects, eg rime or inversion fog. This means that there needs to be a lot of directed observation, much explanation with ample use of diagrams and pictures, rather than a ritualistic reading of instruments.

150

The instruments required in a Stevenson Screen are an ordinary thermometer, maximum and minimim thermometer, wet and dry-bulb thermometer. A rain gauge should be placed nearby. If possible, a sunshine recorder should also be installed in a suitable place in the school (though it has very specific requirements), and a barometer in the geography room is desirable. Unfortunately the cost of setting up a weather station is high. It is most useful to have meteorological instruments available to be taken away on field courses. Some of the most effective weather observations can be made away from the towns, where pupils have a chance really to see and feel the weather.

A few pupils make weather studies their hobby. This can be put to good use in those public examinations which allow individual projects to be presented.

8 Audio-Visual Aids

When producing his own teaching materials, the teacher has to consider where to concentrate his efforts. There is an enormous amount of commercially produced material on the market, much of it very good indeed, and there is no point in trying to duplicate this. The teacher's own materials will rather illustrate his own individual knowledge and perceptions of geography, and will be used to give added point and relevance to the commercial items. If a syllabus is to be anchored firmly in local examples – and most syllabuses will be – then the teacher will always have to produce most of his teaching materials on the local area. Whatever items he decides, or is required, to produce, it is desirable that they should be technically excellent.

The most important items are 35mm slides, overhead projector acetates, sound tapes, materials produced with various kinds of duplicator, items for wall display, and class models – the list is not intended to indicate an order of importance.

USING COLOUR SLIDES
Colour slides bring factual immediacy into geography teaching and they are also invaluable for demonstrating change or processes, in space or in time. The teacher who can take his own photographs has the advantage of introducing his own geographical experience to his pupils and of designing courses based on that experience.

Slides can show a total landscape or townscape, and so provide starting-points for region-based and systematic studies of many kinds. They can be used to pick out significant detail in landscapes and townscapes, and can illustrate the appearance of different urban zones. Shots taken from tall buildings or from the air can be combined with those taken at street level. Longer-term, continuous change in landscapes and townscapes can be illustrated. Examples include urban development on the edges of a town; city centre renewal, with sets of 'before and after' pictures; or the skyward leap of a central business district, eg Sydney 1960–70. It is helpful to include a clearly recognisable fixed point in successive pictures.

Sets of slides can be built up for various purposes: to show the characteristic components of a regional landscape; or the sequence of processes taking place in a commercial undertaking. Thus a visit to a tea estate might yield pictures of tea picking, pruning tea bushes, tea being delivered to the factory by conveyor belt, withering, rolling, fermenting, drying, grading, packing and labelling. Case studies can be illustrated. A farm visit may be photographed in step-by-step detail and perhaps related to a map and a tape-recording.

Slides can be used to remind pupils what they saw on a field excursion, for revision purposes; if visibility at the time was poor, they can be shown what might have been seen. Aspects of places visited on field courses can be illustrated under conditions at other times of year, eg mid-winter. The teacher can take his camera to places where he cannot take his pupils, and certainly not large classes, on many successive occasions, and the resulting slides enable him to share his geographical experience with them.

The seasonal change in a landscape can be very effectively illustrated, especially by a series of slides taken from precisely the same point at different seasons. Examples of meteorological conditions and cloud forms can be collected in slide form over a period of years. Pupils can be shown examples of extreme conditions, eg rivers, waves, weather, holiday traffic, which they cannot readily observe for themselves.

With younger pupils especially, slides help to build up a geographical vocabulary. The meaning and relationships of conventional map signs can be demonstrated by photographs of the actual features.

Close-up photography allows the illustration of physically small items before a whole class, allowing detailed comment by both teacher and pupils, and close-up slides are also valuable for more penetrating individual study. Examples include geological specimens, fossils, soil samples, insects (eg locusts, safari ants), birds, animals; picture postcards, especially old issues which can be of great historical interest; very small illustrations in books, even such things as letter-headings on firms' note-paper, which may include useful illustrations; and details of early town panoramas, which can be studied in detail when projected, and possibly used to prepare pupils for an urban field-work project.

Slides can be made of close-up photographs of illustrations and documents which can be borrowed, eg from the schools' museum service, or from parents and friends. Small sections of Ordnance Survey and other maps can be photographed to make slides for whole-class study. Permission to copy must of course be obtained for all maps less than fifty years old.

Practical operations can be demonstrated in close-up, which may be difficult to show to large groups in any other way. Examples include handling weather recording instruments, taking a soil sample, or model-making. Blackboard and other kinds of ephemeral work may be recorded for future use. This is a very useful technique, which is developed later in this chapter.

Slides can be made by cutting up filmstrips. This allows them to be used in any number or order; one or two pictures from several strips can be conveniently used in one lesson, which is not otherwise possible. Several inexpensive types of slide-mount are available.

In the case of half-frame filmstrips, it can be useful sometimes to put two pictures into one full-size mount, so that they can be projected together. Examples might include a map and a picture, two pictures of the same landscape in the wet and the dry season, or two contrasting parts of the same country.

PHOTOGRAPHY FOR SLIDE MAKING

Many schools now possess, or have access to cameras, and geographers make more use of these than do most other subject specialists. The geographer thus needs to know exactly what he wants a camera to do, and requisition accordingly. But before doing this he is recommended to buy a comprehensive photographic manual, such as M. J. Langford, *Visual Aids and Photography in Education: A Visual Aids Manual for Teachers and Learners* (London and New York, 1973). The free educational leaflets issued from time to time by Kodak Ltd are also useful.

It is always advisable to invest in a photographic system, not just a camera. The camera selected should have interchangeable lenses, and be adaptable for close-up work. Three useful lenses are the 50mm for normal outdoor work, the 35mm wide-angle for work where space is restricted, and the 135mm long-focus which acts as a small telescope and is able to pick out particular items in a general landscape, and to bring distant and sometimes inaccessible objects into close range. Close-up attachments take the form of supplementary lenses, which fit over the 50mm lens.

Cameras have two types of viewfinder, those which are separate from the lens and those which work through the lens. The second are termed single-lens reflex cameras, and have great advantages over the separate viewfinder type, especially in close-up work. They automatically overcome the problem of parallax, whereby the image seen by the lens and viewfinder, where the two are separate, cease to coincide at close range. It is possible, say, to photograph a small section of a map with a single-lens reflex and be sure of the exact boundaries of one's picture.

For close-up work, a tripod is necessary, and its use is to be recommended when a long-focus lens is used. The slightest movement of such a lens, focused on a distant object, will blur the picture. In fact, a tripod should be used with any lens whenever a shutter speed slower than 1/125th second is necessary. Time exposures always need a tripod, or an equivalent, eg a table-top, window ledge or the top of a wall.

A single-lens reflex camera and its accessories are expensive but, if a school intends to produce large numbers of slides, and really make use of the teaching potentials of photography, they will prove a good long-term investment. High-quality cameras are generally more reliable and robust than cheap cameras. Before ordering any of the bargain-price cameras which appear on the market from time to time, a school should check whether accessories, spare parts and repair facilities are available; and, that the equipment is strong enough to stand up to the wear and tear of multiple use, indoors and out. If funds allow, the requisition of a polaroid camera for use by the pupils is to be recommended. This allows the older pupils to take their own geographical pictures, and to see the results immediately.

Much of the geographer's photographic work will be with colour film, and it is a good idea to use the same make of film all the time. The colour renderings of different makes of film vary considerably, and to change from one colour to another in the course of a lesson can be distracting. Those makes of film which are returned in cardboard mounts after processing have an advantage over others, because the mounts can be used for concise teaching notes. The school, or perhaps the education authority on behalf of all its schools, should negotiate preferential terms with the manufacturers or wholesalers of the film finally selected.

Effective teaching pictures

The good teaching picture is first of all a good picture in its own right. It must be correctly exposed, sharply focused and well composed. A picture with these qualities will to some extent teach automatically; it makes its point visually, is pleasing to look at and may even be remembered for its photographic as well as for its geographical content. In contrast, the wrongly exposed, blurred and badly composed picture irritates rather than instructs. The viewer has mentally to structure the unstructured picture before considering its geographical content. To do this repeatedly during a lesson or lecture is surprisingly exhausting, and causes most pupils to lose interest. Moreover, at school level and probably at college and university levels also, most pupils and students lack the background experience which would enable them to carry out this restructuring process; so, the point of the picture is lost.

Equally important, the good teaching picture makes a clear teaching point. Before taking any picture, the geographer has to be certain what precisely it will show and what it will add to the understanding of a particular group of pupils. A great many potential slides can be eliminated by examining these points, and the teaching quality of those remaining improved. Experience in schools suggest that about a dozen slides, each with a specific teaching point to make, are enough for one lesson, and that two or three, worked over in detail, can be even more effective. The problem is to obtain slides of the requisite technical and geographical quality, capable of being worked upon in this way. Sometimes it may be necessary to show three slides to make one teaching point, because the ideal picture cannot be taken.

Various principles of picture-making are relevant to the illustration of geographical subjects for teaching purposes by means of slides. A projected picture should make the beholder feel that he could if he wished step through the screen into the city street or the rain-forest which is being shown. This feeling of participation can be achieved in two ways. The picture should be composed so that the eye of the beholder is led by strong visual lines from the margin to the centre, so that he forgets the frame; and people may be placed in the picture so that the viewer can imagine that he could step into the picture beside them.

The teaching effectiveness of a picture may often be increased if it shows somebody actually doing something. Geographers tend to take too many static pictures; they photograph factories or industrial plant from the outside, when their significance lies in what happens inside. A picture of a glass-blower at work is far more instructive than a picture of a glass works, especially if the works look exactly like any other kind of light industrial plant.

Composition

One of the most fundamental rules about making acceptable pictures is to avoid dividing them into halves, or even quarters, by strong vertical and horizontal lines. Straight horizons which run across the centre of a picture are unpleasing; the only possible reason for taking such a picture would be to demonstrate the flatness of a land-surface, or the existence of a high-level peneplain. Even then, a more pleasing effect is to be obtained by placing the horizon about one-third of the distance from either the top or bottom of the picture. This can often be done by taking the picture from a slightly higher point, such as the top of a church tower, even the roof of a vehicle. Strong vertical lines are best kept somewhat to left or right of centre, otherwise an unpleasing effect of sub-division into two or more separate pictures may be produced.

The focal point of every picture needs to be decided before the shutter release button is pressed. The picture should be composed so that the eye of the beholder is led by converging lines towards that point. Pictures without a clear focal point are always ineffective as teaching pictures, because the pupil is not told, visually, what he is supposed to look at.

Large areas of blank foreground, such as asphalt, grass, a beach or a flat water surface are to be avoided. In cases where they cannot be avoided in the original photograph, they should be masked out before projection. Sometimes it is possible to cut out foreground at the photographing stage by using a 135mm long-focus lens. A general rule is to take photographs as close to the subject as possible.

The sky may be a pale blue or grey blank in a picture, in which case its area should be reduced to a minimum; or it can be a powerful element in the composition, and make a teaching point. It is not always possible to wait for ideal sky conditions before taking a picture, but very often, by waiting half an hour, or returning another day, a somewhat dull picture can be transformed by including a visually interesting sky. Clouds can give a sense of depth and distance to the most uninteresting terrain. Sometimes the sky itself can make an important teaching point; for example, summer afternoon thunderstorms are an integral part of the Finnish or English Fenland scene, and a picture showing a black sky behind a brilliantly sunlit foreground can convey this aspect of the region's geography in a memorable manner.

Depth

Projected pictures are two-dimensional, while the real world is three-dimensional, and has many other qualities as well, such as sound and scent, which the picture cannot show. To counteract the flatness of a picture, certain photographic devices can be employed to suggest depth. The use of clouds has already been mentioned. Patches of sunlight and shadow can be used to bring out the receding planes in a landscape, and strong side- or front-lighting can produce a three-dimensional effect.

Differential focus can be used to pick out the important parts of a picture in sharp relief; and the colour red, which for physiological reasons always looks nearer to the eye than other colours, can sometimes be used to convey the illusion of depth. A strategically placed figure in a red anorak can give a three-dimensional quality to a mountain scene.

Scale

It is always difficult to convey a sense of scale through a picture. Probably it can only be done with complete success when the viewer and the photographer have similar background experience. The difficulty of scale appreciation increases with the unfamiliarity of the scene. Thus, pupils who have walked in Snowdonia may be able to interpret slides of the Scottish Highlands quite accurately, but they will find Alpine scenes more difficult, and Himalayan almost impossible. An added difficulty is that the colour slide compresses all scenes, small and large, into the same frame, and much of the effect of changing scale, as between British, Alpine and Himalayan mountains, is lost. The scale problem can never be solved completely, but the inclusion of people and familiar objects in teaching pictures always helps.

Movement

It is also difficult to convey a sense of movement through a still picture, but usually this does not greatly matter. Indeed, an advantage of the still picture is that it 'stops' the world which is always changing and allows some aspect of it to be studied in detail.

Generally speaking, it is better to arrest movement completely by using a fast shutter speed (eg 1/500th to 1/1,000th second) than to allow blurring. Landscape photographs taken on windy days can be most unsatisfactory, aesthetically and from a teaching point of view, if all the vegetation is unsharp. In the case of waterfalls, waves and other moving water features, a speed of about 1/250th second gives acceptable results.

Correct exposure

Exposure must be used in a positive way to enhance the teaching effect of photographs. Over-exposure is always a mistake, because it burns detail out of the film which cannot be recovered. But a judicious use of under-exposure, especially when combined with strong front or side-lighting, can increase a picture's three-dimensional effect. A lens-hood should always be used when photographing towards the sun; and the sun *must never* be looked at through the viewfinder.

Manipulation of exposure can sometimes be used to add 'atmosphere' to a picture, and this may enhance its teaching effect. Like the painter, the photographer should not content himself with merely recording what he sees. Sometimes he will want to make his own statement about it. This is done by a careful selection of subject; by choice of appropriate lighting, time of day, time of year, and by adjustments to exposure. The geographer with a camera need not always be coldly clinical about his pictures. Sometimes he should use his photographic skill to convey to his pupils something of his feeling for places and people.

Close-up photography

Given a camera and accessories which make close-up work possible down to a range, say, of 120mm, a whole extra range of possibilities for making teaching pictures opens up. The close-up lens can photograph a small object, such as a geological specimen, or a picture as small as a postcard, and this can be projected to fill the whole screen, making its detailed study by a whole class possible.

There are several technical points to note in close-up work. Daylight is nearly always the best form of illumination; it allows ordinary daylight-type colour film to be used, and eliminates the need for equipment any more elaborate than a camera tripod and a sheet of pin-board or a table top on which to mount the items being photographed. Correct exposure should be obtained with a light-meter pointed at the object, or area of a map or picture, being photographed, from a distance of about 100–150mm.

A slow shutter speed should be used, say 1/30th second or more. This is because the depth of field of a lens working at close range is only a few millimetres, but it can be increased slightly by stopping down (ie reducing the size of) the lens aperture. Close-up photographs which have to be taken without a tripod (or its equivalent) need the fastest possible shutter speed, say 1/500th second, to minimise camera shake.

Photography throughout the year

Because of the normal timing of field courses and teachers' private holidays, most teaching slides are taken in summer, or in the tropics, during the dry season. Summer photography is often unsatisfactory because abundant vegetation obscures landscape detail, and the uniformly intense greens of summer may be monotonous and unpleasing. Clearly, summer sunlight has great advantages for indoor and close-up photography using daylight, and for urban work. Dry-season landscape photography in the tropics also suffers from the disadvantage of monotonous colouring, but at least foliage is at a minimum and movement through the country at its easiest.

There are several reasons why pupils should not only see summer (or dry season) slides. For example, pupils and students on summer field courses can gain no impression of the severity of winter conditions, which control man's activities in many favourite field-work areas of highland Britain. In summer, the high Pennines or Cairngorms look deceptively inviting; the Roman Wall, marching across the uplands of Northumbria, may impress pupils as a comfortable place to eat lunch. In January, these places are dramatically different. Therefore, as often as possible, the places which pupils visit need to be illustrated by winter photographs.

It is also important to collect slides which show extreme physical conditions, such as rivers in spate or winter storm waves. Physical landforms develop mainly in response to extreme conditions, and these need to be emphasised in illustration. On fair-weather field courses – which all teachers hope for – they may never be observed.

MAKING SLIDES WITH BLACKBOARD AND CAMERA

The blackboard is ideal for quick sketching and also for more elaborate drawing. It is easier and very much quicker to sketch acceptably on the blackboard, given practice, than to produce a high-quality pen-and-ink drawing. Moreover, the blackboard sketch can be added to and subtracted from very easily, so that sets of drawings showing development can be produced and photographed.

Such is the ease of making colour slides from blackboard sketches that a simple, quick but significant illustration will often be produced, perhaps conveying a single idea, which one would never have time to compose at the drawing board. For best results, an absolutely black and unpitted board is required. This is particularly important when the simplest kind of blackboard-and-camera slide is produced by mounting a black-and-white negative between two pieces of glass. The black background of the board then becomes the white background of the slide, and clearly the whiter this is the better.

The board should be large enough to make the use of a close-up attachment on the camera unnecessary, and also to make lettering easy. A size of about 90 × 120cm suits most forms of drawing. Sunlight is the best illumination, and the board should therefore be portable. The camera should be mounted on a tripod, and the fastest exposure given commensurate with a lens aperture of about f.4, which is close to the optimum optical performance of standard lenses. Correct exposure is determined most accurately by means of a light-meter, which should be held about 10cm from the brightest part of the drawing. If a slight under-exposure is then given, the surface of the board will be rendered completely black.

The base of the blackboard should be placed at an angle of 45° to the sun's rays. This minimises shine on the board and also removes the danger of the photographer's shadow falling unnoticed across the drawing. Hazy sunshine gives a more even illumination than bright sun in a clear sky. Early morning or late evening sunlight should be avoided; it gives a reddish tinge to the chalk colours and makes white, yellow and orange almost indistinguishable.

It is helpful to use a consistent style and use of chalk colours, so that one drawing can be compared visually with another. Colours such as blue and purple, which do not show up well when used directly on the blackboard, perform perfectly well on film. Red has the optical property of appearing closer to the eye than other colours, and can therefore be used for special effects. A possible rule-of-thumb use of colours might be: blue for water features, including names of these; brown for hills and mountains; green for lowland and for all forms of agricultural information; red for towns and railways; orange for industry and roads; white for glacial features and also for most labelling; purple to be held in reserve; yellow to be used for emphasis.

Chalk colours can be mixed, especially when shading, merely by holding two or more sticks of chalk together. Mixing improves the visual effect of a drawing by softening the harsh colours of standard chalks. Mixing can also be used to convey an impression of depth and perspective. For example, on a relief drawing which is mainly brown, the more significant features, or perhaps those which are near at hand, can be strengthened in orange and a small amount of yellow, so producing an almost three-dimensional effect.

Examples of the technique

The photographer always sees more in his picture than do other viewers. The teacher views the slide from a background of first-hand experience, and still 'sees' the three-dimensional reality through the flat picture. The class, however, may very well not do this. Indeed, the picture which a teacher talks about in his lesson or lecture may be that which exists in his mind rather than that which is actually projected. It is useful therefore to prepare drawings which select significant aspects of colour slides for specific teaching purposes.

A labelled drawing which shows the scene presented on a slide can therefore be very useful. An example is illustrated in plate 2, with reference to a physical landscape in the Malvern Hills. It accompanies a colour slide taken from the grid reference noted at the base of the drawing, and picks out the geological outcrops to the west of the hills. Sketches of this kind may be either drawn by eye, or traced from the image of the original slide projected on to the blackboard.

Drawings can be produced which show the relief of a selected area in the form of a bird's-eye view. This technique is particularly useful with town sites. It is difficult to discern the map contours in a heavily built-up area, and in any case the contour interval of maps is often too coarse to show significant relief detail. Plate 3 shows a bird's-eye relief drawing of the site of Newcastle upon Tyne. It emphasises the deep valleys, cut by small burns, which shaped the development of the medieval street plan and the alignment of the city walls. These micro-relief features hardly appear on the 1:63360 Ordnance map; in fact, some of the valleys have been filled in; but they are important in explaining the layout of modern Newcastle.

The bird's-eye view technique may be applied to much larger areas. Plate 3 shows a panoramic sketch of northern Tanzania. It was developed by eye from the 1:500,000 map and is designed to bring out the significant relief elements of the region. A drawing of this kind can be used as a location diagram to familiarise a class with the layout of a region. Small sections of the drawing can be photographed in close-up, and used to introduce air and ground pictures of particular features.

Panoramic drawings can usefully be developed from viewpoints unfamiliar to pupils. For example, it is perhaps appropriate to show a panorama of Russia as it might appear in the mind's eye of a Russian citizen, rather than that of an inhabitant of western Europe. For those with some talent for realistic sketching, the panorama technique can be extended into the building up of synthetic regional landscapes. Drawings of this type are built up in stages, each set of additions being photographed.

Building up drawings in stages offers much scope for illustrating

164

the development of both physical and cultural landscape features. Three stages in the building up of a drawing to show the glaciation and deglaciation of an upland area are illustrated in plate 4. Sequential drawings of this type can be used to show, for example, the recession of a waterfall, the construction of a moraine, the formation of rias, raised beaches, and river terraces; also stages in the growth of a town, in the building of a major engineering project such as the Snowy Mountains hydro-electric and irrigation scheme, or the sequence of processes in an industrial enterprise. Each stage on the diagram will be matched with slides.

USING FILMS

An enormous number of films exist, covering a wide range of geographical and allied topics, and at first sight they would appear to be a most valuable teaching resource. However, before using a film, the geographer would be well advised to ask what precisely it can do which cannot be done at least as well by other means; and also, what constraints the use of hired or borrowed films will impose on his course planning.

Films can show things which neither teacher nor pupil can see for themselves. They can be extremely good at conveying general background impressions of far-off places and peoples: the turmoil and immensity of the Victoria Falls, the distinctive colours and the endless spaces of central Australia, the varied life of a city, the bursting of the wet monsoon; but as serious teaching tools films are often less satisfactory. There are several reasons for this.

First, commercial films can never be made with a specific teaching situation in mind. They try to provide something for a wide range of situations, and so rarely give a teacher just what his class needs. Second, films show what their makers decide should be shown, and few film-makers are either teachers or geographers. Even the best films tend to have irritating omissions and to include scenes with no teaching value.

Commentaries are also a problem, because they are aimed at a general audience, probably a cinema audience which pays to be entertained rather than instructed. They also assume a quite specific level of background knowledge, which may not suit a particular class. Again, where films are instructional, sequences are often uncomfortably rapid because of the high cost per unit length of film.

It follows that film use has to be prepared very carefully. If a film is to be studied in detail, it is best used with a class in the geography room, rather than shown to a mass audience in the school lecture hall. It is also possible to make certain modifications to the standard product. For example, one can stop a film at key points, so that an important picture can be looked at in detail. One may use part of a film, and perhaps repeat it. Clearly, one does not want to take a class into a lecture hall to see five minutes of film, yet that five minutes, repeated and worked upon, may be a uniquely valuable piece of teaching material. Again, the sound-track of a film may be turned down and replaced either by direct comment by the teacher, or a taped commentary. Obviously, the teacher has to preview all the films he uses.

There are certain topics which ciné film illustrates particularly well, such as how people live and work in different parts of the world, or natural processes in which movement is the essence of the explanation. Time-lapse photography can be especially effective, eg showing glacier movement. Agricultural and industrial processes are good subjects, especially in cases where danger, noise or distance make direct observation by pupils impossible. A class cannot get close to a blast-furnace when it is being tapped; the official cameraman, equipped with telephoto lenses, can appear to get very close indeed.

The medium is very suitable for topics which can be explained most clearly by the use of animated diagrams or working models, eg wave-action, or small objects in close-up, eg aspects of bio-geography. Archive materials such as old films, photographs, drawings, maps, which no one teacher could possibly bring together, can be filmed by a ciné cameraman who can make visits to art galleries, museums, archives and libraries on behalf of the teacher.

When films are hired, they usually have to be booked months in advance, and it is normally too expensive to hire a film for more than one day. Hence the teacher is compelled to build his course to some extent around the fixed points of film bookings. This problem can be overcome to a considerable degree by education authorities and libraries building up collections of films for school use. Borrowing may then be possible at short notice. Once used, films *must* be returned promptly. Failure to do so can cause great inconvenience elsewhere.

RADIO, TELEVISION AND VIDEOTAPE

Radio and television programmes are useful aids to teaching geography, especially when they are recorded. They can then be inserted into courses at the appropriate points, instead of constraining the teaching programme by their inflexible timings.

Most types of tape-recorder can record broadcast programmes without difficulty. The only problem is usually the lack of a technical assistant, available to make recordings during school hours. To overcome this difficulty, the British Broadcasting Corporation and many other broadcasting authorities and companies make some of their educational broadcasts available on tapes, which may be borrowed by schools for an extended period.

Television programmes can also be recorded, but this requires access to a videotape machine, which is a far more elaborate and expensive piece of equipment than an ordinary tape-recorder. Video machines are obtainable which record both in black-and-white and colour. There are many different makes on the market, usually incompatible with one another.

Sound and television broadcasts bring an extra dimension of immediacy into geography lessons. Probably their greatest value lies in their capacity to bring into the classroom influential people from the world outside. A class may hear and see a cabinet minister, a scientist of international repute, a trades union official, the managing director of a large company, a top technical expert talking about their work and their current problems and goals. Their contributions are likely to be backed up with up-to-date facts and figures. Broadcasts of this kind help to make geography a 'real' subject.

As with all aids to teaching, broadcast programmes have to be prepared for, both by teacher and pupils, hence the advantage of having them in recorded form. Both the public and independent broadcasting bodies in Britain publish prospectuses of their school programmes well in advance, also booklets which may be ordered in class sets. These often provide admirably up-to-date teaching material. The teacher has to decide his objectives in using a particular programme, how he will prepare his pupils for it, how he will follow it up. He has to define his own tasks in the teaching unit of which the broadcast programme forms a part.

Schools which are equipped with videotape cameras can make their own programmes. For satisfactory results, a properly blacked-out studio, studio lighting, at least one fixed and one movable camera are required, together with qualified technical help. It is unlikely that many schools will have these very expensive facilities, but they may become quite widely available through teachers' professional centres and schools' television centres, maintained by education authorities.

The video camera can be used to record a selection of regional and national weather synopses, which can be used as film to illustrate lessons about depressions, fronts, occlusions, anti-cyclones and related meteorological topics.

If there is a studio available, the geographer can produce his own set piece lessons, which will usually be used more than once. Possible techniques using videotape cameras include:

Recording oral exposition – the teacher or visiting speaker should remember to look at the camera.
Photographing blackboard work as it is built up step by step; if a blackboard drawing is used, the camera can zoom in to specific detail as required.
Photographing slides, filmstrip pictures and OHP acetates, projected on to a screen.
Photographing clips from ciné film and combining them with other items in a sequence.
Recording display work, large posters, charts and diagrams; the camera can 'track' across these, to give an illusion of movement.
Close-up photography of sections of maps, diagrams in books and

specimens, using special lenses; there is no difficulty in recording a map section the size of a postcard. The camera can 'track' across a still photograph to give an impression of movement; it can follow a route across a map.

Video programmes can be stored indefinitely, but the high cost of tape makes this uneconomic, except for exceptionally useful items. The main disadvantage of videotape, from the programme production point of view, is the difficulty of editing it. On the tape, the recordings of vision and sound are about 20cm apart, and the tape cannot be cut and spliced as can ciné film. Editing can only be done by re-recording on to a second machine. If one wishes to combine sections of two tapes, then three video machines must be assembled, two to play and one to record. Clearly, this cannot be done very often.

Purchase of videotape apparatus is really justified only when schools are wired for closed-circuit television (CCTV). This enables recorded television programmes, and also direct broadcasts, to be viewed through receivers placed in classrooms. With this system, the opening lesson in a team-teaching project can be viewed in a normal classroom situation, instead of being given 'live' to a large gathering of pupils in the school hall or lecture theatre. The whole or parts of the lesson can then be repeated if necessary, to one class or several. Similarly, visiting speakers' talks and demonstrations can be recorded on videotape and played again for further study.

The development of portable video cameras has opened up many possibilities for outdoor work. Many portable cameras require a mains supply, but they can still be used out-of-doors in urban areas by enlisting the help of a well-placed shop, or even a private householder, and taking along plenty of extension cable. Battery-powered cameras allow much greater freedom. In all cases, it is highly instructive to involve the pupils in deciding what to record and how best to do it. Portable video cameras are especially useful for recording interviews in the field, and street and industrial scenes which may be noisy, uncomfortable and even dangerous, but which require detailed study and discussion.

GENERAL DISPLAY WORK

From time to time, the geographer finds it useful to prepare a large, bold map or drawing to illustrate some aspect of his teaching. Display work of this kind is best done with fibre-tipped pens on non-absorbent paper. A wide range of colours and several thicknesses of pen are obtainable, and very pleasing and effective results can be achieved with practice and the adoption of certain techniques.

Display work should always be as simple as possible. Simplicity is especially important if pupils are going to copy a drawing; they must be able to see how the drawing has been done. The size and boldness of all display work should suit the purpose for which it is intended. Either it is designed for close-up study or it is planned for distant viewing by large numbers – but not for both.

Drawings can be sketched with a soft pencil before being inked in. A minimum of colours should be used. There is always a temptation to use too many colours, with consequent diminution of teaching impact. The significance of all colours should be decided before a display is started. The rule followed by interior decorators, that three colours are quite enough for most rooms, is to be recommended in display work.

The art teacher's advice to pupils to use the whole of their paper also applies to display work. Lettering should be kept horizontal by the use of feint ruled lines. Uneven lettering in the teacher's display work sets a poor example to pupils.

Sometimes it is helpful to the pupils if the teacher builds up display work step by step during the lesson, so that they can learn how it is done. If a sequence of drawings is required, developing in stages from one basic drawing, the latter may be traced to form the basis of later drawings. Tracing will be done on a tracing table lighted from below through ground glass, if one is available; failing this, it can be done by using a convenient window, fastening the pairs of sheets to the glass with masking tape.

In the upper classes of secondary schools, large maps and diagrams of an accurate and formal kind are needed. These are greatly improved by the use of stick-on letters, numerals, symbols and shading and by stencils, which allow even the modest draughtsman to achieve quite good results quickly.

Drawings can be traced from projected slides and filmstrip frames. By this means, surprisingly professional-looking display work can be produced. A reminder of teaching points contained in a projected picture can thus be left on display, for comment in full daylight.

USING PICTURES

A wealth of geographical information exists in the form of printed pictures. Examples include travel brochures; illustrative materials produced by government agencies and public and private corporations, individual firms, advertisers; pictures in journals such as the *Geographical Magazine* and the colour supplements of newspapers; and picture postcards. The teacher's problem is usually to obtain the right picture at the right time, and the only hope of being able to do this is to begin collecting useful pictures in one's student days and continue until retirement!

Pictures are only effective educationally when pupils are taught how to study them. If pictures are displayed on a wall, they need to be integrated into the work of the class, by the use of worksheets, for example, and by annotating the pictures themselves.

How may pictures be used? Pupils may obtain information from them, answer questions about them. Often it is useful to point out, by marker pins and threads, exactly what the pupils should look at. As in the case of slides, it is easy to assume that pupils will see in a picture what their teacher sees, and will automatically connect the words he uses, orally or in his worksheets or annotations, with the appropriate parts of the picture. They may also have difficulty in interpreting the flat picture in terms of three dimensions and correct scale. For this reason, it is sometimes advisable to ask very simple questions about pictures, such as, What is this? (a rock outcrop, grass, cornfield); Is this building higher than our school? How far away do you think this object is, and how long might it take you to walk to it? Is the ground flat or sloping in this part of the picture, and which way is it sloping? Which way is the river flowing, and how do you know?

171

Small pictures, eg picture postcards, can be mounted as work-cards, for use by small groups and individuals. Work-cards may contain information, instructions, references or questions related to the picture.

Pictures, such as postcards, are often most valuable when they are displayed or otherwise used in sets, so that several pupils can work simultaneously on related aspects of one topic. For example, a set of postcards can be used to illustrate a tour round a town. Excellent cards for this purpose are produced for many major cities. Quite naturally, however, the publishers of commercial postcards rarely include pictures of gasworks, power stations and factories in their sets, and the teacher will have to fill in these gaps by approaching public and industrial concerns. It is helpful to link sequences of pictures together by relating them to a map and perhaps to an aerial photograph.

Sets of postcards can also be obtained fairly easily to show different kinds of scenery, eg glaciated mountain scenery in the English Lake District, limestone scenery in the West Riding of Yorkshire. Even better as teaching aids are the superlative mountain views published in some Alpine countries. From the Alps too come mountain panoramas, outstanding among which are those drawn by Heinrich Behrann. Some of Behrann's panoramas can be used for quite detailed work on Alpine physical and human geography.

Old postcards can be useful in studying changes in landscapes and townscapes. Sometimes they can be matched with contemporary maps.

A teacher may sometimes take his own black-and-white photographs and make large prints for teaching purposes. These need to be mounted on stiff card, and protected from finger-marks by plastic film. It can be useful to have colour slides and large prints of the same subjects; the latter can then be left on display for consolidation and revision.

This discussion has concentrated on work done by the teacher. However, much educationally valuable display work is done by pupils. Whenever possible, particularly when working with the younger age-ranges, a teacher who is keen and competent at display

172

work, and who can find the necessary time and materials, will make the preparation of class displays an important teaching method. It will not matter very much if nobody but he and his class look at the results. It is the doing that is educationally worthwhile.

FLANNELGRAPHS

The flannelgraph is a simple and cheap form of visual aid, developed originally in church Sunday schools to teach Bible stories. Recently, it has been much used by teachers of English as a foreign language. It has many uses in geography teaching, because it can show development; and it is particularly useful for this when local conditions make the use of projected materials impossible.

The principle of the flannelgraph is that blotting-paper will stick to flannel. The basic requirement is a sheet of white flannel, large enough to be seen by all the pupils being taught. Drawings and lettering are then prepared on drawing paper, to the back of which strips of blotting-paper are stuck. Better still, specially manufactured 'flock-dot' paper may be used; this is drawing paper backed with small discs of fibrous material, which sticks to the flannel sheet.

If necessary, the rough surface of the flannel can be coloured, either with chalks or crayons. Surplus chalk dust should be shaken out before any pictures are stuck on the flannelgraph. The use of crayons allows a certain amount of background detail to be drawn on the flannel itself. Lettering and drawing on the flock-dot paper (or drawing paper) may be done in chalks; in pen-and-ink or pencils; or with fibre-tipped pens, which give the most effective results.

The possibilities of the flannelgraph are illustrated by the following example, depicted in plate 6. The picture represents a Chagga smallholding, called a *kihamba*, on the slopes of Kilimanjaro in north Tanzania, and is built up as follows:

1 The basic flannel sheet is coloured in crayon, one-third blue for the sky, two-thirds green for the ground. The upper part of the green section is shaded in heavily to represent the rain-

forest, about six miles from the *kihamba*. Two streams are shown, flowing in deep gorges. Below the rain-forest, a distant view of the cultivated zone is suggested, with hut roofs showing among the vegetation.

2 The first stick-on drawing to be put on the flannel shows the two volcanic peaks of Kibo and Mawenzi, and the moorland zone below them, coloured brown.

3 Clouds are then added, a reminder that Kilimanjaro is a weather-generating centre; also to emphasise that the many streams which flow down the mountain come from rain falling on the forest, not from the melting snows of Kibo.

4 Details of the Chagga *kihamba* are then added to the foreground. First comes a traditional dwelling, conical in form, thatched and with a paraffin-tin chimney; this is called a *msonge*. Substitution of a same-size drawing shows its interior arrangements: fireplace, stalls for the small stature cows, a sleeping space. A second *msonge* is added, suggesting the large families found in the Chagga country.

5 Drawings are added to show the principal crops: bananas for food, beer-making, animal feed and litter, twine and many other uses; coffee for cash.

6 Next comes a new bungalow, built out of the profits from the good coffee prices of the 1960s and 1970s. (Most *msonges* are now more or less abandoned.)

7 Near the huts is a home-made coffee-stripping machine, which looks like a mincer and extracts the beans from the red coffee cherries. This coffee, which is only for home use, is seen drying on the ground. (The bulk of the crop is taken away by the co-operative organisation in cherry form, for central processing.)

8 Small patches of other crops are added, eg maize, sugar cane, pineapple, pawpaw, potatoes, cabbage.

9 A water 'furrow' is placed near the hut. This brings water from a mountain stream to the *kihamba*.

10 The path leading to the *kihamba* is drawn in reddish-brown, to suggest the colour of the mountain's volcanic soils. Drawings representing *dracaena* hedges are placed alongside

the path, and around the huts and bungalow. (This plant had customary and religious significance among the Chagga people.)

11 Finally, a number of figures are added: a boy carrying a water-can on his head; girls bringing banana leaves to the cows in the *msonge*; and women carrying maize cobs from the fields on the lower slopes of the mountain.

The flannelgraph has many applications. Some are plainly generally educational, as in building up pupils' geographical vocabulary, using drawings, or teaching conventional signs used on maps. With younger pupils they can be used to illustrate stories, or as the starting-point for a simulation game. Other applications can be specifically geographical, especially concerned with change or process, eg showing how meteorological processes work, the development of a depression, frontal rain, the föhn effect; illustrating urban replacement, for example in the form of street frontages; making substitution drawings to show the outside and then the inside of buildings; building up synthetic landscapes, item by item; showing how physical features develop – for instance, a glacier can be 'removed' and replaced by a drawing of identical size which shows the form of its underlying valley.

MODEL-MAKING

Model-making is traditionally associated with junior schools, but it has applications at all levels of education. The problem in secondary schools is usually to find time and space in which to do it, and to combine it with examination work. Recently, the growth of individual project work leading to the CSE has produced something of a model-making boom in parts of Britain.

Models can help to show three-dimensional relationships. A teacher may pride himself on his '3-D' blackboard drawings, but these may not convey an impression of depth to pupils unused to the convention, or unable to grasp it at a certain stage in their mental development. Models can show what the drawings mean. Thus a model of karst scenery can show disappearing streams, pot-holes, a limestone pavement, dry valleys, underground streams and caves and a vauclusian spring, all related to one another.

Through making models, pupils can sometimes learn how real things are made. For example, if a model is made of a conical African hut, using twigs and other natural materials, the method of construction is likely to resemble that of the original. Modelling can also teach lessons about relationships between design and function. Pupils can work out, from a description of the operations to be performed, how best to design a milking parlour for a farm, how to lay out the various parts of a pulp mill, given site details, or how to arrange different kinds of shops, offices and other services when designing a new shopping-centre.

Generally speaking, model-making is most valuable when pupils are involved at the design stage. The work then becomes a kind of simulation exercise; indeed, simulation and model-making can often be used together.

When a whole class works together on a co-operative project, an elaborate model can be produced with surprising speed, given good organisation. Suppose a model of a synthetic regional landscape is to be made. The class will divide into seven or eight groups, each with specific jobs to perform. One will prepare the land surface, using papier mâché, plastic filler or wire-netting covered with paper. Another group will paint a back-drop around three sides of the model. Other groups will model buildings, transport features, and so on. The results may be put together with striking effect (plate 5).

This whole-class approach to modelling calls for very detailed organisation. All pupils must know exactly what they have to do, and how their tasks contribute to the finished project. Tasks allocated to groups must all require about the same time for their completion. A number of spare tasks should be held in reserve, for groups who finish early. Arrangements for giving out and collecting materials must be carefully thought out. Poorly organised co-operative work of this kind is a sure prescription for chaos.

It may be noted that modelling by itself is seldom effective as a teaching method. It has to be followed by a teaching session, in which the ideas learned are made explicit and recorded in permanent form.

Materials for model-making

A wealth of publication exists about model-making; model railway enthusiasts alone have a complete literature. However, many of the techniques and topics suggested in published work are far too elaborate for the geography teacher, whose concern is primarily with the learning which takes place as the model is being made. Indeed, he will normally dispose of models soon after they are finished, because they are rarely of value to those who have not made them.

Models are of two basic kinds: those which are fully three-dimensional, and those which consist of silhouettes mounted one behind the other in diorama form. Dioramas are really drawings cut out and mounted.

Simple materials are the rule. For most models, nothing more elaborate is needed than a baseboard, adhesive paste, stiff card, fibre-tipped pens or coloured pencils, and natural materials, such as soil, moss and stones.

Most models require a firm base. An old blackboard is ideal for a class model, a tray may suffice for smaller models. The simplest way to represent the land surface is by using natural materials, soil, moss, stones, etc. Alternatives include: (1) layers of polystyrene glued one on top of another, trimmed with a sharp knife or hot wire, and rounded out with plastic filler or putty; (2) chicken wire or fine metal gauze, shaped over the top of cardboard cross-sections. Tissue paper is then pasted over the wire and, when dry, a land surface is added in plastic filler or papier mâché – shredded newspaper mixed with adhesive paste; (3) newspapers can be tightly bundled and used to support a land surface made of drawing paper; (4) modelling clay may be used, but this is extremely heavy and cracks as it dries.

Where natural materials are used, colouring the surface is unnecessary. In other cases, powder paint is the most useful medium. Powder colours always improve in appearance if they are mixed with white, producing an effect rather like oil paint.

Water surfaces will normally be shown in blue powder paint. Sometimes a mirror or a piece of glass can be used to represent a pond or lake. Glass allows underwater details to be shown, eg the form of a delta or the cross-section of a fiord.

For vegetation, natural materials, twigs and leaves, may be used. However, when particular types of plants are to be shown there is an advantage in having the pupils draw these on card with fibre-tipped pens or crayons. These drawings are cut out and mounted as silhouettes. Undifferentiated vegetation and hedgerows can be made from plastic sponge dipped in green ink or paint.

Buildings and man-made features can be drawn on card and mounted as silhouettes or they may be fully modelled in three dimensions. In the second case, the building has to be reduced to a series of flat shapes, which are then cut out and stuck together. A detachable roof shows the interior of a building. Full use should be made of matchboxes, cotton reels, matchsticks and all other ready-made shapes. Matchsticks can be used for all kinds of framework construction, eg an oil rig.

Many models, especially those of landscapes, are much improved by the addition of a back-drop around two or three sides. This can be drawn with fibre-tip pens or paints on stiff card, and can show distant features which cannot be included in the model itself.

USING THE TAPE-RECORDER

Apart from its use to record broadcasts and play them back later, the tape-recorder may be used to produce teaching materials of many kinds.

A teacher can add his own commentary to slides or a filmstrip and put it into cassette form for use by groups and individuals. Teaching notes, provided with commercial slides and strips, are a useful basis for such a commentary. Sometimes the teacher will add to the published notes and bring them up-to-date; in other cases, he may simplify them, and use a more limited vocabulary.

Whenever group work and individual investigations are carried out, there is a consolidation problem. It is necessary to make sure that the whole class learns about all significant aspects of the work.

Contributions from each group and individual may be recorded, thus providing a synopsis of the work and a useful basis for revision.

In cases where a class can discuss reasonably well, the salient points from a discussion can be recorded. This can be an invaluable aid to clarifying pupils' ideas. The method of recorded discussion can be used to consolidate points learned during a simulation game; it can be used to follow-up field work; and it can help to make explicit the geographical ideas extracted from a statistical exercise.

If a portable tape-recorder is available, recordings can be made in the field and brought back into school to be edited. Sometimes field recordings will be made by the teacher alone; he may have access to people and places to which he cannot take his pupils. Sometimes, field recordings will be made by the teacher with the pupils present; sometimes, the pupils themselves may make the recording. Recordings made in the field in one year may provide excellent classroom teaching material for the next.

A more ambitious use of the tape-recorder is to prepare dramatic presentations which illustrate aspects of the course. Presentations are of two kinds, those prepared by the teacher, often with the help of colleagues, and those prepared by the pupils. In both, the teacher has to study his source materials and decide how it can be put into dramatic form. An example illustrates this.

Case study: a Kikuyu farmer in Kenya

Suppose the teacher wishes to tell his class – in this case a sixth form – about the Kikuyu farmers of Kenya. He can teach a straightforward lesson about them, using slides and maps, or he can try to get his pupils to imagine themselves members of a Kikuyu community, by involving them in a dramatic presentation. The cast for this might include the following, the pupils playing all the parts:

Mr Jacob Kanyama, Kikuyu smallholder, owning 4 hectares of land in the Kikuyu highlands about 80 kilometres north-west of Nairobi. His part is to describe his holding, his crops (tea as a cash

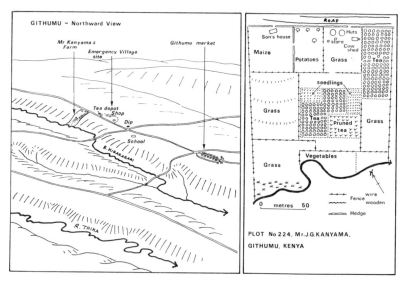

Plan of Mr Kanyama's farm in Githumu, with a sketch panorama of Githumu District to show location.

crop, maize, potatoes and a variety of other subsistence crops) and his dairy cattle (he has two 'grade' cows, and sells milk), and to introduce his family.

Members of the family – these include two daughters at secondary school, one of whom is now at home picking tea; an eldest son, in a government office in Nairobi. Conversation between family members will describe how the smallholding is run and introduce the problem of population pressure in the Kikuyu country.

Chief Francis, chief (government administrator) of the district. His part is to explain about tea collection and marketing through the co-operative organisation; also to mention the government regulation that holdings must not now be made smaller than 5 hectares (in this district) through sub-division.

Two old men, who will talk about changes in land use in the district, with wattle growing being replaced by tea and milk production.

A veterinary officer, who will explain why it is compulsory for all

180

cattle to be dipped weekly, and who will talk about stock improve-ment. He will explain that 'grade' cows are european-zebu or zebu-indian cross-breds, and say why cross-breeding is necessary in Kenya.

A visitor, perhaps several, who will put questions, describe the scene, and keep conversation flowing. The visitors' final questions will introduce the topic of settlement schemes on the former 'white highlands', to be discussed next lesson.

Of course, with many teaching groups, it can be a major achievement to produce a coherent tape of as little as three minutes' duration; but this can be well worthwhile.

DUPLICATED MATERIAL

Many types of duplicating equipment give the geography teacher various kinds of teaching material. He can, by copying items of reference material of which he has only one copy, make them available to the whole class. He can produce large numbers of copies of reference materials which he has written or drawn him-self. Work done by one pupil can be made available to a group or whole class. When he wishes, the teacher can replace teaching by learning from prepared materials, leaving himself free to supervise that learning. The use of duplicated materials also allows multi-activity work to be planned – duplicated material is a necessary basis for all small group and mixed-ability teaching.

The main pitfall to be guarded against when using duplicated material is that pupils will file it away unread. The precise way in which it is to be used by pupils has to be thought out in advance.

Recently there has been some attempt to organise the exchange of duplicated items between geography departments in different schools, most notably the *Setwork Network*, involving about 500 schools, based near Oxford. Other exchange networks seem likely to emerge, probably based in teachers' centres.

Exchanges between schools are especially to be recommended in developing countries, where books are in short supply and teachers work in great professional isolation. The idea has been developed in Tanzania, where sample studies based on local field work have been circulated to schools by the Ministry of Education.

Types of duplicators

Most duplicating equipment will normally be held centrally in a school, and ideally it will be operated and maintained by a trained technical assistant. But, whatever the central facilities may be, the geography department needs a hand-operated spirit duplicator to produce class-size batches of material at short notice.

The spirit duplicator works by transferring a carbon impression from a stencil sheet to special paper, the spirit acting as a solvent. A maximum of about seventy-five copies can be made before the carbon is exhausted.

Stencils for spirit duplicators can be hand-written, typed or drawn with a stylus or ball-point pen. Several colours can be obtained on one sheet by changing the carbon under the stencil. Boxes of assorted coloured carbons are obtainable. The use of different colours needs to be planned in advance. It is almost impossible to tell from the carbon impression which colour one has used, and it is disconcerting to find that, when a map is run off, some of the railways are in red and some in brown.

To put maps and drawings on a stencil, the item to be copied is first drawn or traced on to tracing paper in soft pencil or fibre-tipped pen. The tracing paper is then fixed to the stencil with sticky tape, and the drawing cut through on to the stencil with a stylus or ball-point pen. Where several colours are used, it is helpful to mark these on the tracing with fibre-tipped pen. Each colour can then be traced through in turn, using the appropriate carbon. One clear copy of the duplicated drawing should be filed for reference. It can be traced on to a new stencil if required.

A heat-transfer machine makes stencils from printed items, such as the page of a book, tables of figures, typescript or line drawings in indian ink.

Ink duplicators work by forcing ink through cuts in a wax stencil on to special paper. Most schools have at least one such machine, usually power-operated. Up to 1,000 copies of any item can be made with no loss of quality. Stencils can be stored in newspaper and re-used several times; it is sensible to index the stored stencils.

Typing produces the best results on a wax stencil, but handwriting can be satisfactory if done on a hard surface, eg formica or glass, using a stylus or dry ball-point. To prepare drawings on a stencil, the drawing is first prepared on ordinary white paper, in pencil, ink or fibre-tipped pen. A wax stencil is then fixed over the drawing, and this is lightly traced on to the stencil in soft pencil. The original drawing is removed, and the pencil tracing is cut into the stencil with a stylus or ball-point. If desired, lettering and figures can then be typed on to the stencil.

It is possible to use several colours on an ink duplicator, but this involves changing the inked rollers and re-running each sheet. Wax stencils can be made from printed materials, such as the pages of a book, typescript or line drawings (ink) by an electric stencil cutter. This is an expensive machine which will be held centrally, in a school or teachers' centre.

Photo-copying can be done by a variety of machines, but is always expensive. It is prohibitive to produce a class-set of material by this method. The photo-copier is a resource for the teacher, not the pupils. Many libraries and record offices offer a photo-copying service.

The offset litho machine will reproduce not only print but also photographs, eg from newspapers, and make very large numbers of copies. This is another expensive machine whose hire or purchase can only be justified by continuous (ie well-planned) and imaginative use. A geography department alone is unlikely to have such a machine. The offset litho is necessary equipment in a large school where the work is resource-based. It is also the piece of duplicating equipment most likely to bring the school or education authority into conflict with the laws of copyright.

183

9 Field Work

In schools, field work is a teaching method. Sometimes teachers confuse it with research, which it is not, because pupils only find out what, in outline, their teachers already know. Field work is a method of planned discovery, whereby the teacher prepares situations from which his pupils learn geographical facts and ideas for themselves.

Geography is both a body of knowledge and a distinctive method of study, and field work is the best and most immediate means of bringing the two aspects of the subject together in the experience of the pupil. Therefore, field work is a necessary part of geographical education; it is not an optional extra. The English philosopher A. N. Whitehead wrote in his *Aims of Education* that 'the second-handedness of the learned world is the secret of its mediocrity', and teachers know that there is an uncomfortable core of truth in his statement. Whitehead implies that the teacher of geography or any other subject will only be fully effective when he speaks in some measure from his own experience and understanding; and when those whom he teaches obtain some of their evidence at first-hand from the world outside school.

Traditionally, field work has been associated with visits by school parties to exciting hill and mountain country, often during holiday periods. A few teachers, including some geographers, still equate field work with strenuous physical activity in wild country, but there is no necessary connection. Field work can be done anywhere, in any kind of landscape or townscape, and it does not necessarily involve long journeys or large amounts of time to make it worthwhile. A valuable teaching point can sometimes be made by an exercise lasting half an hour within walking distance of the geography room.

Field work will sometimes be concerned to teach factual information, because this is the raw material upon which reasoning has to be based. It will also be designed to teach pupils about spatial relationships; it will provide opportunities for principles already known to be applied and tested; it may be used to present a collection of facts for analysis, or it may take the form of an exercise in synthesis. Often pupils will be asked to evaluate the relative importance of what they observe and record. Bloom's *Taxonomy of Educational Objectives* is just as useful to the field worker as to the classroom teacher and examiner. Further advances in field work methods, in schools and at higher levels, depend upon a more careful and precise definition of teaching objectives than has traditionally been practised.

As with all kinds of teaching, the detailed preparation of field work is most important. A few educational authorities now make financial provision for teachers to make reconnaissance visits when planning field work. It is urgent that this practice should become the standard. No teacher, however experienced, can extract the full teaching potential from an area unless he has studied it in the field beforehand.

There is also a need for more systematic training in field work techniques. In Britain, for example, in-service training provision has so far taken the form of a limited number of Department of Education and Science courses, supported by courses and conferences run by such bodies as the Geographical Association and the Geographical Field Group. Attendance at all such courses is voluntary on the part of teachers. Further improvement requires a more systematic effort at the local level, involving many more teachers, and with the circumstances of particular schools kept firmly in mind.

Field work is invaluable as an educational method, in the widest sense. By working together out-of-doors, staff and pupils come to know one another in a way almost impossible to achieve in class. Many young teachers have found their disciplinary problems solved, or at least greatly mitigated, as a result of the enterprise and competence they have demonstrated during a field course. Field work gives opportunities for pupils and staff to learn together, instead of the teacher always expounding and the pupils listening. It gives opportunities also for the social development of pupils, teaching them consideration for others and the art of living together; and it can help to promote self-confidence, the ability to communicate with strangers, and independence of thought. Above all it can be active, clearly important because it deals with real people and real geography, and thoroughly enjoyable.

PURPOSES

Teaching geographical vocabulary

An important function of field work, especially with younger pupils, is to transform words into experience – to show them the things which words describe. Pupils have always learned and used some words without having more than the haziest notion about what they mean, and manipulated words to pass examinations. The problem of knowing what words mean is particularly severe for pupils who come from culturally deprived backgrounds; and this is a sizeable proportion of all pupils in school in all countries, whether 'advanced' or 'developing'. Vocabulary work in the field is therefore always important.

For example, it emerged during a lesson in a Gateshead school that at least one boy believed that the word 'hill' meant a steep street with terrace houses on both sides. Presumably therefore, when hills were mentioned in Australia or South America, he visualised Gateshead-type streets. The teacher always has to be on guard against his pupils' misunderstandings of even the most basic terms, which can turn his best-planned lessons into nonsense. This problem can never be fully overcome, but field work which includes a carefully thought out vocabulary-building element can be a great help. No opportunity should be lost of asking pupils, directly or indirectly, to describe what they see and to assign words to landscape and townscape features.

Giving experience of distance, slope, height

Direct experience of distance, angle of slopes, height, direction can be got from practical school work out of doors. To widen this

186

geographical experience beyond the immediate school vicinity pupils must do as much field work as possible on foot. Riding in a coach along tarmac roads is not a substitute. Only walking is slow enough to make detailed observation, discussion and thought possible, and it allows distance, slope angles and heights to be felt. If pupils do their own map reading while walking, they rapidly develop a heightened sense of direction, of the relative positions of observed objects, and of relief. None of these impinges very strongly when one is riding in a motor vehicle. Indeed it might be argued that the motor car and its road systems seal off the environment from close observation; and that one of the geographer's principal tasks is to restore his pupils' capacity to observe closely.

Pupils' understanding of slope angles and heights can be improved by, say, a walk up a chalk escarpment, a river-to-ridge walk in a valley, or a scramble up coastal cliffs of various angles and rock materials.

Comparing the ground with the map

Another important function of field work is to cause pupils to compare the ground with the map. The topographical map, eg the Ordnance Survey 1:63360, 1:50000 or 1:25000 series, is a form of landscape model, because it represents reality in a conventional and highly selective way. It is important from an educational standpoint to remember also that the map is a purely descriptive document; it shows effects, not causes. Through field work, pupils can begin to discover some of the causes of what the map depicts.

Field work can help pupils to appreciate the significance of map scales. If a square kilometre of country is sketch-mapped inside a centimetre square, the absolute need for aspects of the landscape to be omitted, and for others to be represented by conventional signs, quickly emerges. Sometimes, pupils may be asked to add significant detail to published maps from field observation. An example might be minor breaks of slope along a river valley, important to the location of settlements, but concealed by the contour interval of the map.

187

Developing an appreciation of surface forms

Most pupils find difficulty in relating contour patterns to the forms of the ground, and field observation and sketch-mapping in an area of marked relief can help greatly in this respect. Local field work can show pupils that there *are* relief features where they live; many pupils seem to think that 'relief' is only found in country areas, and are surprised to find that river terraces and flood plains, for example, can be traced through a built-up area, and related to the siting of industries, power stations and different kinds of residential area.

Pupils' awareness of surface conditions will be heightened by a walk across a limestone pavement, a peat moss, coastal dunes, salt marshes, even along public rights-of-way through farmland. Walking through forest can be a memorable experience for a boy or girl brought up in open country. It is useful to remember that many pupils in town schools walk almost exclusively in streets, and hardly ever come into contact with the natural surface.

Introduction to imperfect examples of landforms

An important purpose of field work is to bring pupils into contact with examples of landforms which are less distinct and regular in shape than the textbooks (and especially textbook diagrams) sometimes suggest. Lateral and terminal moraines, eskers, drumlins, raised beaches and so forth are seldom clearly separate from other features, and pupils find this overlapping difficult to interpret. The Lauterbrunnen and Yosemite valleys are not *typical* glacial troughs, though they are often cited as such; they are incredibly spectacular examples of such valleys. The pupil, schooled in the texts, often fails to identify landforms he knows about in theory, even when he is standing on them, because they are imperfect. A function of field work is therefore to point out the imperfect example. Ideally, the concept of the ideal form will be developed from observations of the imperfect, but time rarely allows this to be done.

Understanding areal differentiation and the nature of boundaries

One of the geographer's functions is to observe, describe and explain differences between areas. Such differences are especially instructive when, for example, two areas have a comparable geological basis and yet have developed quite differently. An important purpose of field work is to help pupils to recognise and define the characteristics of areal differences, in both physical and man-made landscapes, including towns.

The geographer is also concerned with the position and nature of boundaries. The problem of drawing sharp boundaries between almost any sets of phenomena can be demonstrated most convincingly in the field. Pupils may be asked, where precisely is this geological boundary, which looks so clear on the map? Where does one draw the boundary between town and country in this area, where thousands of townsfolk live in country villages and commute daily, and farmers' wives shop weekly in the town's supermarkets?

Introducing new ideas

One of the most effective ways of introducing an important new idea or principle to pupils is to have them discover it for themselves in the field. Most new ideas thus introduced are part of a sequence, which will be discussed before the field work starts. Thus, preparation for a farm visit might deal with the natural conditions favoured by certain crops, and the methods of cultivation and husbandry used in the district. It might then be arranged with the farmer that most of his comment would deal with such things as price fluctuations, national or world market conditions, transport problems and costs, the need to mechanise because of rising wage-rates and the drift of men to the towns. A much wider concept of the word 'environment' would thus emerge.

Interpreting air photographs

Field work can be used to train pupils in rudimentary interpretation of air photographs. Most pupils seem to find air photos, even verticals, easier to understand than Ordnance Survey or similar maps, but detailed interpretation presents them with many problems. If a set of photos can be taken into the field, and pupils

189

can walk over the area, comparing the ground with the photo, they begin to recognise the 'conventions' of the latter – the meaning of its various textures, its shades of grey, the shapes of buildings seen from overhead, the order of superposition of transport networks, the characteristic appearance of age and function zones in towns.

It may be noted that, where stereoscopic pairs of photos are available, they can be viewed three-dimensionally without the aid of a stereoscope, given a little practice. This is a useful skill for pupils to master when they are using photos out-of-doors.

METHODS

Field work begins with the observation and recording of data. A first requirement is therefore to train pupils to observe accurately and record what they find by appropriate means. Observation can be trained by asking pupils searching questions about what they see, whether by word of mouth or by the use of worksheets, maps and diagrams, which they have to annotate or complete in the field.

The geographer records his observations in the following ways: making maps by measurement, using pacing, home-made survey instruments or those which are commercially produced; sketch-mapping; field sketching, which will normally be annotated and related to the map; note-taking; counting and measuring; tape-recording, eg interviews with people met in the field. These methods will be developed throughout the school course.

Observation and recording are followed by interpretation. This calls for thought processes and such skills as describing systema-tically; analysing or synthesising the results of observations; separating and classifying different kinds of data; evaluating the relative importance of different items observed; explaining from field evidence what has been discovered.

Field work may sometimes consist of pupils being asked to compare reported facts with field observations. This type of work is a useful introduction to more closely structured hypothesis testing, but it is valuable in its own right at all teaching levels. For example, a generalised regional description taken from a textbook may be compared with field observations. Questions may

190

be asked, such as: what percentage of all buildings in this 'stone-built' West Yorkshire town are in fact built of stone? What percentage of the town's total area is occupied by stone buildings? What percentage of the inhabitants of this country village work in the country? Is heavy industry really dominant in this supposedly heavy industrial area? Are textbook statements about relationships between altitude, slope and land use in this area borne out by observation? Conversely, having studied several market towns, perhaps working in groups, pupils may be asked to draw up a theoretical model of the typical market town of the region.

There is an extensive amount of literature on field work methods and examples, of which the whole range is too great to be surveyed here. In the sections which follow, some guidelines are given for the teacher who is developing his own field work programme.

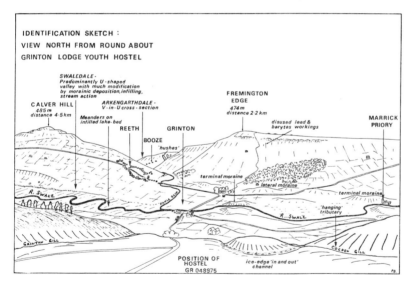

Landscape identification sketch, showing some of the details and information which pupils might observe from the vicinity of Grinton Lodge Youth Hostel, Yorkshire. The sketch would be given to the pupils unlabelled. 'Hushes' are gulleys produced by lead extraction.

191

Teaching in the field

Teaching in the field may be defined as the exposition of landscape in the field. It consists of getting pupils to see what is there, and in giving them an appropriate amount of information to stimulate sensible questions about it. It is to be distinguished from field work, which is work carried out by pupils; both activities are necessary. Field teaching will probably be used to introduce the local area, the local region (however defined), and the general geography of more distant areas. A field course in a new area will generally include an element of landscape exposition, to bring together the various elements of the field work.

The skills of field teaching are those of all good teaching; they include the clear identification of teaching points; clarity and audibility of exposition; choice of appropriate language; and the achievement of a cumulative structure to the exposition, with many internal links and references back. Good field teaching depends upon a very thorough knowledge of the landscape.

Geographical walks

A field work programme may begin with a local walk. This may be led by the teacher, if the group is small, or it may be guided by worksheet and map issued to the pupils. Introductory walks are to be recommended in both rural and urban areas. They need to have clearly defined teaching objectives; usually they set the scene for more detailed work.

Walks will have objectives such as the following: to point out local relief and drainage features; to examine one street in detail – often this is a kind of urban detective work; to trace the growth-stages of a town outwards from its centre; to look at a view from a high point, then to walk down into it, and identify important features; or to pick out important physical and man-made landscape features in an area.

When conducting a walk, economy of comment is the rule. The well-prepared enthusiast can easily fall into the trap of telling his pupils all he knows, instead of contriving ways of their finding it out for themselves. Decide in advance how pupils will record their information; unrecorded information is soon forgotten.

Coach-and-foot reconnaissance

These are general surveys of larger areas than can be covered on foot; usually they involve the use of a coach. A teacher planning a survey of this type has first to decide his main teaching points. Then he has to plan a route and select a number of stops, which provide field evidence to support these points. For each stop, he must decide how to convey his points most effectively, whether by exposition or through a short field work exercise. The well-planned survey will include a variety of methods. An alternative programme must be prepared in case of bad weather conditions, especially poor visibility. Pupils will be required to make observations of the landscape while the coach is travelling between stops. Refreshment and toilet stops will be built into the programme, which will be timed as precisely as possible.

The major pitfalls of the reconnaissance survey method are: to make it too long, so that pupils become exhausted – about five hours, with plenty of changes of activity, is about the maximum; to try to teach too many different things; and to do too much oral exposition while giving the pupils too little to do.

Coach-and-foot reconnaissance surveys may be used for:

Transects across the geological 'grain' of a piece of country, to examine relationships between rock type, structure, soils, land use, settlement sites and forms.

Routes through physically delimited areas, such as river basins, to examine their characteristics in association.

Routes through areas delimited by man's activities, eg a county or other administrative area, a coalfield, a frontier area, an area whose accessibility has recently been changed by the building of a bridge or motorway, or the removal of a railway.

Routes through towns and conurbations, to demonstrate zonation and variation in development.

Thematic studies, in which certain aspects of landscape are picked out over a wide area. Examples include the distribution and relation of glacial landforms, of hydro-electric installations in a valley system, the impact of tourism on settlements.

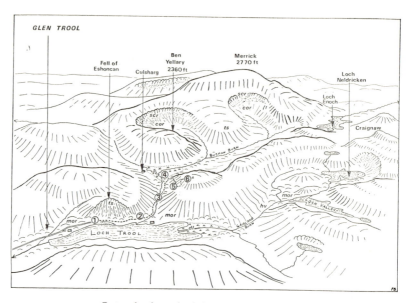

GLEN TROOL

Introducing glacial geomorphology.
Plan for a walk in Glen Trool, Scotland; distance 3km.
(Ben Yellary 719m; Merrick 844m)

1 From the lookout point near Glen Trool coach park, altitude 93m,
identify U-shaped trunk valley of Glen Trool; glacial basin now
occupied by Loch Trool; truncated spurs (ts on the drawing); hanging
tributary valleys (hv), especially Buchan Burn, followed by the subsequent walk; varieties of morainic deposit (mor).
2 At foot of Buchan Burn valley, identify features associated with adjustments to present-day climatic and biotic conditions, such as:
screes (scr) being fixed by vegetation; soil creep; V-in-U cross-profile
of Buchan Burn valley, and other valleys; deeply incised streams,
sometimes following fault-lines.
3 In Buchan Burn valley, note how stream is modifying its long-profile,
eg minor waterfalls have worked upstream. Suggest that boulders in
stream bed, too large to be moved even under present-day flood-
conditions, are evidence of more rapid and powerful run-off under
glacial and periglacial conditions. Find examples of perched blocks,
attributable to glacial action. Identify change-of-load terraces.
4 Here the steep 'hanging' section of Buchan Burn gives place to the
level floor of an infilled glacial lake, across which the burn meanders.

Teaching through question sheets

Another useful field work method is to send out pupils with a list of questions, to which they have to find the answers by observation and measurement. For example, a group may be sent along a town street with a duplicated map and the following questions:

How many houses in this street used to be shops? How do you know? Mark them on your map in red.

How many houses used to be other kinds of buildings, apart from shops? How do you know? What were they? Mark them all in blue on your map. Why do you think they are all houses now?

Are all houses in the street the same age? Make a list of all the dates you can find on the houses, then mark on your map:

the oldest houses, in brown
the next oldest, in green
the newest, in yellow
(Give the age of each category in your key)

Are there any houses which do not fit into this scheme? What can you find out about them?

There is a factory at the end of the street. Was it there when the street was built? How do you know?

Questions can be used, in conjunction with duplicated drawings and maps, to help pupils identify landforms, seen from a vantage point.

---

5 Examine slopes of Buchan Hill for evidence of past and present movements of material, eg erratics, screes, rocking stones. Note glacial smoothing and plucking of rock spurs. Find exposures of bedrock, marked by glacial striae.

6 From summit of Buchan Hill, altitude 484m, all the country shown on the drawing is visible. Identify further examples of glacial features, eg corries (cor) on slopes of Merrick, Loch Valley and Loch Neldricken. Note that Loch Trool is the partly infilled remnant of a larger loch, and that Water of Trool is building a delta (dl) into it at its head. Summarise the observations made, and discuss their possible significance in terms of past events and present-day processes.

Using questionnaires

Questionnaires are structured lists of questions which pupils use at an interview, with farmers or shoppers, for example. Clearly, the use of questionnaires needs to be carefully controlled, otherwise annoyance can result. It seems reasonable to suggest that a long questionnaire should only be used to interview a farmer or other busy person with his prior approval, obtained by the teacher.

At school level, certainly below the sixth form, the questionnaire is a teaching method, not a method of research. The purpose of a questionnaire is to teach pupils to formulate questions in relation to the specific kinds of information that are needed. The teaching objectives of a questionnaire must always be worked out. Why will these questions be asked, and others omitted? What will the pupils learn from answers to their questions?

The design and use of questionnaires may be illustrated with reference to a farm visit. First, the teaching objectives of the whole operation have to be defined by the teacher. These are likely to be to show pupils that a farm is a complex organisation, operating in a complex environment, and not a static object on the landscape.

Next, the co-operation of an interested and articulate farmer, or farmers, must be secured. The government agricultural advisory service can usually help here. At school level, it is far more important that the farmer should be able to talk well than that his farm should be a random sample. To select an unsuspecting farmer, descend upon him with thirty pupils, and expect him to teach them, all unprepared, is both discourteous and pedagogically unsound. Whenever possible, the teacher will be well advised to visit the farmer beforehand, discuss with him the points to be made, and ask him to check through the proposed questionnaire. He may well improve it.

On the visit, all the pupils, equipped with the full list of questions, note down all the farmer's answers; but certain groups of pupils will be given special responsibility for asking particular questions. This prevents an irritating repetition of questions by successive groups.

The extent and type of information to be sought through the questionnaire will be determined by the learning context of which the farm visit is part and by the age and ability of the pupils. The following suggestions for format of questions are comprehensive and not selected for a specific study context.

Name of farm, name of farmer. Locality, position (grid reference). Area of farm. Is a farm plan available? If not, the farm and fields may be surveyed rapidly, eg by pacing if it is small enough.

Land use. How does the farmer use his land: what crops are growing now? What are the areas of each? What have been grown during the past twelve months? Is any land fallow? What are the most important crops in (1) area, (2) yield, (3) profitability?

What animals does the farmer keep? What are their uses? Details of breeds, age-structure, housing and feeding arrangements and general animal husbandry may be asked for.

Method of cultivation: what tools, machinery, fertilisers are used? Are any special cultivation methods used, eg terracing, irrigation?

Houses and buildings: what buildings are there on the farm, and what is each used for? What building materials are used? How old are the buildings? Have any older buildings disappeared? Are plans of the buildings available? If not, a plan will usually be drawn, measured by pacing.

Population and labour force: who lives on the farm, and what are their relationships? Is there any employed labour? Any part-time labour, throughout the year or at particular times? It may be useful sometimes to list the farm population under sex and age-groups: 0–15 years, 16–30, over 30, etc.

Population movements: if grown-up children have left the farm, where have they gone, and what kind of jobs are they doing?

Tenure and farm history: does the farmer own his farm, is he a tenant, and if so, of whom? How long has the farm been in his family? Is it part of a larger unit which has been sub-divided? Are there any inheritance customs which may cause it to be sub-divided in the future?

Sales and purchases: what does the farmer sell? How does he sell his various products, eg through a co-operative, through a local mart, to a frozen foods factory? What is the annual output of the farm, in numbers of animals and quantities of crops sold? What does he buy each year?

Other points of interest: these might include questions about water supply, fuel, common grazings, uses of a forest for gathering feeding stuffs, bee-keeping, the growing of experimental crops; also the provision of services to the farmer, and his view of these. Discussions of change, recent or in progress, can be useful.

With older pupils and students, it is worth asking a farmer's views about: obtaining maximum output per unit area; obtaining maximum output per unit of labour. Related questions can then be asked about his views on mechanisation and intensification, or obtaining more land where this is possible, ie through amalgamation. Answers can differ very much between developed and developing countries.

Preparation for industrial visits

Field work includes visits to industrial plant, mines, quarries, power stations, shipyards, docks and other forms of commercial enterprise. The problem in such cases is to make the visit both geographical and educational. Often, school parties are taken round by professional factory guides, or by relatively junior technical staff, who know little of locational and policy matters. Explanations tend to be almost exclusively technical, concerned to describe the processes which are going on, and often these are too difficult for the pupils to grasp. Another difficulty is that what is seen may not be at all self-explanatory. Although, for example, an hour's visit to a tea factory is easy to follow, because the tea can be seen passing through the various processes, a half-day tour of a steel works or an atomic power station may be very difficult. The teacher has the task of adding a geographical dimension to the visit.

This may be done in various ways. It may be possible for the teacher to interview a member of the senior management before the visit, to discuss broad issues of location and policy. The results of such an interview can be turned into notes and questions for the pupils to bear in mind. It can be useful to obtain descriptive literature about the plant, and produce pupils' notes from this. A simple systems diagram, showing inputs to the plant, the sequence of processes, and the outputs, can be especially helpful.

What may be termed the 'geographical dimension' may be set out under such questions as:

What do the terms 'steel works', 'cannery', 'power station', etc, actually mean, in terms of people doing things with materials and machines? In other words, how does it work, what does it do?

What are the needs of the plant in, eg labour (numbers, male, female); raw materials; energy; water; space; transport? Where do these inputs come from?

What does the plant produce? Where do its products go, what are they used for, with what do they compete?

Why is the plant located where it is?

Does the plant continue any traditional crafts in the area? Was it placed here originally because of a local entrepreneur, and if so, why did he choose this site?

What relationships has this plant with others? Is it part of a regional, national, multi-national group?

How does it influence the area, in terms of supporting other industries, creating jobs, upgrading various facilities?

Studies of process

Much field work is concerned with the study of process, both in the physical and socio-economic fields. This aspect of field work has increased in importance since about 1965 with the general introduction of quantification, systems thinking and the use of dynamic models into geography.

In the field of physical geography, teaching objectives might be: to show that landforms are the products of processes and events; to develop with pupils the concepts of process-landform interaction; process interaction; and the balance of processes, or dynamic equilibrium, related ultimately to climate.

It is always important to establish the basic idea of the continuity of processes; many pupils have a very static view of physical landscapes. Field work in geomorphology may begin with pupils being sent out to find all the evidence they can that changes are taking place. They will look for such things as soil creep, even on gentle slopes; loose scree; breaks in the vegetation cover; unstable stream and river banks; flood deposits; signs that river meanders have migrated downstream; unstable sand dunes; rock surfaces attacked by frost; and so on.

Some of these observations lead on to measurement. For example: current speeds in the middle of a stream and near its banks can be measured by floating ping-pong balls downstream and timing and mapping their movements. The behaviour of currents at bends can be observed by this means. The amount and speed of erosion and deposition along different sections of a river bank can be measured by inserting marked stakes horizontally into the bank at water level and observing the depth of material removed or added in a given time, say a week. Where a stream is shallow enough for wading, cross-sections of its bed can be drawn, using a marked pole. Simple levelling with home-made instruments can be used to map river terraces. In cases where a stream can be observed regularly throughout the year, its water levels, rates of discharge, and the size and weight of particles it carries can be recorded, and perhaps related to meteorological conditions.

More geographers than ever before are now competent to introduce simple biogeography into their field work. The main purpose of such studies is to show that plants, animals, insects and other living forms exist in complicated associations; that these are dynamic and liable to change if interfered with. Possible observations include studies of lichen and plant colonisation on bare rock surfaces, on scree or an abandoned quarry face; changes in vegetation brought about by changes in grazing, or by the elimination of a pest such as rabbits; studies of the distribution and relationships of plant associations on salt marshes; studies of sand dune development, from sand patch to fully developed dune; studies of the colonisation of abandoned building sites by plants.

The concepts of change and tension can be used as starting-points for field work in the socio-economic field. Thus, urban field work may also begin with a search by pupils for evidences of change and signs of tension in the urban system. They may for example be asked to locate, map, count per grid-square as appropriate, such items as empty houses awaiting demolition; private houses which have changed their function, eg become shops or flats; new buildings replacing old in the central business area; streets where shops appear to be doing badly, or have recently closed; streets obstructed by parked cars or delivery vehicles; large lorries in narrow streets; and so on. Sometimes the notion of change and tension can be introduced by discussing the advantages and disadvantages of living in this part of town now, fifty, and a hundred years ago.

Hypothesis testing and the use of models

Field work can also be used to show pupils how to test the truth of a hypothesis, and to compare theoretical models with reality. It is wise to introduce this approach with caution. At the secondary school level, pupils in general have little background knowledge and experience on which to erect conceptual frameworks. They may very well not understand the reasons which lead to a hypothesis being proposed; and they may find more difficulty than the teacher expects in relating a model to a number of actual cases. But, as with other kinds of teaching, one tries the method until the pupils grasp it.

The hypothesis-testing approach proceeds by a series of steps:

1 First the teacher has to formulate a geographical idea or principle which can be posed in the form of a hypothesis.
2 He then has to plan work which will enable his pupils to formulate this hypothesis for themselves.
3 Then he has to design a piece of field work, which will show the pupils whether or not the hypothesis is correct, or in what ways it is inadequate.
4 The results of this field work will then be discussed, and conclusions drawn. The hypothesis may be re-formulated, and the process of field testing repeated. In theory, and if time

201

allows, this sequence will continue until the hypothesis fits the observations.

5   Finally, further work will be built on the conclusions drawn.

Some examples, taken from various aspects of geography, will show what is meant. It might be hypothesised that a hollow in a hillside is a corrie, and once held a glacier. Pupils will look for evidence for this, eg a terminal moraine at the corrie mouth, breached by a stream; an old lake-bed; screes and a steep back-wall with bare rock surfaces. They may level the long-profile of the corrie to test for overdeepening.

Another example is to hypothesise that in a particular area large farms are more efficient than small farms. Efficiency might be measured by livestock density or numbers of machines per unit area of each farm, or variety of crops grown. In many areas, the obvious conclusion, that large size equals greatest efficiency, will be found to be wrong, or at least, a gross generalisation about a complex situation.

Starting from the hypothesis that the heaviest motor traffic in a town will be found in the central business area, it may be seen that this is not the case, and the related field work may introduce pupils to aspects of town planning.

Field work based upon comparisons of theoretical models with reality, or attempts to deduce such models from observations, are similar in principle to hypothesis testing. Usually, however, they ask pupils to consider the validity of widely accepted models.

In recent years, the search for general patterns has led geographers to formulate 'laws' of spatial behaviour, especially in the socio-economic field. Several widely used models can easily be field-tested. Examples include von Thünen's model of rural land use around a town (brought up-to-date and regionally adapted); Burgess's model of concentric urban zones, and modifications by Hoyt and Ullman; Christaller's model of settlement hierarchy and spacing, and its development by Bracey and others; Reilly's and Huff's models, which deal with patterns of retail distribution and the spheres of influence of market centres; and gravity models, which try to predict the flows of traffic between centres.

None of these is, of course, exclusively a field work topic.

Probably the most productive use of a model is to work out a justification for it in the classroom; send pupils into the field to discover discrepancies from it; then begin to explain these discrepancies in the classroom again.

In the last resort, the teacher has to decide, within the contexts of limited time and transport, which models are worth testing in the field. It would appear to be unsound pedagogically to concentrate all one's field work efforts on any single method.

ORGANISATION

It is wisest to work through a series of steps when planning a field course away from the school, and involving overnight accommodation. Not all the steps will be necessary for every course, and their order will vary with particular circumstances.

It is important to decide latest dates for the completion of each important step, especially when several staff are involved. In the case of very complicated courses and expeditions, it may be useful to apply critical path analysis to the planning operation.

A planning outline

1 Decide the educational objectives and desirable duration of the course. Consider how it will relate to the rest of the work in geography. If the course is to be multi-disciplinary, how will it relate to each contributing specialist syllabus?

2 If the course involves leading pupils in mountainous country, make sure that at least one member of staff is qualified to do this. Some education authorities have regulations on this point.

3 Identify a number of possible areas where the course objectives might be achieved. Narrow the choice to areas which staff either know well, or can reconnoitre, and which are adequately documented.

4 If staff reconnaissance is necessary, ask the education authority for financial support, detailing a programme.

5 Obtain lists of accommodation and prices in the proposed areas.

6 Identify suitable centre/s in one or more of the proposed areas. Criteria for selection include (a) good food, (b) adequate drying facilities, and (c) a work-room for use in the evenings. Make a decision about the area, and book accommodation provisionally.

7 Begin to work out course details, with wet weather alternatives, to announce to pupils, head, colleagues, parents. Decide firmly which members of staff will take part, and allot tasks to each.

8 Establish what financial help, if any, is available to pupils in need.

9 Obtain written approval for the course, presented in detail, from the head or education authority as appropriate. Practices vary widely here. It may be sufficient for the head of department to obtain outline permission at the start of each school year for all courses proposed. In other cases, heads, governors and education authorities require full details of every course.

10 Obtain costs of alternative methods of transport.

11 Advertise course to pupils, announce firm cost, and obtain parental approval in writing for each pupil taking part. This is best done by the head, using a standard letter. If necessary, obtain a deposit.

12 If the course is an elaborate one, planned and prepared for over a lengthy period, dates for subsequent and final payments will be announced. A savings scheme may be set up. Funds collected may be deposited with a building society, where they earn interest.

13 It may be useful to form a staff–pupil planning committee.

14 Make all transport reservations. If appropriate, find out the earliest dates in the year on which bookings can be made, eg for ferries and trains, and book on these dates.

15 Investigate insurance position thoroughly. Find out what insurance is provided by the education authority – there is rarely any form of all-purpose insurance. Make certain that all staff members are adequately insured against claims, loss and accident. Teachers' professional associations will advise. Generally speaking, where a field course is an approved extension of normal school work, the education

authority is deemed to bear ultimate responsibility for it.

16 Sometimes it may be appropriate to carry out some publicity for a course, especially if it is voluntary and has the character of an expedition. Some schools print their own expedition stationery, approach firms for funds and equipment, and ask parents' associations for help. Requests for help need to be specific. Where help in kind is requested, there must be space to store the items given.

17 If membership of the Youth Hostels Association is necessary, make sure that all pupils, and staff, enrol in good time.

18 Work out, as soon as possible, what special clothing – if any – will be needed. Arrange a display of items. Parents need to be told about such requirements as early as possible. Even if details cannot be given, it should be announced that certain items will be required when a deposit is asked for.

19 Determine what maps, compasses, other equipment will be needed by the party as a whole. Obtain these. Ordnance Survey maps will be requisitioned direct from the offices of the Survey at Southampton, using the special schools' discount form provided.

20 Plan the journey in detail, where this is appropriate. Give all members a copy of the arrangements. On a long journey, it is necessary to anticipate all contingencies as well as needs. Will packed food be necessary? Are hot drinks available on the train? Can breakfast be ordered in advance to be consumed during a stop in the early hours? If a member gets detached from the party, what procedure should he follow?

21 If the visit is overseas, make sure at an early date that all members, pupils and staff, have a valid passport. Check current international health regulations, and take appropriate action. Find out about currency regulations, from a bank or travel agency, and take necessary action.

22 At an early stage, establish with participants what norms of behaviour will be expected. Give early thought to the sanctions which will be imposed if these norms are not adhered to. Give all pupils and parents a copy of agreed 'Notes on Personal Conduct'.

23 In all cases, but especially if the course is to be strenuous and exacting, get to know the pupils well. It can be useful to arrange an overnight expedition, eg to a youth hostel, in order to get the party together and give them brief experience of things – such as walking – they will encounter. No group should be taken to a foreign youth hostel before they have been to one at home.

24 About one week before departure, assemble the whole party with all its clothing and equipment. If some members seem to have brought everything they possess, help them to decide what to leave behind. Check all documents. Allocate responsibility for carrying items of course equipment.

25 Confirm all travel and accommodation arrangements one week before departure, using first-class mail or telephone.

26 If self-drive transport is to be used, eg education authority minibuses, have this serviced thoroughly. Have garage make up a spares kit.

27 On departure day:
    (a) assemble party early;
    (b) make sure all documents, tickets, vouchers are to hand;
    (c) at crucial transfer points on the journey, eg at railway or coach stations, ask all members to hold their luggage and items of equipment for which they are responsible. Check items against list.

Air charter arrangements

It is sometimes possible for a school, or a group of schools, to charter an aircraft, either for a short observational flight, or to travel to a distant centre. An aircraft charter agreement has to be signed by an individual, who then becomes responsible in law for payment. A teacher should never sign such an agreement, and pay the 10 per cent deposit normally required, until he has obtained (1) bookings and substantial deposits, which should be announced as non-returnable; (2) a form of indemnity from all adults taking part, and the parent of every pupil, absolving him from personal liability should any claim arise in consequence of the flight. The advice of a solicitor should be taken.

10 New Approaches to Familiar Themes

During a period in which many new geographical ideas are being developed, largely owing to the application of a wide range of new research techniques, the geography teacher in schools is called upon to adopt new approaches to meet the rethinking that is occurring. In the fields of regional and urban geography and geomorphology, to give three important examples, there are various ways of introducing new ideas into school teaching, some of which are suggested here. They can be developed further by ingenuity and practice.

REGIONAL GEOGRAPHY

To make sure that pupils know what other parts of their own country and the world are like, and how other people live and work, is a principal service function of geography in schools. No other subject specialist is concerned directly with these matters. In a world in which an event in one place can be known by and may effect the whole world community, this knowledge of places and peoples is more important than ever.

Teaching regional geography may be defined as the application of geographical modes of thought to specific areas. These modes of thought are concerned, as we have seen, with spatial ordering and spatial interaction. Therefore, faced with the task of teaching pupils what some part of the earth's surface is like, the geographer will take as his starting-points the area's surface phenomena and their distributions. He will look for pattern and significance in these distributions and try to explain them. In the process he is likely to touch upon aspects of economics, history, culture, perception, geology, political systems, which are not in essence spatial at all, though they play a part in shaping the regional system.

A regional study will often start with the teacher asking himself what it is important for pupils to know about the region. The answer to this question often points the way to an appropriate structuring of the regional study.

Sometimes, the obvious starting-point will be relief and geology. In other cases, climatic regime may dominate the regional system. More often than not, however, studies of the most important economic activities of a region will be the starting-point. These may include work on location, relative accessibility, transport systems, trade links, markets, capital investment, national and international interests, and so on. Another possibility is to begin a regional study with the population map. Arguably, the population density map of East Africa is the most significant map of that region. At all costs, a ritualistic rehearsal of regional information under standard headings needs to be avoided.

Regional geography teaching may also be approached by considering regional problems. Areas may be selected for study because they represent cases of general problems, such as rural depopulation, population pressure, overdependence upon extractive industry, dramatic contrasts between wealth and poverty, an enclave economy with modern industries set amidst subsistence farming, an ageing and partly obsolete industrial structure, problems of multi-racial cities, and so on. There is no shortage of problems, and many are well documented. However, too great an emphasis upon problems can be depressing. Sometimes the problems of a region can be posed in statistical form, the pupils being asked to identify the problem and suggest possible solutions.

Assembling materials for regional studies

The following list of points may help in planning a regional study and gathering materials:

Location. Where is the region? What are its boundaries, and on what basis are they drawn? How is it related to other parts of the

208

earth's surface? What connections are there with the home region?

Distinctiveness. On what basis is this region distinguishable from others? Is it a sample of a larger unit, or class of units? Why ought pupils to know about it?

Appearance. What does the regional landscape look like? What are the components of this landscape? What do its villages and towns look like? Can its towns, its industrial structure, its farms be represented in model form?

People's life and work. What do people do for a living? Statistical data can be useful here, eg official employment figures. What is the annual rhythm of their farming? With younger pupils, details about food, dress, houses etc need to be mentioned.

Biography. Have any interesting people, such as inventors or entrepreneurs, lived in this region? Have there been regional writers who have described it well?

Maps. What topographical maps and plans exist, and to what extent will the pupils be able to interpret them directly?

Teacher's and pupils' source materials. What good, up-to-date texts exist for this region? What class texts and reference books are available for the pupils? What illustrative materials can be obtained, eg slides, filmstrips? Is there any detailed case study material? Are specimens of important products obtainable?

METHODS IN REGIONAL GEOGRAPHY

There are various possible approaches to the teaching of regional geography. Three are discussed in detail and illustrated by examples: landscape phenomena in regional context; model landscapes; and case studies.

Landscape phenomena in regional context

In this approach, a particular feature or object on the earth's surface is selected as a starting-point from which to explore, through its origins and functions, the characteristics of the region of which it is a part. Such features and objects may be landforms, such as a moraine, a dry valley in limestone, a waterfall; a small area of rain forest, modified by partial clearance and burning; a Mediterranean beach crowded with holidaymakers from many countries; a group of houses in a particular part of a town, or an open space, whether temporary or permanent; some aspect of industrial archaeology, such as an abandoned mine or railway station; or Sydney Harbour Bridge.

For an example of the application of this method, one might select a computer bureau located in a single-storey building on the government-sponsored industrial estate at Shannon Airport, Ireland. The regional context of this bureau is wide-ranging and complex; it includes historical, social, economic and technological elements. To some degree it is also physical, in that the precise location of Shannon Airport was decided by the limited availability of flat ground in an area of many glacial hillocks.

A computer bureau transforms statistical information into forms usable by computers. Various processes are carried out, notably the making of punched cards or tape from raw data. Unlike most aspects of computer operation, punching has to be done manually, and requires large numbers of trained personnel. So far, no electronic device has been invented which can turn raw data into computer form, except at the crudest level, and it seems unlikely that such an invention will be made. A computer bureau is likely to have international links. It may process and perhaps store data for clients in many countries, probably using signals bounced from satellites. It would seem therefore that a bureau might be located anywhere. Why was Shannon chosen?

The answer lies first of all in the general reasons for the growth of the Shannon estate, which is illustrated in plate 7. After the Second World War, trans-Atlantic aircraft, then piston-engined, had to refuel as far west as possible before leaving Europe. Shannon fulfilled this requirement admirably, and an important international airport developed. As the range of aircraft increased, and jets were introduced in the mid-1960s, landing at Shannon became less and less necessary. To prevent the decline and possible closure of a very profitable airport, the Irish government decided to create a new reason for landings. A customs-free industrial estate was established, designed to exploit the spare load-carrying capacity of trans-Atlantic aircraft. This capacity exists because of the determination of many national airlines to maintain a stake in the North Atlantic traffic, with a consequent over-provision of services.

Several somewhat unusual enterprises rapidly established themselves on the new estate, including a computer bureau. This made use of the fact that Irish female labour is both plentiful and willing to perform the tedious manual tasks of computer work at one-third the wages expected in North America. Soon it became the practice for raw data to be flown to Shannon from Boston and other North American east-coast cities, there to be punched and immediately flown back.

Shannon had additional advantages. Often it was necessary to telephone to North America to clarify items of data. From central London a delay of up to three hours might be expected on such a call, and from central Dublin, one hour. From Shannon there was virtually no delay at all.

This is still not the whole story. Shannon's comparative advantage was enhanced by industrial developments around the fringes of Boston, where a whole new zone of computer-using industries sprang up. These obtained their very large numbers of card-punchers and other skilled personnel from the ranks of those who formerly travelled daily from the suburbs to the central financial area of Boston. Boston businesses found themselves starved of computer personnel, and so the advantages of flying data to Shannon became even clearer.

This explanation can be developed into a study of the regional characteristics and development problems of western Ireland, at a depth appropriate to the class. The teacher might go on to examine the physical layout of the lower Shannon valley and of the upland areas to east and west, and discuss the consequences at the present time of the region's peripheral position, relatively far away from the main centres of population and industry both in Ireland and England. He might analyse some of the causes of rural depopulation in the region, and describe its effects upon rural living conditions. He might discuss some of the problems of attracting new industries to Limerick, the regional capital, and show how Shannon could become the springboard for a degree of social and economic resurgence in the region.

Model landscapes

A major problem in regional teaching is to make the study realistic and interesting, and for most pupils this demands abundant illustration at some stage. A second problem is how to combine the parts of a regional study so that the pupils perceive the whole as well as its parts. Interesting work may be done on farming, towns, communications, physical features, yet the overall picture of the region may never emerge. In order to achieve this overall impression, the writer sometimes uses the model landscape method whereby a regional landscape is built up in pictorial form from its component parts. Such models are sometimes called 'synthetic', 'composite' or 'potted' landscapes.

It may be objected that the model landscape method relies too much upon a teacher making the right selection of material to present to his class. This may be true, but a similar charge of selectivity can be levelled against the writers of textbooks, the makers of filmstrips and those who set questions in public examinations. Clearly, the teacher has to be aware of this danger, and inform himself as accurately as he can about the regions he intends to teach. The model landscape method can be an interesting way of presenting a regional synthesis, from time to time.

The model landscape may be drawn on a blackboard, or presented on a series of overhead projector overlays. The landscape picture is built up step by step as the work proceeds. Alternatively, one may begin with the completed picture, and break it down into its component parts, usually for revision. With younger pupils, the model landscape may take the form of an actual model, made by the class working in small groups.

The details from which a model landscape picture is constructed may be given to pupils in several ways. The teacher's own slides, taken specially for the purpose, are the most useful. These can be taken to show exactly what is required, and to exclude irrelevancies. Commercial filmstrip frames and slides can be used; so can picture postcards, industrial brochures and other kinds of picture,

212

mounted and suitably annotated. Drawings can be made of items for which there are no photographs. Large-scale maps and air photos can help to bring the various landscape components together.

The methods used will depend upon the teacher's skill in drawing quickly on the blackboard or overhead projector acetate. If he finds this difficult, he may prepare most of his drawings beforehand, and in the case of blackboard drawings, turn them into slides. Shortage of time is also a problem.

The method, like many others, is better suited to a timetable which allows long rather than short teaching periods. Two examples, one of a large region, the other of a small one, will illustrate it.

The large region selected is central Honshu, Japan, of which the model was built up from slides produced by a West German firm, together with pictures and wall posters from the Japanese official information agency. The following details are represented:

1. A mountainous inland landscape with steep slopes and a distant view of Fujiyama – the pilgrims' path to the top may be seen.
2. On the lower slopes of Fuji a mountain resort clusters around hot springs.
3. In the central mountains, another resort (eg Nikko) has shrines, a lake, waterfall, and ski-lift for winter use.
4. In a high valley there is a multi-purpose reservoir, used for water supply, hydro-electricity power generation, fishing and recreation.
5. A forest industry and saw-mill utilise steep forested slopes.
6. At lower levels, hillsides are terraced for rice and wheat cultivation (the terraces are to some extent relict features).
7. Tea gardens utilise a south-facing slope.
8. At still lower levels, there is intensive double-crop rice and rice-and-wheat cultivation; also citrus orchards and mulberry plantations.
9. Villages cling to rocky outcrops, avoiding use of the valuable farm land.

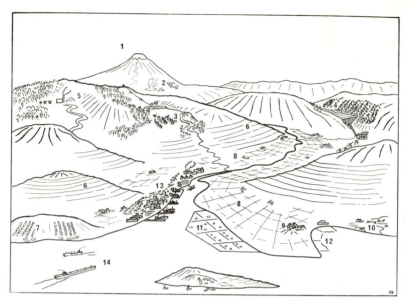

Synthetic or model landscape, central Honshu, Japan. The key to the composition of the drawing is given in the accompanying text.

10 Near the coast, earthquake damage, especially marine flooding, can be seen.

11 Population pressure has led to a new polder being reclaimed from the sea, with Dutch technical assistance. Holdings on the polder are of several different sizes, experimenting to find out which is most economic.

12 Culture pearls are produced in oyster beds in sheltered locations.

13 A major seaport city occupies the centre of the drawing. This has a central business district with steel-and-concrete blocks (no skyscrapers, except in central Tokyo, because of the earthquake threat); a surrounding zone of low buildings in traditional Japanese styles and materials; industrial zones – steelworks and the rectangular buildings of a major electronics concern are suggested; shipyards.

14 Ships approaching the port include oil tankers from the Middle East and Indonesia, iron ore carriers from Australia.

214

Ships leaving may be presumed to carry manufactured goods for the world's markets.

Clearly, additional items can be added; no attempt has been made to show a road system, for example. The drawing can be produced at many different levels, to suit the capabilities of particular teaching groups.

The small region selected as an example is the south-west peninsula of England. The drawing of the model landscape shown in plate 2 has been used with a third form to summarise the regional characteristics of Devon and Cornwall.

Case studies

Case studies are another way of approaching a regional study through a selected aspect of the region. Sometimes this is called, inaccurately, the sample study method, but few published case studies are representative samples in any strict, statistical sense. They are more likely to have been selected because of the presence, for instance, of a co-operative farmer or factory manager, willing to give time to answering questions.

The idea of the case study is to examine a particular feature – farm, smallholding, estate, village, factory, city street, fishing port; and from this to build up a general account of its region. A close-up study of this kind can be realistic, detailed, personal, things which appeal to pupils and students of all ages. The teacher's problem is to get the necessary information. A number of possible sources are listed on pages 256–7.

It is necessary to sound a warning note about the selection of case studies. Teachers of geography have to beware of the picturesque and unusual and find ways of making the typical interesting. Cases should as far as possible reflect normal, not exceptional conditions in the region being studied. Where the use of cases known to be somewhat exceptional cannot be avoided, their departure from general regional conditions should be made clear. Thus, a council housing estate at Fort William or a Sydney suburb are more representative of their respective regions than a Highland croft or a sheep station on the frontiers of settlement.

Consideration of an example – a farm on Mainland, Orkney – will show the kind of detail which is required. It will, of course, be presented at a level appropriate to the capacities and experience of a given group of pupils.

Information will be needed on:

The farmer's name. Details of his family, with names, ages and relationships.

Location of the farm, in Scotland, in Orkney, and in the immediate area. Site details, with sketch-map. Soils, slopes, aspect, elevation, drainage, etc. Appearance of the local landscape.

Size of farm. Details of land use, with map. Numbers and types of livestock.

House and other buildings on the farm with uses of each. Plan of the buildings. Building materials, approximate dates of buildings and additions. Conditions inside the house, eg mains electricity, mains water, telephone, cooking arrangements, deep-freeze, family diet, television.

Farm economy. A description of how the farmer makes his living. Items produced, methods of sale; items bought on to the farm. Methods of agriculture, stock husbandry. Machinery used, whether owned or hired. Number of people working full-time and part-time on the farm. Cycle of the farming year.

Services available to the farmer and his family: farming advice, artificial insemination, co-operative purchasing, cattle marts, shipping services to the Scottish mainland, buses, travelling shops, clinic, schools, health centre, library, etc.

Problems of the area, which may or may not affect this particular farmer: freight rates, difficulty of finding employment off the land, shortage of jobs for those most highly qualified, drift of young people to the towns.

This model may be adapted for use with various types of farm and smallholding. The study may be acted out by pupils and tape-recorded.

Today, the emphasis in geography is upon the formulation and refinement of general statements, the identification of general processes, the analysis of regional systems of processes and relationships. This kind of geography can appear to be very abstract to the secondary school pupil. Case studies have a most important part to play educationally in keeping geographical generalisations firmly anchored in reality.

Other aids to regional geography teaching

Background 'colour' for regional studies can sometimes be provided by readings from appropriate literature, including fiction. Where several subjects are being taught in a combined course, readings can provide historical, social, technical, biographical, as well as geographical information in a most useful way.

A pioneer attempt to collect and arrange short literary passages for use by geographers was the late Margaret Anderson's *Splendour of Earth*; but all teachers will have their favourite extracts to add to this collection.

Literary extracts have to be used with care. For one thing, they tend to be historical, and the pictures they paint, eg of Lancashire cotton towns (a favourite topic for descriptive readings) are often badly out-of-date. Again, many potentially useful passages are written in too elaborate a style to be read aloud to the younger pupils. Sometimes their language can be simplified by the teacher, who knows just what a given class can absorb. He may also decide to write descriptive passages of his own, based on a literary text. Variety can be given to a lesson by recording the passages on tape; if a speaker with the appropriate regional accent can be found, so much the better.

Some teachers use musical extracts to give background atmosphere to regional studies. These can be very effective, but again, a word of warning is necessary about the low level of musical receptivity of many pupils. The teacher may believe that Vaughan Williams' *Sinfonia Antarctica* gives a wonderful picture of men struggling through a wilderness of wind and ice, but his pupils may gain no such impression. However, the idea is always worth trying and there can be striking successes. Records of traditional instruments, such as the Paraguayan harp or African drums, can be useful. Folk and pop music can sometimes help to create regional

217

atmosphere. Thus, 'High Life' music is an inescapable part of West African town life, and records are easily obtainable. Finally, it is reasonable to hope that pupils will hear the language spoken of some of the major regions they study.

THE GEOGRAPHY OF TOWNS

Towns have traditionally been neglected in geographical teaching in schools. All too often, a town of, say, a million people is represented by a dot, with a list of associated products. Geographers in an urban society have to treat towns more seriously than this.

The first and most important step in planning the urban component in a school course is to decide what ideas, or concepts, can be communicated to the pupils. Because all towns are parts of regional, national and global systems of relationships and processes which are always changing, these ideas must be dynamic, not static. Teaching about towns, therefore, has to show that towns are functional entities, not mere structures. A number of ideas about towns may be compiled as basic to teaching about them. Further ideas can be developed from these:

Towns stand, and develop upon, physical sites. The form of the site may shape the town's development.

People inhabit towns. Other people visit them, daily and at less regular intervals. People move about within towns, at different times, by different means and for different purposes.

People have needs, such as food, drink, clothing, shelter, work, recreation, which towns help to supply.

Providing for these needs involves people in work and movements, and requires space.

These activities, or urban functions, are sometimes complementary, sometimes competitive. Often, they compete for limited, desirable space.

Towns are of different sizes.

Towns grow, and sometimes they decline.

Different parts of towns date from different periods of growth.

Towns are zoned according to function. Functional zones are

often related to age-zones, but the two may not coincide exactly. Towns have central business districts, which may not be central in a geometrical sense. Normally located in the central business district are the largest buildings, the town's administrative offices and the most important concentration of large shops and major commercial functions; also, the heaviest pedestrian and – perhaps – vehicular traffic.

The functions of zones within towns may change with time.

The range of functions in a town is related to its size; also to its relations with other towns, and to the size, population and wealth of the area it serves.

In a country or a continent, there tends to be a hierarchy of towns – large, medium and small. There are usually more small towns than medium, more medium than large.

The layout of different parts of towns is often related to the technology of the time at which those parts were built, especially to transport technology. For example, many English towns have suburbs related to tramway and private-car usage.

Dominant building materials may be zoned within a town. The use of materials also reflects technological changes. Thus, the railways diffused the use of Welsh roofing slates throughout Britain late in the nineteenth century.

The way in which towns are zoned varies from one part of the world to another. Differences relate to the functions of towns, and to the socio-political systems within which they have grown.

In all countries, even the USSR, towns are zoned according to wealth, social status or social 'class'. Multi-racial towns are partly zoned according to ethnic groupings.

Boundaries of all kinds within towns are never static.

Introducing urban studies

Probably the best way of introducing urban studies is through a local example. The initial teaching problem is to get pupils to perceive the town as a whole – normally, most of them will know only a few streets, shops and bus routes. Next, pupils have to be shown how to unscramble the bewildering conglomeration of buildings, streets and functions which make up the town. They need to begin to ask and answer the question, are there any patterns in all this confusion?

If possible, this question should be considered first through simple field work. The idea of the Burgess concentric zone model may be introduced by walking pupils along a carefully chosen route, along which they record such things as numbers and types of shops: heights of buildings; numbers of banks and insurance offices; names and types of industrial firms; and types of houses. They need to be questioned about what they see, both orally and by work sheet. All information will be mapped, and the existence of distinct zones noted. Explanation can then begin.

Where pupils cannot be taken out of school, a similar process of exploration can be attempted, using maps and pictures. The teacher may have to take most of his own photographs, because few sets of commercial slides or filmstrips on individual towns exist. However, some Geographical Association branches and teachers' centres are now producing sets, which can be bought or borrowed. The set produced by the Geography Teachers' Association of New South Wales, *Sydney's Central Business District*, is an outstanding example of local initiative.

In presenting a town study, the following steps may be recommended, given time:

1 Show slides of the significant sub-divisions of the town.
2 Match each picture against a mounted section of the 1:10560 map, and/or sections of air photographs.
3 Attempt, through discussion, to formulate broad descriptive statements about each section according to its characteristics, eg, this is the city-centre shopping district, this a suburban shopping centre, this an area of terrace houses, this an area with large houses standing in gardens, and so on.
4 Differences will then be discussed. Are houses in this area older or newer than that? What can be said about street plans, street widths, the regularity and spacing of buildings in the following sections? Do building materials vary?

5   The whole town will be studied on the 1:63360 or 1:50000 map. Although the scale is small, it is possible to make out the broad patterns of urban development, especially on the Ordnance Survey New Popular edition (1947, later revisions). Comparisons between latest and older editions of maps can also be helpful. If possible, the relevant sections of these maps will be made into slides, so that the whole class can study them at once.

6   A blackboard sketch can be built up step-by-step to show the growth of the town. Alternatively, OHP overlays may be prepared. Old postcards can be useful, illustrating each growth stage.

7   Finally, a concise, reasoned description of the town will be prepared, accompanied by a map or maps. This will identify and relate significant aspects of site, growth and function.

This final account will then be used as a model, against which other towns, at home and abroad, are compared. Wherever the necessary information, maps and pictures can be obtained, town studies in other parts of the country and the world will include a short form of the process described.

Urban social geography

Another approach to town studies is through work in social geography. Some of the world's most intractable human problems have to do with large towns. The unplanned growth of Calcutta, the mass squatting in Manila, the migration of millions of poor, uneducated negroes and Puerto Ricans into New York since the mid-1950s, the mushroom growth of shanty-towns in Latin American cities – these and many other examples immediately spring to mind, but they are no more than extreme cases of world-wide problems, often found near home.

Until recently, geographers have neglected this part of their field, which overlaps with sociology. Now attitudes seem to be changing, and an important new trend may have been set by such publications as G. M. Lewis's paper, 'Levels of living in the North-eastern United States c1960' in *Transactions of the Institute of British Geographers* (45, 1968), by the same writer's work on patterns of race-related violence in United States cities and, at the school level, by Martin Simons's *Poverty and Wealth in Cities and Villages* (1972). Social topics also receive much attention in the Schools Council Project, *Geography for the Young School Leaver, 1970–5*. It might be argued that, because the multi-racial city is becoming a world-wide phenomenon, it should be included in every geography syllabus as a particular subject, also that the distribution of wealth could be regarded as a basic geographical study.

School work in social geography may include items such as:

Mapping the distribution of shops, open spaces and other facilities. Frequency of their provision in different parts of the town may then be quantified.

Mapping the homes of all pupils in a school, in a year group or a house. This map can be compared with urban zones already delimited. The homes of pupils from two or more schools can be mapped and compared. Some interesting socio-economic relationships may be revealed, which – like most topics in this sensitive field – have to be discussed with consideration and tact.

Catchment areas of neighbouring comprehensive schools can be mapped and related to urban zones.

Relationships can be defined and measured between the spacing of houses per unit area, physical site and height above sea-level, distance from the central business district, distance from factories.

Introducing planning concepts

Closely related to social geography are questions of town planning. Today, virtually every town in the world has a planning problem, and geography courses should take note of this fact.

If possible, it is helpful to base work about planning firmly on local examples, to use large-scale maps and air photos and official facts and figures, and to make numerous visits and field studies. Types of work which may be attempted include:

Vehicular flow studies. Measurements of traffic movements into and through a town, at different times of day, week, year. Identification of problems.

Studies of alternative traffic circulation schemes, in terms of the altered accessibility of shops, offices, bus stations etc. Topological maps can be useful here.

Car park location studies: where ought they to be built? Why? Should they be built at all?

Studies of pedestrian zone projects: where will the vehicular traffic go?

Studies of the effects of new road building through and around towns. How many shops, houses are destroyed? How far away does the effect of a major scheme extend?

Studies of how planning causes 'blight', either by developers accumulating land or by long-postponed road plans.

Studies for the location of new shopping areas, out-of-town shopping centres. Where should they be?

Studies of industrial locations in and around a town. Locations may relate to former transport requirements and cause contemporary or future problems.

Studies of the persistence of old patterns within towns, eg the line of a city wall, medieval street widths, even old field boundaries.

New town studies. On what principles have they been designed? What would it be like to live in Washington, Brasilia, Canberra, if one were very rich, well-off, or poor? How would you set about planning a new town?

Pupils may be asked to study and discuss such questions as:

Which takes precedence and why – a new motorway or somebody's house?

Under what circumstances should a beautiful old building be preserved or demolished?

Does planning mean that people *must* be moved from the inner area of the town or city to housing estates, either in other parts of the town or distant from the centre?

Do people really want to live in tall blocks of flats? What are the alternatives?

What does the ordinary citizen want from official planning?

It is essential to include urban studies in geography courses. So large a proportion of the world's peoples live in towns, in all parts of the world, and the problems of urban populations are so widespread and serious in their implications, that to omit their study from any course, designed to educate future citizens, is at least unrealistic. It is particularly important to allow pupils to question some of the glib assumptions of the present time about urban planning: for example, the necessity and desirability of modifying towns to suit the convenience of vehicular traffic rather than pedestrians. Urban studies sooner or later bring pupils face to face with some of the most pressing ethical questions about wealth and poverty and social justice, and they are doubly valuable on that account.

GEOMORPHOLOGY

Some geographers advocate the dropping of geomorphology from geography courses, on the grounds that it cannot easily be integrated with those parts of the subject involving man. Whatever the pros and cons of this view at the university level, there would appear to be at least three strong arguments in favour of retaining a geomorphological component in school courses. In the first place, the environment in which the child grows up is based upon a physical surface; any attempt to teach from that environment must take account of the forms of that surface and associated physical, biotic and chemical processes. Next, the study of geomorphology, if properly presented, helps the pupil to enjoy landscape in an informed way, and this is surely a worthwhile educational purpose. Thirdly, geomorphological studies can provide an excellent intellectual training, with ample opportunities for the application of scientific method.

Geomorphology concentrates today upon the explanation of surface phenomena in terms of processes. The historical approach to landscape study, especially as developed by W. M. Davis and

224

his followers, remains important – with modification – but is far less dominant than it was in the years up to about 1960. Past conditions and events often have to be taken into account when present-day surface features are being studied, but the emphasis tends to be placed firmly upon an elucidation of what is happening in the landscape *now*. The geomorphologist thinks in terms of dynamic adjustments of surface forms to a present-day balance of processes. He tries to disaggregate the complex processes at work, and wherever possible to measure their effects and rates of operation.

Teaching geomorphology at the school level involves three important tasks. First, pupils have to be made aware of the existence of landforms and of the processes which produce, maintain or change them. Second, pupils have to be shown how to order the array of landforms which present themselves, to relate one form to another, and to relate groups of forms to appropriate processes and events. Third, this process of mental ordering has to be induced without suggesting that all the answers are known; some well known textbooks fall into this trap. The task is to produce a state of informed doubt in the pupil, coupled with a wish to know more. Of course, the achievement of informed doubt is a well-nigh impossible aim with many pupils; but the aim is nevertheless worth attempting.

At least two special problems make the achievement of these tasks difficult. Perhaps the hardest problem concerns the nature of geomorphology itself. Unlike the other physical sciences, it is rarely possible to subject geomorphological theories to experimental proof. It is, however, possible to demonstrate some of the basic processes in a stream- or wave-tank, and wherever possible, such a tank should be set up in school. Pupils can then see for themselves how a waterfall retreats upstream, how a delta is built, how transported materials become graded, or how waves break along a coastline.

A further problem concerns the absence of a general theory of landscape development. A seemingly complete theoretical model was provided by W. M. Davis and his followers – the model was formulated in complete form before 1890 – and dominated geomorphological teachings in the English-speaking countries for about fifty years. It still appears in the older school textbooks. It is now most important that the teacher of geomorphology, even at an elementary level, realises the implications and shortcomings of the Davisian model. It would be unjust to Davis to try to summarise his tremendous contribution to landscape study in a few short sentences, and then to criticise it, but certain points may be picked out as especially important.

New concepts in geomorphology

The Davisian model presented physical landscapes as natural systems which were 'running down'. An initial uplift of the land, or fall in sea-level, was followed by three 'stages' of development: youth, in which streams were fast-flowing, valleys deep-cut, slopes steep; maturity, in which valleys were wider, divides much reduced, and slopes less steep; and old age, in which the surface had been reduced to a near-plain, rivers meandered, and the slopes of such hills as remained, left behind temporarily by the general process of denudation, were extremely gentle. According to this model, landforms were primarily time-dependent, and the main task of the geomorphologist was to unravel the sequence of events which had led up to the present. Unfortunately, the more closely actual landscapes were examined, the less they were found to resemble the Davisian scheme. For example, slope steepness was found to be unrelated to the supposed 'stage' of a land surface.

The modern view is to emphasise the concept of dynamic equilibrium, between processes tending to produce change, and those tending to maintain the *status quo*. Examples of the former on a valley-side slope will include gravity, water percolation and run-off, freeze-and-thaw and chemical weathering; of the latter, the holding power of vegetation and the reduction of soil particle-size, leading to greater cohesion. Clearly, this balance is primarily dependent upon climate, and especially upon micro-climate. It will vary from one climatic zone to another, and it will change with changes in climate. Slope angle may be seen as a dynamic adjustment to processes induced by climate, not as a function of 'stage' at all.

226

A point inadequately dealt with by the Davisian theory is that a great many landforms are relict features, referable to climatic conditions which have long ceased to exist. In Britain, for example, many forms are the products of glacial and peri-glacial conditions. The present may therefore be looked upon as a period of dynamic adjustment of old forms to new conditions. Hence the force of the suggestion, made in Chapter 9, that field work should often begin with pupils being sent out to find evidence of change taking place in a landscape.

The word 'normal', used by Davis and his followers to describe the supposed 'cycle' of landscape development under moist temperate conditions, now has to be abandoned. There is no reason to suppose that the balance of climate and process found in such regions is more normal than any other. Indeed, as information about the landscape-forming processes of the humid sub-tropics has increased, it has become clear that they may have the greatest claim to be considered normal. It may be useful to regard the process-balances of other parts of the world as variations from this norm, in the directions of greater aridity, lower temperatures, and so on.

The present task in schools is to construct new syllabuses which incorporate the new geomorphological ideas. Attempts to graft these into structures which remain essentially Davisian will not do. Teaching methods, including field work, which make the new ideas effective then have to be devised. It is helpful to begin by listing the basic geomorphological information and ideas which pupils will be expected to know and understand as a result of their courses. The following are suggestions for such a list:

Knowledge and ideas in geomorphology

The earth as a planet. Proofs and consequences of the earth's shape, rotation, tilt, movements in space. A general foundation to all work in physical geography, of which geomorphology forms part.

Major earth structures. Evidence for the nature of the earth's interior. Distribution and outline structure of continents and ocean basins. Isostasy, continental drift. World climatic variations.

227

The geological background. Geological time and its conventional sub-divisions. Mountain-building movements and the distribution of different types of mountains. Palaeogeography – geographical conditions in selected, important geological periods.

Rocks. Characteristics of major rock types, with examples. Notes on distributions. Recognition of rock specimens and rocks in the field.

Rock types, structures and relief. Examples and explanation of some important relationships. Limitations of structural explanations of relief forms.

Geomorphological processes. Description, observation (where possible) and explanation of major physical, biological and chemical processes, related to landforms.

Description, explanation and classification of landforms. The study of forms in associations, rather than singly: whole-landscape studies. Classification related to process. Landforms and time.

Thereafter each geomorphological topic can be analysed into a similar, though more detailed sequence of information and ideas, and these sequences become the basis for course and lesson planning. For example, the following sequence develops the topic of rock types, structures and relief with respect to limestones and limestone scenery:

Limestones are sedimentary rocks of a particular kind. They consist of organic remains which accumulated in warm, shallow seas into which few rivers discharged.

There are many varieties of limestone, formed in many geological periods and found in all continents.

Limestones are soluble. Rainwater, which is weak carbonic acid, attacks them.

Limestones are permeable. Often they are also well jointed and bedded.

Because of their solubility and permeability and the presence of joints, water which falls on limestone surfaces immediately percolates down to the water-table (assuming that this is below the surface). In consequence, limestone surfaces are dry, and there are no surface streams.

Streams which flow on to limestone surfaces from outcrops of impermeable rocks disappear underground by sinks or swallow-holes.

Systems of underground streams, flowing in caves, form at the level of the water-table.

Where such systems of caves and underground channels are found in limestone areas with arid climates, eg New Mexico, they indicate wetter conditions at their time of formation, usually the Pleistocene period.

Dry valleys occur in many limestone areas; they exhibit a dendritic pattern characteristic of normal stream systems. These valleys are relict features, dating from the Pleistocene period and the cold periods which followed the last glaciation. They were formed when streams flowed on the surface of ground which was saturated and frozen, and therefore temporarily impermeable.

Deep, narrow limestone gorges were once thought to be produced by cavern collapse. Some small gorges may perhaps have been formed in this way, but most probably result from rapid down-cutting by surface streams, following faults or fissures.

Additional concepts can obviously be added. Specific lists of concepts can be drawn up for particular teaching situations, eg for a day's field work in a limestone area.

11 Looking Ahead

In conclusion, it may be useful to try to identify some trends in geographical education which are already apparent, and others which may be expected to develop over the next few years; and also to pinpoint some major constraints upon development, which it would be foolish to ignore.

JOINT RESEARCH AND CAPITAL INVESTMENT

It is evident that major advances in curriculum design and implementation can only come through joint research, backed by substantial capital investment. Of course, the individual thinker and innovator will always be important; but it now requires an extended effort on the part of a full-time research team to work out the implications of all the new ideas for schools, to turn the ideas into syllabuses, and to prepare and test teaching materials. The first, and in many ways the most impressive example of major progress being achieved in geographical education since the Second World War was the American High School Geography Project, 1961-71. This was financed in the first place by the Ford Foundation, and organised under the auspices of the Association of American Geographers, with support from the National Science Council.

A team of university geographers, psychologists and school teachers was asked to translate some of the new ideas in academic geography into forms usable with pupils aged 14-16 years. From a massive piece of thinking and research, an array of publications emerged, taking their final form in six units entitled *Geography in an Urban Age*. These are available internationally through the Macmillan Company. The units are: (1) *Geography of Cities;* (2) *Manufacturing and Agriculture;* (3) *Cultural Geography;*

(4) *Political Geography;* (5) *Habitat and Resources;* and (6) *Japan.* The American High School Project materials are usable in other parts of the world; but the ideas they contain are probably more useful than the materials themselves, which are distinctively North American. They have already had a considerable effect upon curriculum projects in Britain.

In Britain, a number of curriculum development projects involving geographers have been, and are being, carried out under the auspices of the Schools Council. These include *Geography for the Young School Leaver,* based at Avery Hill College of Education, London; *Geography 14–18 Years,* based at the University of Bristol School of Education, and *History, Geography and Social Science, 8–13 Years,* based at the University of Liverpool. Geographical elements have also been included in a number of Humanities and Science projects. Only the *Young School Leaver* project has been completed; it is aimed to meet the needs of the 14- to 15-year-olds who have little success or interest in school work. Three units are published by Thomas Nelson, London, entitled *Man, Land and Leisure; Cities and People;* and *People, Place and Work.* These materials are lavishly illustrated, and include slides, OHP acetates and tapes; many items are suitable for local adaptation.

NEW TEACHING AND LEARNING METHODS
Many ideas about how to teach and how to get pupils to learn have been discussed and demonstrated during the past few years. Teachers now have the job of mastering the pedagogic skills which the new methods require. This will be quite a difficult, certainly an expensive, process.

The new methods and forms of pupil organisation require of teachers a higher level of professional skill than ever before. It still remains to be seen how widely some of the more difficult new methods will be adopted. For example, mixed-ability teaching calls for outstanding curricular and managerial skill, and for many teachers, it implies a period of in-service training. Above all, it needs to be supported by an adequate investment in materials and apparatus. We do not yet know whether the taxpayer will be prepared to pay for general mixed-ability education.

SCHOOL AND UNIVERSITY LINKS

It is most important that the development of new syllabuses and methods in the schools is based upon an active debate between university and school geographers. There are already many signs that the drift apart of university and school geographers has been reversed; in the late 1960s, this looked like being a serious problem.

Much unrealistic writing and talking can take place when those who are not themselves faced with the problems of schools speculate about developments in school geography. Conversely, teachers tend to underestimate their own capacity and that of their pupils to master new methods, and they are quite reasonably apprehensive about changes they do not fully understand. A major reason for launching the Geographical Association's second journal, *Teaching Geography*, was to provide a forum for university and school debate.

EVOLUTION, NOT REVOLUTION

At certain times during the 1960s, it seemed that the 'new' geography – seldom defined – would totally replace the old. It now seems clear that the subject will develop by integration rather than replacement.

Extreme positions are now much easier to recognise, and often they are being modified. New ideas and approaches will generally be found to complement and expand what has gone before; throwing out the baby with the bathwater will not be found an appropriate model for the development of geography. Rather will there be a continual re-working of new and old ideas, an exploration of new connections, and continuous activity on the boundaries of the subject.

NON-DIRECTIVE CURRICULUM DEVELOPMENT

There seemed to be a tendency in the early stages of the curriculum development movement to try to tell teachers what and how to teach. It is now clear that teachers will not accept the imposition of curricula from outside the profession.

Teachers need to be involved at all levels of discussion about the design and implementation of new curricula. At the same time, they cannot be expected to produce the new materials for themselves. The task of project teams is therefore to generate non-directive curriculum materials, and to provide exemplars of how to use it; but to leave the teacher in the classroom to make the final decisions about method.

MAKING AVERAGE TEACHERS EXCELLENT

Curriculum projects and associated in-service training courses will have to improve the educational performance of non-exceptional schools, staffed by average teachers, if they are to be worthwhile.

The central problem of educational reform is to find ways of making the average teacher, and therefore the average school, excellent. This process has been carried out in most major industries, such as farming and engineering. The brilliant farmer of 1910 would be regarded as very average today; many of the skills of last century's master craftsmen in wood and metal have been automated, so that quite unskilled men can do them faster than any craftsman could. But this process has not yet been applied to teaching. Its achievement will require sustained and highly capitalised team efforts, just as it did in farming and industry.

CURRICULUM REFORM

Major advances in geographical education can only take place within a general reform of curriculum content and process. It is impossible to revise the teaching of one subject in isolation. Changes have to be agreed throughout the school in timetabling, for example. There may have to be changes in school and community relationships. Certainly there will have to be changes in the structure and methods of public examinations.

THE LEAST ABLE PUPILS

Despite the efforts of such projects as *Geography for the Young School Leaver*, the problem of how to make school worthwhile for pupils in the bottom 20 per cent of the ability-range remains unsolved. Many of these boys and girls are apathetic or hostile towards school. Many habitually play truant, or are away with trifling excuses. The problems of many stem from unsatisfactory homes. Schools have only a marginal effect upon their education.

It helps to clarify the problem if one realises that no curriculum materials of the conventional kind, however attractively packaged, will meet the needs of most of these pupils. What is needed is a fundamental re-thinking about the nature of school as a whole, and an acceptance by society at large that these young people are a corporate, and not just a school, responsibility. There is as yet no general agreement about the kind of curriculum these pupils need, but geographers will be much exercised, with other teachers, in tackling this problem over the next few years. Geography, with its emphasis upon practical and field work, and its concern with urban and rural environments, clearly has a contribution to make.

The next decade will undoubtedly be a strenuous time for teachers of geography.

Bibliography and Sources

Teachers struggling to keep abreast of work in the midst of a busy term have little time left for extended reading. Those who do not themselves teach in schools seldom realise how little time is available for such reading once the term has begun, especially for senior staff. This bibliography is classified with the aim of making consultation easier for the busy teacher. Part 1 provides a guide for day-to-day questions on teaching geography and organising the subject in school, and Part 2 lists material for vacation and in-service course reading. Part 2 may be used as a requisition list for a school staff library or for the library of a teachers' professional centre.

A few titles of books of outstanding merit for use by pupils below the sixth form have been listed but, as it is dangerous to suggest a book for a teacher or a class unless one knows them personally and how they propose to work, there is no extended list of recommended textbooks. Many of the titles in the bibliography can be used – selectively – as sixth-form reference material.

Teachers are recommended to make full use of publishers' inspection copy services, to read the reviews in journals such as *Geography*, and to attend publishers' exhibitions whenever possible. The annual book exhibition arranged in London by the Geographical Association is invaluable.

The addresses of organisations of interest to geography teachers can be found in *Handbook for Geography Teachers*, edited by M. Long (London, 1964). Because so many relevant articles are published in its journals *Geography* and *Teaching Geography* and for its interest in the teaching of the subject, it is useful to mention here the address of the Geographical Association, 343 Fulwood Road, Sheffield S10 3BP.

The following summary of the contents of this bibliography is intended to facilitate reference to specific topics:

PART 1

PART 2

236

PART 1

TEACHING GEOGRAPHY IN SECONDARY SCHOOLS

General works on teaching geography, and sources

Bradford, E. J. G. *School Geography: A Critical Survey of Present-day Teaching Methods* (Exeter, 1925)

Gopsill, G. H. *The Teaching of Geography* (London, 1956)

Graves, N. J. *Geography in Secondary Education* (Geographical Association, Sheffield, 1971)

Grenyer, N. 'An introduction to recent developments in geography teaching: an annotated bibliography', *Geography*, 57 (1972), 333–6

Hancock, J. C. and Whiteley, P. F. *The Geographer's Vademecum of Sources and Materials* (London, 1971)

Hopkins, M. F. S. *Learning through the Environment* (London, 1968)

Incorporated Association of Assistant Masters. *The Teaching of Geography in Secondary Schools* (London, 1952, later eds)

Jay, L. J. 'The British Isles in the classroom: a review', *Geography*, 57 (1972), 135–9

Lines, C. J. and Bolwell, L. H. *Teaching Environmental Studies in the Primary and Middle School* (London, 1971)

Long, M. (ed). *Handbook for Geography Teachers* (London, 5th ed 1964, and later eds)

Long, M. and Roberson, B. S. *Teaching Geography* (London, 1966)

Morris, J. W. *Methods of Geographic Instruction* (Blaisdell Mass, 1968)

Naish, M. C. 'Some aspects of the study and teaching of geography in Britain: a review of recent British research', *Teaching Geography No 18* (Geographical Association, 1973)

Sporck, J-A., Tulippe, O., Pinchemel, P., Graves, N. J. *et al Unesco Source Book for Geography Teaching* (UNESCO, 1965)

Teaching methods

Bailey, P. J. M. 'Teaching regional geography: the synthetic landscape method', *Geography*, 48 (1963), 285–92

237

Biddle, D. S. (ed). *Readings in Geographical Education* vol 1 (Sydney, 1968); vol 2 (with Deer, C. E.) (Sydney, 1973)

Brearley, D. 'The use of charter flights in the teaching of geography', *Geography*, 51 (1966), 42–9

Dreghorn, W. and Large, N. F. 'Some models for teaching physical geography', *Geography*, 52 (1967), 182–5

Dury, G. H. 'Rivers in geographical teaching', *Geography*, 48 (1963), 18–30

Everson, J. A. and Fitzgerald, B. P. *Settlement Patterns* (London, 1969); also *Inside the City* (London, 1972)

Fairgrieve, J. 'Can we teach geography better?', *Geography*, 21 (1936), 104–9

Forster, C. A. 'Monte Carlo simulation as a teaching aid in urban geography: evaluation of an example', *Geography*, 58 (1973), 13–28

Frey, A. E. 'The teaching of regional geography', *Geography*, 58 (1973), 119–28

Geographical Association, Sixth-Form and University Standing Committee. 'Regional geography in the sixth-form course: a report', *Geography*, 56 (1971), 206–15

——. 'Climatology in the sixth-form course: a report', *Geography*, 55 (1970), 34–9

Graves, N. (ed). *New Movements in the Study and Teaching of Geography* (London, 1972)

Griffin, P. F. and Chatham, R. L. 'The still picture in geographical instruction', *Journal of Geography*, 66 (1967), 222–30

Hanwell, J. D. and Newson, M. D. *Techniques in Physical Geography* (London, 1973)

James, P. 'On the origin and persistence of error in geography', *Annals Association of American Geographers*, 57 (1967)

Keeble, D. 'School teaching and urban geography: some new approaches', *Geography*, 54 (1969), 18–33

Long, M. 'The interests of children in school geography', *Geography*, 56 (1971), 177–90

Maund, D. J. and Jenkins, R. 'Central place study in a secondary modern school', *Geography*, 55 (1970), 434–40

Natoli, S. J., Cason, R. M. and Castner, J. *Activities Selected from the American High School Geography Project* (Washington DC, 1970)

Oliver, J. L. 'Directories and their use in geographical inquiry', *Geography*, 49 (1964), 400–9

Palmer, J. and Sutcliffe, B. 'What should we teach in sixth-form geomorphology?', *Geography*, 56 (1971), 89–95

Pinder, D. A. and Witherick, M. E., 'The principles, practice and pitfalls of nearest-neighbour analysis', *Geography*, 57 (1972), 277–88

Proctor, N. 'Using block diagrams in teaching geography', *Geography*, 48 (1963), 393–8

——. 'Philately and geography teaching', *Geography*, 50 (1965), 134–41

Pugh, J. C. 'Some avoidable errors in physiographic studies', *Geography*, 49 (1964), 44–9

Robinson, R. J. 'Latin America's economic situation – the use of the rank correlation coefficient', *Teaching Geography No 13* (Geographical Association, 1970)

——. 'Teaching a geographical idea: the friction of distance', *Geography*, 58 (1973), 142–7

Simons, M.'What is a geographical factor?' *Geography*, 51 (1966), 210–17

Small, R. J. 'Some criticisms of the teaching of geomorphology at A-level', *Geography*, 51 (1966), 29–37

——. 'The new geomorphology and the sixth-former', *Geography*, 54 (1969), 308–18

Stamp, Sir Dudley. 'Philatelic cartography: a critical study of maps on stamps with special reference to the Commonwealth', *Geography*, 51 (1966), 179–97

Thomas, W. S. G. and others. 'Implications for geography teaching in the Newsom Report', *Geography*, 52 (1967), 186–92

Tidswell, W. V. 'An introduction to the analysis of road networks', *Teaching Geography No 15* (Geographical Association, 1971)

Toyne, P. and Newby, P. T. *Techniques in Human Geography* (London, 1971)

Walford, R. A. (ed). *New Directions in Geography Teaching* (London, 1973)

Whipple, G. 'Geography in the elementary social science program: concepts, generalizations and skills to be developed' in James, P. E. (ed), *New Viewpoints in Geography* (Baltimore Pa, 1966) 112–43

White, R. L. and Hardy, G. B. 'An instructional exercise in industrial location: the electricity industry', *Teaching Geography No 17* (Geographical Association, 1972)

Selected books for pupils below the sixth form

Beddis, R. A. *Focal Points in Geography, Books 1–4* (London, 1967–72)

Briggs, K. *Introducing Transportation Networks* (London, 1972)

Cole, J. P. and Benyon, N. J. *New Ways in Geography*. Introductory Book, Books 1 and 2, Teacher's Book, pupils' workpads (Oxford, 1969)

Graves, N. J. and White, J. T. *Geography of the British Isles* (London, 1971)

Rolfe, J., Dearden, R., Kent, A., Rowe, C. and Grenyer, N. *Oxford Geography Project:* 1 *The Local Framework;* 2 *European Patterns;* 3 *Contrasts in Development* (London, 1974)

Simons, M. *Poverty and Wealth in Cities and Villages* (London, 1972)

An outstanding series of 'regional' reference books are the *Problem Regions of Europe* series, from Oxford University Press. Titles include: Clout, H. D. *The Massif Central* (1971), Mountjoy, A. B. *The Mezzogiorno* (1972), Lawrence, G. R. P. *Randstad Holland* (1972), Turnock, D. *Scotland's Highlands and Islands* (1974), Mead, W. R. *The Scandinavian Northlands* (1973)

FIELD WORK

Techniques

Archer, J. E. and Dalton, T. H. *Fieldwork in Geography* (London 1968)

Baraniecki, M. M. and Ellis, D. M. 'A market survey: techniques and potentialities', *Teaching Geography No 12* (Geographical Association, 1970)

Boardman, D. J. 'The place of the school field centre in the teaching of geography', *Geography*, 54 (1969), 319–24

Briggs, K. *Field Work in Urban Geography* (London, 1970)

Bull, G. B. G. 'Field work in towns. A review of techniques for sixth forms and technical colleges', *Geography*, 49 (1964), 206–21

—— *A Town Study Companion* (London, 1967)

Chapallaz, D. P. and others. 'Hypothesis testing in field studies'. *Teaching Geography No 11* (Geographical Association, 1970)

Cross, M. F. and Daniel, P. A. *Field Work for Geography Classes* (London, 1968)

Everson, J. 'Some aspects of teaching geography through field work', *Geography*, 54 (1969), 64–73

Himus, G. W. and Sweeting, G. S. *The Elements of Field Geology* (London, 1965)

Hoskins, W. G. *Field Work in Local History* (London, 1968)

Large, N. F. 'The pit heap as a venue for geographical fieldwork', *Geography*, 54 (1969), 193–7

Long, M. 'The status of field work. The attitudes of examination boards and local education authorities', *Geography*, 47 (1962), 72–84

Morrison, A. 'Traffic study as quantitative field work', *Teaching Geography No 14* (Geographical Association, 1970)

Mottershead, R. and Owen, M. D. 'Some problems arising in field work in modern geography', *Geography*, 57 (1972), 232–4

Newman, R. J. P. 'Field work using questionnaires and population data', *Teaching Geography No 6* (Geographical Association, 1969)

Sinker, C. A. 'Vegetation and the teaching of geography in the field', *Geography*, 49 (1964), 105–10

Ward, C. and Fyson, A. *Streetwork: The Exploding School* (London, 1973)

Wheeler, K. S. and Harding, M. *Geographical Field Work: A Handbook* (Leicester, 1965)

Wheeler, K. S. *Geography in the Field* (London, 1970)

Wilks, H. C. 'Recent books about fieldwork: a review', *Geography*, 58 (1973), 355–9

Wilks, H. C. 'Geography fieldwork: a continuous and graded course', *Geography*, 53 (1968), 387–90

Yates, E. M. and Robertson, M. 'Geographical field studies', *Geography*, 53 (1968), 55–66

Planning and organisation

Bailey, P. J. M. 'African setting', *Journal Institute of Education*, University of Newcastle upon Tyne, 18 (1966), 19–22

Barnetson, P. *Critical Path Planning* (London, 1968)

Bedford, B. L. *Mountain Safety – Summer*. Notes to accompany filmstrip DW 160, Diana Wyllie, for British Mountaineering Council (London, 1973)

Blackshaw, A. *Mountaineering – From Hillwalking to Alpine Climbing* (Harmondsworth, 1973)

Schools Council. *Out and About: A Teacher's Guide to Safety on Educational Visits* (London, 1972)

GEOGRAPHY ROOM APPARATUS AND EQUIPMENT

Bayliss, J. M. *Running a School Weather Station*, Filmstrip and notes, Diana Wyllie (London, 1962)

Geographical Association. *The Geography Room and Its Equipment* (Sheffield, 1972)

Giffard, E. O. *Geography Rooms* (London, 1961)

Hookey, P. G. 'Do-it-yourself weather instruments', *Teaching Geography No 2* (Geographical Association, 1968)

Taylor, A. and others. *Communications Media Handbook*, Communication Committee, Faculty of Education, University of Wales (Cardiff, 1972)

Wyatt, H. 'A resource centre in geography teaching', *Geography*, 58 (1973), 260–2

PREPARATION OF TEACHING MATERIALS

Anderson, E. W. 'Hardware models in geography teaching', *Teaching Geography No 7* (Geographical Association, 1969)

Bailey, P. J. M. 'Blackboard and camera: some combined uses in the teaching of geography', *Geography*, 46 (1961), 232–7

Langford, M. J. *Visual Aids and Photography in Education: A Visual Aids Manual for Teachers and Learners* (London and New York, 1973). Comprehensive guide to photographic techniques.

Mowbray, W. L. and Galley, M. 'Relief models using new materials', *Geography*, 53 (1968), 308–9

Smith, G. R. *First Models in Cardboard* (Leicester, 1963)

Taylor, L. C. *Resources for Learning* (Harmondsworth, 1971)

Thomas, D. W. 'Overhead projector transparencies for geography teaching: a review', *Geography*, 53 (1968), 400–3

Treasure Chest for Teachers: Services Available to Teachers and Schools, the most useful single reference, published by the Schoolmaster Publishing Company (London, 1960, frequently revised)

White, A. T. *Modelling Relief Maps* (Leicester, nd)

White, J. T. 'The uses of manila card in the classroom', *Geography*, 50 (1965), 142–4

DEPARTMENTAL ORGANISATION AND MANAGEMENT

Bailey, P. J. M. 'The functions of heads of departments in comprehensive schools', *Journ Educational Administration and History*, 5 (1973), 52–8

———. 'The organisation and management of geography departments in comprehensive schools', *Geography*, 57 (1972), 226–31

Freeman, J. *Team Teaching in Britain* (London, 1969)

Heamon, A. J. 'Geography teaching in a comprehensive school', *Geography*, 42 (1957), 244–9

Marland, M. *Head of Department: Leading a Department in a Comprehensive School* (London, 1971)

EXAMINATION AND ASSESSMENT

Bruce, G. *Secondary School Examinations: Facts and Commentary* (Oxford, 1969)

Clarke, E. (ed). *Objective and Completion Tests in O level Geography: Physical and General Geography 1–15* (London, 1973)

Eggleston, J. F. and Kerr, J. F. *Studies in Assessment* (London, 1969)

Gronlund, N. E. *Measurement and Evaluation in Teaching* (London, 2nd ed 1971)

Hones, G. H. 'Objective tests in geography', *Geography*, 58 (1973), 29–37

Jones, S. and Reynolds, J. 'The development of a new O-level syllabus', *Geography*, 58 (1973), 263–8

Prudden, H. C. 'Some problems of external examination questions', *Geography*, 56 (1971), 28–31

Roberson, B. S. 'Geography examinations at O- and A-level', *Geography*, 56 (1971), 96–104

Roe, P. E. 'Examining C.S.E. geography', *Geography*, 56 (1971), 105–11

Vernon, P. E. *The Certificate of Secondary Education: An Introduction to Objective-type Examinations*, Secondary Schools Examination Bulletin No 4, HMSO (London, 1964)

REFERENCE WORKS
Dictionaries, glossaries and gazetteers

Monkhouse, F. J. *A Dictionary of Geography* (London, 2nd ed 1972)

Moore, W. G. *A Dictionary of Geography* (Harmondsworth, 1972)

——. *The Penguin Encyclopedia of Places* (Harmondsworth, 1971)

Stamp, L. Dudley (ed). *Longman's Dictionary of Geography* (London, 1966)

——. *A Glossary of Geographical Terms* (London, 2nd ed 1966)

Webster's New Geographical Dictionary (gazetteer) (London, 1973)

Factual data

Europa Year Book (London, 14th ed 1973). Vol I: International Organisations, Europe; Vol II: Africa, the Americas, Asia, Australasia

Europa Publications Survey and Reference Books:
Africa South of the Sahara 1973 (London, 1973)
The Far East and Australasia, 1973 (London, 1973)
The Middle East and North Africa 1972–3 (London, 1973)

Fullard, H. (ed). *Geographical Digest* (London, annually in May)

See also: *Statesman's Yearbook* and *Whitaker's Almanac* (London, annually), and daily newspapers such as *The Times* and *The Guardian* (London), *New York Times* and *The Christian Science Monitor* (Boston Mass.)

Book lists and literary sources

Anderson, M. S. *Splendour of Earth* (London, 1954)

Church, M. and others. *A Basic Geographical Library*, Assoc of American Geographers (Washington DC, 1970)

Jay, L. J. 'Geography books for sixth forms', *Teaching Geography No 4* (Geographical Association, 1968, with later revisions)

Lukehurst, C. T. and Graves, N. J. *Geography in Education: A Bibliography of British Sources* (Geographical Association, 1969)

Mills, D. G. 'Teaching aids on Australia and New Zealand', *Teaching Geography No 5* (Geographical Association, 1969)

Viney, D. A. (compiler). *School Books Guide: Secondary Geography 1972* (London, 1972). This useful book lists more than 3,000 titles of books for schools, gives short notes about content and the age-ranges for which books are written. There is a comprehensive index. Regular revision is planned.

PART 2

THE NATURE OF GEOGRAPHY

Abler, R., Adams, J. S. and Gould, P. *Spatial Organization: The Geographer's View of the World* (Englewood Cliffs NJ, 1971)

Bacon, P. (ed). *Focus on Geography: Key Concepts and Teaching Strategies* (Washington DC, 1970)

Berry, B. J. L. and Marble, D. F. *Spatial Analysis: A Reader in Statistical Geography* (Englewood Cliffs NJ, 1968)

Board, C., Chorley, R. J., Haggett, P. and Stoddart, D. R. (eds). *Progress in Geography*, 5 (London, 1973)

Bunge, W. *Theoretical Geography* (Lund Sweden, 1962)

Burton, I. 'The quantitative revolution and theoretical geography', *Canadian Geographer*, 7 (1963), 151–62

Chorley, R. J. and Haggett, P. (eds). *Frontiers in Geographical Teaching* (London, 1965, 1970)

Chorley, R. J. (ed). *Directions in Geography* (London, 1973)

Cooke, R. U. and Johnson, J. H. (eds). *Trends in Geography* (London, 1969)

Fuson, R. H. *A Geography of Geography: Origins and Development of the Discipline* (Dubuque Iowa, 1971)

de Geer, Sten. 'On the definition, method and classification of geography', *Geografiska Annaler*, 5 (1923), 1–37

Haggett, P. *Geography: A Modern Synthesis* (London, New York, 1972)

Hartshorne, R. *The Nature of Geography* (Lancaster Pa, 1939)

——. *Perspective on the Nature of Geography* (London, 1959)

Harvey, D. *Explanation in Geography* (London, 1969)

Taafe, E. J. *Geography* (Englewood Cliffs NJ, 1969)

Wooldridge, S. W. and East, W. G. *The Spirit and Purpose of Geography* (London, 1951)

RECENT DEVELOPMENTS IN THE SUBJECT

Statistical methods: use and limitations of data

Cole, J. P. and King, C. A. M. *Quantitative Geography* (London, 1969)

Cambridge, J. T. (ed). *Count Me In. Numeracy in Education* (London, 1968)

Dickinson, G. C. *Statistical Mapping and the Presentation of Statistics* (London, 1963)

Gregory, S. *Statistical Methods and the Geographer* (London, 1963)

Hanson, E. L. and Brown, G. A. *Starting Statistics* (London, 1969)

Jackson, J. N. *Surveys for Town and Country Planning* (London, 1966)

Meek, R. L. *Figuring Out Society* (London, 1971)

Sauvain, P. A. *Advanced Techniques and Statistics* (London, 1972)

Siegel, S. *Nonparametric Statistics for the Behavioural Scientist* (New York, Tokyo, 1956)

Yeates, M. *An Introduction to Quantitative Analysis in Geography* (New York, 1968)

Applications of statistics and models in geography

Thompson, D. 'A select bibliography on quantitative methods in geography', *Geography*, 54 (1969), 74–83 (the most useful first reference for teachers)

246

For those wishing to investigate more deeply, and to look at some of the primary sources, the following short list may be recommended

Berry, B. J. L. and Pred, A. 'Walter Christaller's *Die Zentralen Orte in Süddeutschland:* abstract of theoretical parts of the work', *Central Place Studies, Bibliography of Theory and Applications*, Regional Science Research Institute, Bibliography Series, 1 (Philadelphia, 1961)

Burgess, E. W. 'The determination of gradients in the growth of the city', *Publs American Sociological Society*, 21 (1927), 178–84

Chorley, R. J. and Haggett, P. *Models in Geography* (London, 1967)

Cole, J. P. 'Mathematics and geography', *Geography*, 54 (1969), 152–64

Gould, P. 'Man against his environment: a game theoretic framework', *Annals Association of American Geographers*, 57 (1967), 290–7

——. *Spatial Diffusion* (Washington DC, 1969)

Hägerstrand, T. *The Propagation of Innovation Waves*, Lund Studies in Geography, Series B Human Geography, 4 (Lund, 1952)

——. *Innovation Diffusion as a Spatial Process*, trans A. Pred (Chicago, 1968)

Haggett, P. *Locational Analysis in Human Geography* (London, 1965)

Harris, C. D. and Ullman, E. L. 'The nature of cities', *Annals American Academy of Political Science*, 242 (1945), 7.17

Hoyt, H. *The Structure and Growth of Residential Neighbourhoods in American Cities*, Federal Housing Administration (Washington DC, 1939)

Lösch, A. *The Economics of Location*, trans W. H. Woglen and W. F. Stolper (New York, 1967)

Morgan, W. B. 'The doctrine of the rings', *Geography*, 58 (1973), 301–12

Rogers, E. M. *Diffusion of Innovations* (New York, 1962)

Sinclair, R. 'Von Thünen and urban sprawl', *Annals Association of American Geographers*, 57 (1967)

Stewart, J. Q. and Warntz, W. 'Physics of population distribution', *Journ Regional Science*, 1 (1958), 99–123

Thünen, J. H. von. *Der isolierte Staat in Beziehung auf Landwirtschaft und Nationalökonomie*, trans C. M. Wartenberg, intro. P. Hall (Oxford, 1966)

Weber, A. *Ueber der Standoort der Industrien* (Tübingen, 1909), trans C. J. Fredrich, *Alfred Weber's Theory of the Location of Industry* (Chicago, 1929)

Zipf, G. K. *Human Behaviour and the Principle of Least Effort* (Cambridge, New York, 1949)

Ecosystem, Environment and systems thinking

Arvill, R. *Man and Environment* (Harmondsworth, 1967)

Barry, R. G. and Ives, J. D. (eds). *Arctic and Alpine Environments* (London, 1973)

British National Committee for Geography. *Geographical Studies of Environmental Pollution*, Review of work by geographers submitted to Royal Commission on Environmental Pollution, *Area*, Inst British Geographers, 4 (1972), 114–21

Chisholm, M. 'General systems theory and geography', *Transactions Inst British Geographers*, 42 (1967), 45–52

Clapham, W. B. Jr. *Natural Ecosystems* (New York, London, 1973)

Cox, C. B., Healey, I. N. and Moore, P. D. *Biogeography: An Ecological and Evolutionary Approach* (Oxford, 1973)

Ehrlich, P. R., Ehrlich, A. H. and Holdren, J. P. *Human Ecology: Problems and Solutions* (San Francisco, 1973)

Emery, F. E. (ed). *Systems Thinking* (Harmondsworth, 1969)

Eyre, S. R. and Jones, G. R. J. (eds). *Geography as Human Ecology* (London, 1966)

Laszlo, E. *Introduction to Systems Philosophy: Towards a New Paradigm of Contemporary Thought* (New York, 1972)

Moss, R. P. and Morgan, W. B. 'The concept of the community: some applications in geographical research', *Transactions Inst British Geographers* 41 (1967), 21–32

Owen, D. F. *Man's Environmental Predicament: An Introduction to Human Ecology in Tropical Africa* (London, 1973)

Riley, D. and Young, A. *World Vegetation* (London, 1966)

Simmons, I. G. 'Ecology and land use', *Transactions Inst British Geographers*, 38 (1966), 59–72

Spencer, J. E. and Thomas, W. L., Jr. *Cultural Geography* (New York, 1969)

Stoddart, D. R. 'Geography and the ecological approach. The ecosystem as a geographical principle and method', *Geography*, 50 (1965), 242–51

——. 'Catastrophic human interference with coral atoll ecosystems', *Geography*, 53 (1968), 25–40

Teather, E. K. 'The hedgerow: an analysis of a changing landscape feature', *Geography*, 55 (1970), 146–55

Thomas, W. L. (ed). *Man's Role in Changing the Face of the Earth* (Chicago, 1956)

von Bertalanffy, L. 'The theory of open systems in physics and biology', *Science*, iii (1950), 23–9

Perception theory, mental maps

Gould, P. 'On mental maps', Michigan Inter-University Committee of Mathematical Geographers, 9 (1966), 1–54

——. 'The structure of space preferences in Tanzania', *Area*, Inst British Geographers (1969), 29–35

Hall, J. M. 'Industry goes where the grass is greener', *Area*, Inst British Geographers, 40–6

Kirk, W. 'Problems of geography', *Geography*, 48 (1963), 357–71

Lowenthal, D. (ed). *Environmental Perception and Behaviour*, University of Chicago Department of Geography Research Paper 109 (1967)

Simulation games

Cherryholmes, C. 'Some current research on the effectiveness of educational simulations: implications for alternative strategies', *Amer Behavioural Scientist*, 10 (1966), 4–8

Dalton, R. and others. *Simulation Games in Geography* (Secondary school level) (London, 1972)

Tansey, P. J. and Unwin, D. *Simulation and Gaming in Education* (London, 1969)

Taylor, J. L. *Instructional Planning Systems: A Gaming-Simulation Approach to Urban Problems* (Cambridge, 1971)

Taylor, J. L. and Walford, R. A. *Simulation in the Classroom* (Harmondsworth, 1972)

Walford, R. A. 'Operational games and geography teaching', *Geography*, 54 (1969), 34–42

——. *Games in Geography* (Secondary school level) (London, 1969)

Wilson, A. *War Gaming* (Harmondsworth, 1970)

Developments in physical geography

Bainbridge, J. W. and Stockdale, R. W. *Weather Study: An Approach to Scientific Enquiry* (London, 1972)

Barrett, E. C. *Geography from Space* (Oxford, 1972)

——. *Climatology from Satellites* (London, 1973)

Barry, R. G. and Chorley, R. J. *Atmosphere, Weather and Climate* (London, 1968)

——. *Synoptic Climatology: Method and Applications* (London, 1973)

Bowen, D. Q. and others. *A Concise Physical Geography* (Amersham, 1972)

Bowen, D. Q. 'Time and place on the British coast', *Geography*, 58 (1973), 207–16

Brunsden, D. and Doornkamp, J. C. 'The unquiet landscape: introduction to the science of landform evolution', the first of 24 articles prepared by the Geomorphological Research Group, *The Geographical Magazine* (May, 1971)

Chandler, T. J. *The Climate of London* (London, 1965)

Chorley, R. J. (ed). *Water, Earth and Man* (London, 1969)

——. *Spatial Analysis in Geomorphology* (London, 1972)

Chorley, R. J. and Kennedy, B. A. *Physical Geography: A Systems Approach* (Englewood Cliffs NJ, 1971)

Cooke, R. 'Systems in physical geography', critique of Chorley and Kennedy, in *Area*, Inst British Geographers, 3 (1971), 212–16

Davis, W. M. *Geographical Essays* (1910, repr New York, 1954)

Dury, G. H. *The Face of the Earth* (Harmondsworth, 1959)

——. *The Land from the Air* (London, 1963)

Embleton, C. and King, C. A. M. *Glacial and Periglacial Geomorphology* (London, 1968)

Gregory, S. 'Water resource exploitation – policies and problems', *Geography*, 49 (1964), 310–14

Hare, F. K. 'Energy exchanges and the general circulation', *Geography*, 50 (1965), 229–41

—— 'The concept of climate', *Geography*, 51 (1966), 99–110

Holmes, A. *Principles of Physical Geology* (London, 2nd ed 1965)

Horton, R. E. 'Erosional development of streams and their drainage basins: an hydrophysical approach to quantitative morphology', *Bull Geol Soc Amer*, 56 (1945), 275–370

King, C. A. M. *Beaches and Coasts* (London, 2nd ed 1973)

Pitty, A. *Introduction to Geomorphology* (London, 1971)

Selby, M. J. *The Surface of the Earth* Vol 2; *Soils* (London, 1971), 108–234

Small, R. J. *The Study of Landforms: A Textbook of Geomorphology* (London, New York, 1970)

Sparks, B. W. and West, R. G. *The Ice Age in Britain* (London, 1972)

Sparks, B. W. *Geomorphology* (London, 2nd ed 1972)

Steers, J. A. *Coasts and Beaches* (Edinburgh, 1969)

Stoddart, D. R. 'Coral reefs: the last two million years', *Geography*, 58 (1973), 313–23

Strahler, A. *The Earth Sciences* (New York, 2nd ed 1971)

Tivy, J. *Biogeography: A Study of Plants in the Ecosphere* (Edinburgh, 1971)

Developments in socio-economic geography

Alexandersson, G. *Geography of Manufacturing* (Englewood Cliffs NJ, 1967)

Ambrose, P. *Analytical Human Geography* (London, 1969)

Bauer, P. T. *Dissent on Development* (London 1971)

Berry, B. J. L. *Geography of Market Centres and Retail Distribution* (Englewood Cliffs NJ, 1967)

Boesch, H. *A Geography of World Economy* (New York, 1964)

Burton, I. and Kates, R. W. (eds). *Readings in Resource Management and Conservation* (Chicago, 1965)

Chisholm, M. *Rural Settlement and Land Use* (London, 1962)

——. *Geography and Economics* (London, 2nd ed 1970)

Chorley, R. J. and Haggett, P. *Socio-economic Models in Geography* (London, 1967)

Cosgrove, I and Jackson, R. *The Geography of Recreation and Leisure* (London, 1972)

Couper, A. D. *The Geography of Sea Transport* (London, 1972)

Dawson, J. A. and Doornkamp, J. C. (eds). *Evaluating the Human Environment* (London, 1973)

Dumont, R. *Types of Rural Economy* (London, 1964)

Dunn, E. S. *The Location of Agricultural Production* (Gainsville Fla, 1954)

Estall, R. C. and Buchanan, R. O. *Industrial Activity and Economic Growth* (London, 1966)

Fryer, D. W. *World Economic Development* (London and New York, 1965)

Ginsberg, N. *Essays on Geography and Economic Development* (Chicago, 1960)

Harris, C. D. 'The market as a factor in the localisation of industry in the United States', *Annals Association of American Geographers*, 44 (1954)

Johnston, R. J. *Spatial Structures* (London, 1973)

Kansky, K. J. *Structure and Transportation Networks*, University of Chicago Department of Geography Research Paper 84 (1963)

Krumme, G. 'Towards a geography of enterprise', *Econ Geog*, 45 (1969), 34ff

McDaniel, R. and Hurst, M. E. Eliot. *A Systems Analytic Approach to Economic Geography* (Washington DC, 1968)

Manners, G. *The Geography of Energy* (London, 1964)

Mercer, D. C. 'The geography of leisure – a contemporary growth point', *Geography*, 55 (1970), 261–73

Morgan, W. B. and Munton, R. C. *Agricultural Geography* (London, 1971)

Morrill, R. L. *The Spatial Organisation of Society* (Belmont Calif, 1970)

Mountjoy, A. B. *Industrialization and Underdeveloped Countries* (London, 1966)

252

Naylon, J. 'Tourism: Spain's most important industry', *Geography*, 52 (1967), 23–40

Odell, P. R. *Oil and World Power: A Geographical Interpretation* (Harmondsworth, 2nd ed 1972)

Patmore, J. A. *Land and Leisure* (Newton Abbot, 1970)

Philbreck, A. K. *This Human World* (New York, 1963)

Rutherford, J., Logan, M. I. and Misson, G. J. *New Viewpoints in Economic Geography* (Sydney, 1966)

Smith, D. M. *Industrial Location: An Economic Geographical Analysis* (New York, 1971)

Smith, R. H. T., Taafe, E. J. and King, L. J. *Readings in Economic Geography: The Location of Economic Activity* (Chicago, 1968)

Taafe, E. J. and Gauthier, H. L., Jr. *Geography of Transportation* (Englewood Cliffs NJ, 1972)

Thoman, R. S. and Conkling, E. C. *Geography of International Trade* (Englewood Cliffs NJ, 1967)

Zelinsky, W. *A Prologue to Population Growth* (Englewood Cliffs NJ, 1970)

Urban geography

Berry, B. J. L. 'Cities as systems within systems of cities', *Papers and Proc Regional Science Assoc*, University of Pennsylvania, 10 (1964)

Bird, J. H. *Seaports and Seaport Terminals* (London, 1971)

——. 'Of central places, cities and seaports', *Geography*, 58 (1973), 105–18

Conzen, M. R. G. *Alnwick, Northumberland: A Study in Town-Plan Analysis* (London, 1960)

Davies, W. K. D., Giggs, J. A. and Herbert, D. T. 'Directories, rate books and the commercial structure of towns', *Geography* 53 (1968), 41–54

Dickinson, R. E. *City Region in Western Europe* (London, 1967)

Dwyer, D. J. 'The city in the developing world and the example of Southeast Asia', *Geography*, 53 (1968), 353–64

Gottman, J. *Megalopolis* (Cambridge Mass, 1964)

Hall, P. *The World Cities* (London, 1966)

Johnston, J. H. *Urban Geography: An Introductory Analysis* (Oxford, 1968)

Harvey, D. *Social Justice and the City* (London, 1973)

Lynch, K. *The Image of the City* (Cambridge Mass, 1960)

Martin, J. E. *Greater London's Industrial Geography* (London, 1966)

Mayer, H. M. *The Spatial Expression of Urban Growth*, Assoc American Geographers Resource Paper 7 (1969)

Mountjoy, A. B. 'Million cities: Urbanization and the developing countries', *Geography*, 53 (1968), 365–74

Murphy, R. E. and Vance, J. E. 'Delimiting the CBD', *Econ Geog*, 30 (1954), 189–222

Murphy, R. E. *The American City: An Urban Geography* (New York, 1966)

Park, R. E., Burgess, E. W. and McKenzie, R. D. *The City* (Chicago, 1925)

Smailes, A. E. *The Geography of Towns* (London, 1953)

Wheatley, P. *The Pivot of the Four Quarters* (Chicago, Edinburgh, 1971)

Wolforth, J. and Leigh, R. *Urban Prospects* (Toronto, 1971)

Source books and papers for regional studies

Behrman, J. N. *The Role of International Companies in Latin American Integration* (Lexington, 1972)

Berry, B. J. L. *The Geography of Market Centres* (Englewood Cliffs NJ, 1967)

Britton, J. N. H. *Regional Analysis and Economic Geography* (London, 1967)

Brunskill, R. W. *Vernacular Architecture* (London, 1970)

Bryan, P. W. 'Geography and landscape', *Geography*, 43 (1958), 1–9

Chisholm, M. 'Must we all live in south-east England? The location of new employment', *Geography*, 49 (1964), 1–14

Coates, B. E. and Rawstron, E. M. 'Regional incomes and planning', *Geography*, 52 (1967), 393–402

——. *Regional Variations in Britain: Studies in Economic and Social Geography* (London, 1971)

Coghill, I. *Australia's Mineral Wealth* (Melbourne, 1971)

Cumberland, K. B. and Whitelaw, J. S. *The World's Landscapes: New Zealand* (London, 1970)

Dawson, J. A. 'Some New Zealand maps and statistical sources', *Geography*, 54 (1969), 198–203

Debray, R. *Revolution in the Revolution? Armed Struggle and Political Struggle in Latin America* (Harmondsworth, 1968)

Dickinson, R. E. *City and Region* (London, New York, 1964)

East Anglia Consultative Committee. *East Anglia: A Regional Appraisal*, HMSO (London, 1969)

Estall, R. C. *New England: A Study in Industrial Adjustment* (London, 1966)

Fisher, C. A. 'Whither regional geography?', *Geography*, 55 (1970), 373–89

Freeman, T. W. *Geography and Planning* (London, 1967)

Friedman, J. W. and Alonson, W. *Regional Development and Planning* (Boston Mass, 1964)

Gourou, P. *The Tropical World* (London, 4th ed 1966)

Harvey, N. *A History of Farm Buildings in England and Wales* (Newton Abbot, 1970)

Herbertson, A. J. 'The higher units. A geographical essay', *Geography*, 50 (1965), 332–42; reprinted from *Scientia* (14 May 1913), 199–212

Hodder, B. W. and Harris, D. R. (eds). *Africa in Transition* (London, 1967)

Hoskins, W. G. *The Making of the English Landscape* (London, 1965)

Houston, J. M. *The Western Mediterranean World: An Introduction to Its Regional Landscapes* (London, 1964)

Huntington, E. *Mainsprings of Civilization* (New York, 1945)

Isard, W. *Methods of Regional Analysis* (New York, 1966)

Lambert, A. M. *The Making of the Dutch Landscape* (London, New York, 1971)

Lewis, G. M. 'Levels of living in the north-eastern United States c1960. A new approach to regional geography', *Transactions Inst British Geographers*, 45 (1968), 11–37

255

Mead, W. R. *Economic Geography of the Scandinavian States and Finland* (London, 1958)

——. 'Frontier themes in Finland', *Geography*, 44 (1959), 145–56

Morgan, W. T. W. *Nairobi: City and Region* (London, 1967)

Mountjoy, A. B. and Embleton, C. *Africa: A Geographical Study* (London, 3rd imp revised 1970)

Parsons, G. F. 'The giant manufacturing corporations and balanced regional growth in Britain', *Area*, Inst British Geographers, 4 (1972), 99–103

Russell, R. J., Kniffen, F. B. and Pruitt, E. L. *Culture Worlds* (New York, 2nd ed 1969)

Sillitoe, A. F. *Britain in Figures: A Handbook of Social Statistics* (Harmondsworth, 1971)

Smith, C. T. 'Problems of regional development in Peru', *Geography*, 53 (1968), 260–80

Stamp, Sir Dudley, and Beaver, S. H. *The British Isles* (London, 6th ed 1971)

Turnock, D. 'The region in modern geography', *Geography*, 52 (1967), 374–83

Watson, J. Wreford, and Sissons, J. B. (eds). *The British Isles: A Systematic Geography* (London, 1964)

Case studies

Black, H. D. 'Case studies: a review of some recently published books', *Geography*, 58 (1973), 148–51

Two collections of case studies intended for secondary school use are published by the Geographical Association:

Dempster, P. and others. *Asian Sample Studies* (Sheffield, 1968)

Hickman, G. M. and others. *Sample Studies* (Sheffield, 1962, reprint with corrections, 1967)

Many of the *Regional Studies* published from time to time by the Geographical Field Group, Department of Geography, University of Nottingham, contain excellent case study material, eg:

Fordham, P. *Rural Development in the Kenya Highlands: A Report of Geographical Field Work carried out during August 1971. Regional Studies No 17* (1973)

Wheeler, P. T. *Viborg and Its Region. Regional Studies No 16* (1973)

The following books and papers contain case study materials suitable for use in schools:

Bailey, P. J. M. 'The changing economy of the chagga cultivators of Marangu, Kilimanjaro', *Geography*, 53 (1968), 163–9

Church, R. J. Harrison. 'The Firestone rubber plantations in Liberia', *Geography*, 54 (1969), 430–7

Highsmith, R. M. (ed). *Case Studies in World Geography: Occupance and Economy Types* (Englewood Cliffs NJ, 1961)

Hutson, A. B. A. *Sample Studies Round the World* (London, 1970)

McCullagh, P. *The East Midlands* (London, 1972)

Marchington, T. and Price, B. P. *Studies in South East England* (London, 1972)

Shepherd, E. and Shepherd, S. *Field Studies in Southeast Asia* (London, 1972)

Comment on the use of case studies in schools may be found in:

Roberson, B. S. and Long, M. 'Sample studies: the development of a method', *Geography*, 41 (1956), 248–59

Stimson, C. D. J. 'Sample studies: their contribution to geographic education', *Australian Geographer*, 9 (1964)

Maps, map work and air photo interpretation

Balchin, W. G. V. 'Graphicacy', *Geography*, 57 (1972), 185–95

Debenham, F. *Map Making* (London, 1936, with later revisions)

Dickinson, G. C. *Maps and Air Photographs* (London, 1969)

Dury, G. H. *Map Interpretation* (London, 4th ed 1972)

Lambert, A. M. 'Early maps and local studies', *Geography*, 41 (1956), 167–77

Lawrence, G. R. P. *Cartographic Methods* (London, 1972)

MacMahan, H. Jr. *Stereogram Book of Contours* (Northbrook Ill, 1972)

Monkhouse, F. J. *Landscape from the Air* (London, 2nd ed 1971)

Monkhouse, F. J. and Wilkinson, H. R. *Maps and Diagrams: Their Compilation and Construction* (London, 3rd ed 1971)

Render, J. *Map Preparation – Some Guidance on Fundamentals* (Portsmouth Polytechnic, 1973)

Robinson, A. H. W. and Wallwork, K. L. *Map Studies, with Related Field Excursions* (London, 1970)
St Joseph, J. K. *The Uses of Air Photography* (New York, 1966)
Wallwork, K. L. 'Map interpretation and industrial location: the example of alkali manufacture in Lancastria', *Geography*, 52 (1967), 166–81

The following books may be noted as directly useful in schools:
Barker, E. J. and Williams, L. H. *Britain From the Air* (London, 1969)
Devereux, E. J. P. and Morgan, M. A. *Mapwork With Pictures* – 6 volumes, eg *Australia and New Zealand*, vol 6 (London, 1970)
Dobson, F. R. and Virgo, H. E. *Map Reading and Local Studies* (London, 1967)
Geographical Association, *British Landscapes Through Maps* series, edited by K. C. Edwards: seventeen titles in print in 1974 include:
Monkhouse, F. J. *The English Lake District* (2nd ed); Embleton, C. *Snowdonia*; Bailey, P. J. M. *The Norwich Area*
Naish, M., Walford, R. A., Long, M. and Roberson, B. S. *Exercises on Ordnance Survey Maps and Extracts: Stow-on-the-Wold; Bishop Auckland; Calne and Stirling. Teaching Geography series, Nos 8, 9 and 10* (Geographical Association 1969)

PUPILS' LEARNING, WITH SPECIAL REFERENCE TO GEOGRAPHY
Dale, P. F. 'Children's reactions to maps and aerial photographs', *Area*, Inst British Geographers, 3 (1971), 170–7
Gildea, R. Y. 'Programmed learning: its relationship to geographical education', *Journal of Geography*, 67 (1968)
Koussy, A. A. A. H. el. 'The visual perception of space', *Brit Journ of Educ Psychol, Monograph Supplement No 20* (1935)
Jahoda, G. 'The development of children's ideas about country and nationality: 1. The conceptual framework', *Brit Journ Educ Psychol*, 33 (1963), 47–66
Long, M. 'Research in picture study. The reactions of grammar school pupils to geographical pictures', *Geography*, 46 (1961), 322–37

Piaget, J. *The Child's Conception of the World* (London, 1964)

Piaget, J. and Inhelder, B. *The Child's Conception of Space* (London, 1956)

Rhys, W. T. 'Geography and the adolescent', *Educational Review*, 24 (1966), 183–96

Rushdoony, H. A. 'A child's ability to read maps: summary of the research', *Journal of Geography*, 67 (1968)

Shulman, L. S. *Learning by Discovery: A Critical Appraisal* (Chicago, 1966)

Slater, F. A. 'Piaget's and Bruner's theories and learning in geography', *Geographical Education*, 1 (1970), 87–97

Smith, I. M. *Spatial Ability* (London, 1964)

CURRICULUM DEVELOPMENT AND GEOGRAPHY

Beauchamp, G. A. *Curriculum Theory* (Wilmette Ill, 1968)

Biddle, D. S. and Shortle, D. *Programme Planning in Geography* (Sydney, 1969)

Blachford, K. *The Teaching of Geography, Unit 1: A Geographic Viewpoint*, Education Dept, Victoria, Australia (1971)

Black, H. C. 'A four-fold classification of educational theory', *Educ Theory*, 16 (1966), 280–90

Bloom, B. S. (ed). *A Taxonomy of Educational Objectives: 1 The Cognitive Domain* (New York, 1956)

Bruner, J. S. *The Process of Education* (Cambridge Mass, 1960)

——. *Towards a Theory of Instruction* (Cambridge Mass, 1967)

Clegg, A. A. 'Developing and Using Behavioural Objectives', in P. Bacon (ed), *Focus in Geography*, 40th Yearbook of the National Council for the Social Studies (Washington DC, 1970), 291–303

Earth Sciences Curriculum Project. *Investigating the Earth* (Boston Mass, 1967)

Fitzgerald, B. P. 'The American High School Geography Project and its implications for geography teaching in Britain', *Geography*, 54 (1969), 56–63

Foss, B. M. *Education as Art, Science and Technology* (London, 1967)

Goodlad, J. and Richter, M. *The Development of a Conceptual System for Dealing with Problems of Curriculum and Instruction* (Los Angeles Calif, 1966)

Gronlund, N. E. *Stating Behavioural Objectives for Classroom Instruction* (London, New York, 1970)

Johnson, M. 'The translation of curriculum into instruction', *Journal of Curriculum Studies*, 1 (1969), 115–31

Kerr, J. F. (ed). *Changing the Curriculum* (London, 1968)

Leeper, E. (ed). *Curriculum Change: Direction and Process* (Washington DC, 1966)

Maclure, J. S. *Curriculum Innovation in Practice* (Schools Council, London, 1967)

Ministry of Education (Great Britain). *Half Our Future – A Report of the Central Advisory Council for Education* (London, 1966)

Patton, D. J. *From Geographic Discipline to Inquiring Student*, History of the American High School Geography Project, 1961–70 (Washington DC, 1970)

Phenix, P. H. *Realms of Meaning* (New York, 1964)

Reynolds, J. 'Schools Council Curriculum Development Project: Geography 14–18 years', *Geography*, 56 (1971), 32–4

Richmond, W. K. *The School Curriculum* (London, 1971)

Rolfe, J. 'The completion of the American High School Geography Project', *Geography*, 56 (1971), 216–20

Taba, H. *Curriculum Development, Theory and Practice* (New York, 1962)

Taylor, P. H. 'Purpose and structure in the curriculum', *Educational Review*, 19 (1967)

Walton, J. (ed). *Curriculum Organisation and Design* (London, 1971)

Wheeler, D. K. *Curriculum Process* (London, 1967)

Whitfield, R. (ed). *Disciplines of the Curriculum* (London, 1971)

Index

262

Filmstrips, 91, 94, 135–7, 149, 154, 209, 213, 220
Flannelgraph, 173–5, plate 6
Furniture, geography room, 132–4

Games, simulation, 41, 73–82
General Certificate of Education (GCE), 121–3
Geographical Association, 144, 185, 220, 235
Geographical Field Group, 185
Geography: contribution to education, 14–16; definitions of, 11; distinctive
   ideas, 18–23; limits of study, 13–14; modern developments related to schools,
   37–82; pupils' learning problems with, 29–36; related to pupils' learning,
   24–7; skills, 16; vocabulary of, 186
Geography room: blackboards and whiteboards, 147–8; blackout and pro-
   jection facilities, 134–9; design principles, 131–2; display space, 142;
   furniture and layout, 132–4; maps and globes, 143–6; model-making
   facilities, 146; projection and other equipment, 139–42; storage 148–50;
   wave and stream tanks, 146
Geology, 54–5, 145, 154, 193, 208, 228–9
Geomorphology, teaching, 18–19, 109–10, 163–4, 186–8, 193–5, *194*, 199–200
   224–9
Glaciated scenery, 188, *191*, *194*–5
Glen Trool, Scotland, *194*–5
Globes, 145
Graphicacy, 16–17
Gravity models, 67–8
Group work, 27–8, 52, 80–2, 103, 109, 111, 113–17, 136, 176, 178

Hägerstrand, Torsten, 79
Hand viewers, 139–40 *see also* Auto-teaching
Head of Department, tasks of, 83–96
Heat transfer machine, 182
Herbertson, A. J., 56, 106
Hettner, Alfred, 11
Hierarchy, settlement, 61–7, *62*
Homework, 96, 112
Hoyt, H., town development model, 60–1
Humboldt, Alexander von, 11
Hypothesis testing, 42, 190–1, 201–3

Ideas-based courses, 105–8
Idea sequences: about limestone scenery, 228–9; about towns, 218–19
Imagination, cultivation of, 30, 41, 108, 217–18
Incremental drawings, 164, 221, plate 4
Industrial studies, 153, 198–9
Ink duplicators, 183
Innovation, diffusion of, 79
Insurance, 204–5
Introductory walks, 192, 194–5

Japanese landscape, 212–15
Job specification within departments, 86–7

Karamojong grazing game, 75–6

263

266